"Tedlock's book should become the classic on...women's place in the shaman's world."
—*Booklist* (starred review)

"In a time where we see so many women engaging in shamanic practice, Tedlock offers valuable insight into the long-standing role of women in this ancient path. I truly loved reading this book!"
—Sandra Ingerman,
author of *Soul Retrieval* and *Medicine for the Earth*

"Wonderful, insightful, and compelling...Barbara Tedlock weaves a story that is both autobiography and persuasive argument for the importance of women as shaman, worldwide and throughout history."
—David A. Freidel, Ph.D.,
University Distinguished Professor of Anthropology,
Southern Methodist University

"Meticulously researched yet delightfully absorbing...If Joseph Campbell or Mircea Eliade had been feminists, this is a book they could wish they had written."
—Alma Gottlieb, Ph.D., president,
Society for Humanistic Anthropology

"*The Woman in the Shaman's Body* illuminates the oftentimes hidden, and sometimes openly suppressed, feminine spirit that is shamanism, that is healing, that is life."
—Bonnie Horrigan, executive director,
Society for Shamanic Practitioners

ALSO BY BARBARA TEDLOCK

Teachings from the American Earth:
Indian Religion and Philosophy
(with Dennis Tedlock)

Time and the Highland Maya

Dreaming: Anthropological and Psychological Interpretations

The Beautiful and the Dangerous: Encounters with the Zuni Indians

The Woman in the Shaman's Body

RECLAIMING THE FEMININE IN RELIGION AND MEDICINE

Barbara Tedlock, Ph.D.

BANTAM BOOKS

New York   Toronto   London   Sydney   Auckland

THE WOMAN IN THE SHAMAN'S BODY
RECLAIMING THE FEMININE IN RELIGION AND MEDICINE
A Bantam Book

PUBLISHING HISTORY
Bantam hardcover edition published March 2005
Bantam trade paperback edition / January 2006

Published by Bantam Dell
A Division of Random House, Inc.
New York, New York

Book design by Katy Riegel

Library of Congress Catalog Card Number: 2004056633

Bantam Books and the rooster colophon are
registered trademarks of Random House, Inc.

ISBN-13: 978-0-553-37971-6
ISBN-10: 0-553-37971-2

Printed in the United States of America
Published simultaneously in Canada

www.bantamdell.com

I dedicate this book to my shamanic partner, Dennis Tedlock, to my grandmother, Nokomis, and to my other shamanic teachers, Essie Parrish, Bayar Odun, Andrés Xiloj, and Talín Peruch.

Contents

PART TWO
SHAMANIC TRADITIONS IN ACTION

PART THREE
THE FEMALE CYCLE: MENSTRUATION, BIRTH, AND CREATION

PART FOUR
The Power of Gender and
Shamanic Revitalization

Illustrations

Acknowledgments

I thank my grandmother, Nokomis, who quietly but firmly showed me the feminine shamanic path of Ojibwe healing. With her encouragement and that of other powerful women shamans—Essie Parrish (Pomo, Northern California), Bayar Odun (Darhat, Mongolia), Nadia Stepanova (Buryat, Russia), and Talín Peruch (Mayan, Guatemala)—I have been privileged to participate in a number of feminine shamanic traditions. I would also like to thank my husband, Dennis Tedlock, who has accompanied me during my field research and encouraged me to sharpen my arguments about the primacy of women in shamanism. Without his support this work would never have been completed.

Thanks also to my graduate-school mentor Peter Furst, who introduced me to the anthropological study of shamanism. His own exemplary work, centering on Huichol shamanism and hallucinogens, is considered classic in the field. Many thanks also to the Hungarian scholar of shamanism, Mihály Hoppál, who invited me to participate in several conferences sponsored by The International Society for Shamanistic Research. To Lawrence Sullivan, Director of the Center for the Study of World Religions, who actively encouraged my research in healing and religion during my Senior Fellowship at the Harvard Divinity School, I say thanks so much for your insightful questions and strong support.

For encouragement, information, and suggestions I am most grateful to David Antin, Mariella Bacigalupo, Marjorie Balzer, Warren Barbour, Charles Bernstein, Ágnes Birtalan, Shelley Bogen, Jamie Borowicz, Erika Bourguignon, Ivan Brady, Michael Brown, Melvin Kimura Bucholtz, Toni Burbank, Allen Christenson, Robbie Davis-Floyd, Lydia Nakashima Degarrod, Sandra Dijkstra, Mary-Charlotte Domandi, Duncan Earle, David Freidel, Eva Fridman, Bonnie Glass-Coffin, Gary Gossen, Alma Gottlieb, Gilbert Herdt, Harry Hunt, Laurel Kendall, Timothy Knab, Gábor Kósa, Carol Laderman, Catherine McCoid, Sally Mennen, Sarunas Milisauskas, Peggy Nelson, Donald Pollock, Marla Powers, Marina Roseman, Jerome Rothenberg, Beth Savage, Stacey Schaefer, Douglas Sharon, Joan Tapper, Edith Turner, Anne Waldman, and David Young together with my late colleagues, Eva Hunt and Linda Schele.

The work of researching and writing this book was supported by the American Philosophical Society in Philadelphia, the School of American Research in Santa Fe, New Mexico, the College of Arts and Sciences at the University of Buffalo, the Institute for Advanced Studies in Princeton, and the Center for the Study of World Religions at Harvard University.

The Woman in
the Shaman's Body

PART ONE

Reclaiming History

ONE

Old Wisdom

HALF A CENTURY ago, as archaeologists worked in the wooded Pavlov Hills of the Czech Republic, they made a remarkable discovery. During the excavation of the Upper Paleolithic site known as Dolní Věstonice, they found a pair of shoulder blades from a mammoth. The bones had been placed so as to form the two sides of a pitched roof, one of them leaning against the other. Beneath them was a human skeleton, and in the earth that covered it and on the bones themselves were traces of red ocher. The body had been painted red before it was laid to rest.

If nothing more had been found in this grave, it would have added little to what was already known about Ice Age peoples and their customs. During the Upper Paleolithic, corresponding to the final years of the Ice Age, about sixty thousand years ago, people already had the same anatomy as modern human beings. In Eurasia, most of them lived not in caves but in the dark coniferous forests and wide-open steppes that lay beyond the reach of the glaciers.

This particular burial was of no ordinary person, though. A flint spearhead had been placed near the head of the deceased, and the body of a fox had been placed in one hand. For the archaeological team, led by Bohuslav Klíma, the fox was a clear indication that the person in the grave had been a shaman; the fox had a long history as a shamanic spirit guide, in Europe and all the way across Asia and into the Americas. It came as something of a shock, however, when skeletal analysis revealed that the shaman in question was a woman.

Why is this find so important? Before the discovery of this woman—and, though it's hard to believe, for a long time afterward—Ice Age shamans were imagined as members of an all-male religious community of mammoth hunters, a sort of *Flintstones* private club in which manhood was celebrated and the transcendental achieved by worshiping, then negating, the feminine. This excavation—which remains the oldest known of its kind—and further work at Dolní Věstonice prove that wasn't so.

A few years later, near the shaman's grave, Klíma discovered an earthen lodge containing a number of bone flutes and a large oven filled with nearly three thousand small pieces of baked clay. Some pieces had been molded in the shape of human feet, hands, and heads, while others were fragments of animal figurines. According to the archaeologist, "this bake-oven is the predecessor of the potter's kiln, serving for the hardening and firing of the oldest known ceramic productions."[1]

In other words, not only do the oldest known skeletal remains of a shaman belong to a woman, but she is also the earliest known artisan who worked in clay and then hardened it with fire. She wasn't making early household utensils; no, she seems to have been making talismans or figurines of some sort, perhaps for use in her rituals and spiritual healing.

How has it happened that we've lost sight of this ancient woman shaman and what she represents? For despite the proof of language and artifacts, despite pictorial representations, ethnographic narratives, and eyewitness accounts, the importance—no, the primacy—of women in shamanic traditions has been obscured and denied. That women's bodies and minds are particularly suited to tap into the power of the transcendental has been ignored. The roles that women have played in healing and prophecy throughout human history have been denigrated. All too often women who enter medicine or the ministry still believe they're stepping into a strictly men's field; in fact, these are historically women's fields that men have since entered. Women have been characterized as mere artisans or craftspeople—weavers and potters—instead of recognized for the creative, life-giving, cosmos-shaping powers these arts represent. Why? The reasons undoubtedly range from misreading of research to sexism pure and simple. But it's time to take another look at the evidence of millennia and of cultures around the globe. It's time to reclaim the woman in the shaman's body.

GRANDMOTHER'S WISDOM

My interest in women as healers and mystics goes back to my childhood. I well remember the late fall mornings I spent at my grandmother's place on the prairie of Saskatchewan. She was an Ojibwe, and her two-room home was built from hewn jack pine logs chinked with mud. The roof consisted of round poles covered with moss and mud. Outside there were tall grasses and wild berries everywhere, and I would accompany her into the woods to gather the special fruits, flowers, twigs, and roots she needed to make her strange and mysterious healing concoctions.

As we followed the narrow trails that only my grandmother knew, she pointed out each edible plant: chokecherries, cranberries, gooseberries, blackberries, raspberries, violets, mints, chickweed, and all kinds of mushrooms. As we sat on boulders by the side of a stream, she told me stories handed down by her people—tales about Old Lady Nokomis, the owner of herbs, and her grandson Nanabush the shape-shifter, who changed at will from a tree trunk to an entire willow tree, then into a beaver, a deer, or a fluffy white cloud; stories about witches called "bear-walkers" who traveled about at night inside glowing balls of light.

My grandmother—whose name was also Nokomis—was raised and practiced as an herbalist and a midwife among Anglo-Canadians as well as with Ojibwe and Cree peoples. Her first husband, like herself, was a member of the group of healing shamans known in English as the Great Medicine Lodge, or in Ojibwe as the Midewi-win, meaning "mystic drum doings." She bore him five children before he died; then to support herself she traveled around the provinces of Saskatchewan and Manitoba visiting schools, churches, and community centers and teaching herbal healing, storytelling, and massage to anyone who was interested.

For "selling" her traditional knowledge, and for healing whites as well as natives, her relatives disapproved of her. My cousins called her a witch and ran whenever they caught sight of her long braid dangling over her basket, which overflowed with peculiar roots and leaves.

Even though she often dressed in black—she wore a long-sleeved blouse, ankle-length skirt, and black shawl with purple fringe—I knew she was neither a witch nor a sorcerer. Her medicine was good, not evil.

But now I've come to think perhaps she *was* a witch—in beaded moccasins. After all, women healers long ago were known as "witches," a word that came from Old English *witan*, which meant "to know" or "to be wise." Like my grandmother, witches were the wise women who had a special knack for revealing life's mysterious truths. I still remember her explaining that our thoughts and emotions overlap and intermingle, and that this mixing of head and heart connects us to future events hidden in the dark womb of time.

My grandmother was a nonconformist, and as her second husband she chose a Scots-Irish traveling salesman whose life she had saved after a moose-hunting accident. By treating his wound she earned not only his gratitude but also his deep affection, and together they had six children.

My mother was the youngest of them, and she had no interest in learning traditional ways. She left for college and afterward married my Irish-American father. A short time later I was born.

Despite my mother's attempt to distance herself from her heritage, I loved to spend summers with my grandmother. She greeted my curiosity about the spirit world with respect and encouraged my questions. And she asked me about my dreams.

DREAM PROPHECY

One day when I was four I told her a dream in which a tiny spotted turtle swam across the pond toward me, slithered out of the water, and plopped down beside me on a log. My dream was lucky, she explained, for Turtle was a spiritual being, a healing *manito*. He had picked me out and brought me a message: One day I would follow him as a healer.

That winter my parents moved to Washington, DC, where I was stricken with poliomyelitis. When my mother called her, my grandmother already knew that I was seriously ill and was preparing to come to my bedside. As I lay paralyzed inside the iron lung, she sat with me, singing songs and knitting socks and mittens for her other grandchildren.

She brought me a beautiful black and gold turtle amulet she had beaded, and hung it on the corner of the mirror suspended above my head. "Now, when you look into the mirror you will see your face with Turtle. And then you will know who you really are," she whispered (figure 1).

Eventually she convinced my parents that warm water, herbs, and gentle massage were a better treatment for my nonfunctioning muscles than immobilization in an iron lung. They finally agreed, demanded my release from my iron carapace, and brought me home to a regimen of daily swims, sweat baths, and my grandmother's herbal compresses and therapeutic massage, which sent bolts of electricity through my paralyzed limbs. In a few months I had recovered enough strength and flexibility to go to school, albeit with metal leg braces.

By the time I was a freshman at the University of California at

1. *Turtle* manito. *A totemic spirit being that symbolizes healing through proper communication among all living beings. Turtle is the most important icon for Ojibwe shamans who are initiated into the Great Medicine Lodge, also known as the Midewiwin, or "Mystic Drum Doings."*

Berkeley, my leg muscles had recovered so thoroughly that I had only the tiniest limp. I studied and enjoyed myself like any other college student, and tried not to think about my grandmother's lessons—until one night she appeared to me in a dream.

I was in a misty wood where long silken tendrils hung from the branches and hid my grandmother's figure. Suddenly she said, "Step where I step." And, although I could not see her clearly, I followed her purple-fringed shawl up and up into the chilly night sky. At dawn we arrived at a large, messy nest filled with serpent bones and bits of broken eggshell. She stirred the debris with a cedar stick till she found what she was looking for—an unbroken light blue speckled egg—and handed it to me, saying, "Here, take this egg; it will be your medicine power when I am gone."

The shimmering egg stunned me. My grandmother's image slowly faded into a fog lined with flickering green and purple lightning. As the mist lifted and the sun streaked across the morning sky, I awoke knowing that she had died. But she had passed on to me some of her energy, her medicine power.

That morning I stayed home from classes, waiting for the phone to ring. When the call came, announcing her death, I cried uncontrollably for hours. As a remembrance, I folded and cut out a paper loon, her clan totem and one of her most powerful guardian spirits, and placed it next to her picture on my desk. In the lonely months that followed, my grandmother often visited me in nighttime dreams and daytime visions. Sometimes she appeared as herself; at other times she appeared as a loon diving into a lake. Once she was a purple coneflower beckoning me to taste her.

A year later, she came to me in a dream as herself. Her long white hair was unbound. She was wrapped in a plaid Pendleton blanket over the shabby housedress she often had worn at the cabin when she wasn't expecting visitors. Smiling, she reached out and almost touched my hand. Then she looked at me and said, "You, my child, must always be *minobimaa tisiiwin* [seeking the good life] and never allow the wisdom of old Indian women to die out. Now, you are free to walk the medicine path."

Yet it would be many more years before I set foot in that direction again.

MAYAN SHAMANIC APPRENTICESHIP

Ten years after my grandmother's death I found myself in the Guatemalan highlands, a doctoral student in anthropology, married to another anthropologist. It was there that I once again entered the world of healers and shamans. I arrived with academic intentions. Like the good scientist I was trying hard to become, I spent my days studying the exterior layers of the K'iche' Maya, photographing and tape-recording as people burned incense at outdoor shrines and danced to the music of flutes and marimbas. In an attempt to understand a group of spirit seekers, I attended a midnight séance, warning the medium in advance that I intended to watch and not participate. That night during the unexpectedly impressive ceremony I smelled a mysterious rancid odor and saw translucent blue-green balls of lightning circle the room. I felt something like electricity enter my stomach and even heard what sounded like the voice of my own dead father. But I was determined to record the event with the distant coolness of a scientific observer.

Not long afterward, however, I came down with the flu. A long way from conventional Western medical help, and giving in to a documentary urge, I hired a local Mayan healer. Don Andrés arrived wearing a wrinkled blue serge suit that hung loosely on his slender frame. His delicate aquiline nose and rose-brown face gave him an air of gentle strength, and I knew he'd recently served as mayor of his town. He set about work at once, dispensing advice about herbs and grasses, and touching my cheeks and neck with his hot hands in order to break my fever. Then he used divining crystals to uncover the source of my illness, taking on another persona as he did so. Giggling strangely and speaking in two voices—one feminine and compassionate and another masculine and stern—he said it was my rude behavior at the shrines that had brought down the wrath of the Holy World. For that transgression I would die and so would my husband, Dennis.

Stunned and scared at this pronouncement, we fled to the capital the next day. After a couple of days of intense coughing I slowly improved, and we decided to return to the village. Perhaps there was something Don Andrés could do to counteract our apparent fate. Indeed, he and his wife, Doña Talín, who was also a shaman, agreed to help us. We would spend the next nine months meeting with them every day, coming to understand the way they saw their world. They started by having us recount a dream; then, heeding their own dreams and intuitions, they went on to suggest that Dennis and I might learn to practice as healers. Don Andrés and Doña Talín had to ask permission of their ancestors, and Dennis and I had to wrestle with our doubts, but in the days and weeks that followed we did indeed cross the invisible line between scholars learning about a culture and apprentices learning how to perform within it. We were no longer ethnographers interviewing subjects; they made us the students. We stopped asking questions and put aside our translating, and they began to pass along little teaching lessons.

Gradually, we learned to enter and control our dreams in a kind of alert sleeping, and to share, interpret, and complete those dreams together. We studied astronomy, hands-on healing, and herbalism. Don Andrés helped us recognize different types of shrines and to pray correctly. He and Doña Talín sent us off to gather flowers and incense and taught us to calculate the Mayan calendar, which was crucial for divination. He showed us how to embrace casual but meaningful coincidences of inner and outer events, thus transcending and improving our emotional and intuitive selves. Finally, Don Andrés taught us about the vital energy that suffuses the material universe; he trained us in bodily awareness and emotional attunement how to recognize the lightning in the body and the "speaking of blood," manifestations of our connection with the cosmos. In this way we would be able to increase our energy and use it to heal others and ourselves. Our teachers took us to other communities and sent us to other shamans for examinations and to see if they agreed that we had the potential to join their ranks.

Our training ended with a final sharing of dreams that culminated in a gorgeous three-day initiation ceremony, during which Dennis and I joined a large group of other celebrants who had undergone similar training and were either receiving initiation as shamans or else renewing their commitment to the shamanic path. A huge feast followed this.

The true "graduation" test for Dennis and me came a few days later. The son of our teachers had recently married, and his father-in-law mysteriously had become paralyzed and mute. Doctors' tests and treatments had had no effect. And Don Andrés and Doña Talín were similarly powerless; they were too close to the victim. Would we try to heal him? This would be the culmination of months of training in calendrical divination, visualization, the speaking of the blood, and the laying on of hands.

In a small room Dennis and I sat next to each other, opposite the sick man, with our new shaman's bundles laid out in front of us. Dennis sensed immediately that the sickness did not come from an animal or from the cosmos but was human work; it was a kind of witchcraft. As he voiced this aloud, the paralyzed man seemed to smile, the first sign of movement anyone had noticed.

Dennis got up and put his hands on the man's temples. He could feel the asymmetrical energy, how out of balance it was. Then I too stood up and described the energy I sensed. Suddenly the man began to speak, telling how Don Andrés and Doña Talín had deceived him about being Catholic, which they had never been. In a psycho-dynamic reaction his anger had gone deep into his body, freezing it. When he forgave the people who'd tricked him, his paralysis melted away. And our initiation was complete.

FEMININE TRADITIONS

What is the relevance of these stories to a lost feminine tradition in shamanism? How does my personal history help reclaim shamanic ministry and healing as legitimately feminine endeavors? I believe that after years of combining my shamanic training with my academic research I have emerged, in nearly equal measure, as an initiated shaman and a scientific expert. For the rest of this book I will rely on the skills of both those callings—argumentative intellectual reasoning and intuitive emotional reasoning—to make my case.

Over the next few hundred pages, I will present the evidence for the existence, importance, and power of women shamans. I will begin by summarizing what shamans do, then look back to their prehistoric beginnings as well as subsequent historical development. I will explain why women's particular physiology and biochemistry exquisitely equip them for the shaman's role. I will describe their transcendent shamanic roles as midwives, warriors, and prophets and the importance of gender shifting, the ability to embrace both masculine and feminine paths in shamanic healing. And I'll assess the revitalization of feminine shamanism around the globe today.

The pathway through this material is neither straightforward nor simple. But perhaps that is as it should be, for shamanic experience itself is neither straightforward nor simple. It is complex, mystical, and awe-inspiring, as befits the integration of the physical and spiritual worlds—two diverse and powerful realms where the shaman practices her calling.

TWO

Healing and the Seekers of Knowledge:

WHAT SHAMANS DO

THERE'S A CONNECTION between the midwifery and herbal healing practiced by my grandmother and the divination and healing of Don Andrés and his wife, Doña Talín. Their blend of physical, psychological, and spiritual healing has come to be called "integrative medicine" or "holistic healing."[1] Such healing depends on emotional and bodily contact between healer and patient. It emphasizes psychological and spiritual components in the causes and cures of sickness. Holistic healers recognize the innate healing mechanisms of the body and insist that an individual has a responsibility for restoring and maintaining health through behavioral, attitudinal, and spiritual balance.

Shamanism is the oldest spiritual healing tradition still in general use today. As a graduate student, I was taught that it began in North Asia more than forty thousand years ago and only later spread into the Americas with the migration of big-game hunters who crossed the low-lying land where the Bering Strait is now. A common point of origin, followed by geographic diffusion, is supposed to account for the similarity of Siberian and Alaskan shamanism.[2]

The problem is, as we'll see in later chapters, that Paleolithic sites on other continents, including Europe, Africa, and Australia, also show evidence of shamanic practices. The countervailing argument—that shamanism was independently reinvented over and over in many places—is supported by research in neuroscience and medical anthropology. These studies reveal that shamanic consciousness and healing practices are based on an understanding of the human immunological system and psychobiology rather than on a narrow set of culture-historical traits or patterns.[3]

HOW EFFECTIVE IS SHAMANIC HEALING?

From my grandmother's care and the work of Don Andrés and Doña Talín, I've seen firsthand the effectiveness of shamanic healing. Part of their success was due to knowledge of herbs and other plants, but something else was also involved. Shamanic healing uses the power of a patient's faith in the healer and the healing process. Like all healers, shamans employ hope, suggestion, expectation, and rituals that elicit a powerful placebo effect. This effect, which has been called "the doctor who resides within," arises from a direct connection between positive emotions and the biochemistry of the body. By reestablishing emotional and spiritual equilibrium a shaman strengthens the self-healing abilities of a patient.[4]

Research has shown that the use of songs, chants, prayers, spells, and music produce emotional states in a patient that affect the way the immune system responds to illness. Within ceremonial performances song and dance intertwine the sensory realms of color, odor, motion, and touch so as to shift participants from illness toward health. Shamans use metaphors—ways of thinking about one thing in terms of another—to describe a mythic world and to help the patient manipulate sensory, emotional, and cognitive information in a way that alters his or her perception of illness. Healers ritually enact their local system of myths and symbols and interpret the patient's condition within that system.[5]

As for the psychological dimension of shamans' work, the repetitive symbolism of their chants, and, in a number of traditions, the use of drums, gongs, bamboo tubes, or rattles helps restore a sense of order that replaces the chaos of illness. In many cultures shamans call up energy from the depths, creating a magical soundscape that awakens and unites. In this environment there's a release of unconscious feelings, in part through a transfer of negative emotions to the healer. Confession and forgiveness, which are central activities in shamanic healing, also elicit repressed memories that resolve conflicts. When Dennis and I worked at healing the paralyzed man as part of our initiation "test," we could see these forces at work. In general, shamans reestablish harmonious interpersonal relations, providing an emotional catharsis, or the remembering and re-experiencing of painful memories. It has been scientifically demonstrated that shamans who encourage their clients to publicly perform their dreams in poetry, song, and dance are 80 percent effective in healing. Psychiatrists, who use psychoanalytic techniques that encourage their clients to talk about, draw, paint, or describe their dreams in private, are only 30 percent effective.[6]

THE PERFORMANCE OF HEALING

Endorphins and other endogenous chemicals generated in the human brain are released into the bloodstream during healing. Pharmacologists and biochemists believe that these natural substances are as effective as Librium or Valium in their tranquilizing effects, controlling pain and anxiety as well as releasing joy and inducing other altered states of consciousness. The reduction of anxiety creates beneficial immunological effects that enhance the body's capacity for resistance and recovery. Entry into an altered state of consciousness gives a person an intimate contact with the spiritual world and in so doing reinforces a shared worldview, which alleviates mental and psychological suffering.[7]

A shamanic healer would nevertheless refer to what happens in quite different terms. Nearly thirty years ago I met Essie Parrish (figure 2), a Native American healer from the Pomo tribe of northern California. She was a woman of simple dignity with a warm, entrancing voice and a penetrating, insightful stare. She wore her long black hair pulled back loosely, flowing over a forest-green sweater on top of an ankle-length purple dress. I asked her how she had become a healer and how she knew what made people ill. In response, she recounted a dream from her youth.

In her dream, she said, she heard singing. As she slept, the song entered her and began singing itself inside her. When she woke up, the song kept singing itself inside her chest until she sang it out loud and found that it was beautiful.

In a later dream she sang the song as she walked in sunlit hills and valleys that were not of this world. She came to a crossroads

2. *Essie Parrish in her ceremonial dress covered with abalone amulets fashioned after ones she saw in dreams. She is holding doctoring staffs topped by the cocoons of monarch butterflies filled with seeds and pebbles. Whenever she moved, the abalone shimmered and tinkled as the seeds and pebbles softly rattled inside the butterfly cocoons, attracting and holding the spirits.*

and turned east along a narrow path between sparkling multi-colored flowers covered with monarch butterflies. When she reached the end, she saw silken strands woven into a web filled with tiny gemstones. As she looked closer she saw bits of turquoise, abalone, and jet swirling around a central white light. Then she heard a raspy noise, something like a cricket, and realized it was the sound of illness.

"Dangerous beings we call 'in-dwellers' are living inside our bodies like insects, like ants," she whispered. "When I sing I can see where they're hiding in their nests. I massage that area and scatter them in all directions."

Essie then went on to describe in detail the way she worked:

My middle finger is the one with the power. When I work with my hands it's just like when you cast for fish and they tug on your bait. The pain sitting somewhere inside feels like it's pulling your hand toward itself—you can't miss it. No way. It even lets you touch it!

I don't place my hands myself. It feels like someone, the disease perhaps, is pulling me. It's something like a magnet.

When power touches the pain you gasp. Your throat closes. You simply can't breathe. When your breath is shut off like that it feels as if your chest were paralyzed. If you should breathe while holding that pain, the disease could hide itself.

As you quiet your breathing you can feel the pain and your hand can take it out. But if you are afraid and your breathing is not shut off, you can't lift out the pain.

When I take it out you can't see it with your bare eyes. But I can see it. The disease inside a person is dirty. I suppose that's what white doctors call "germs," but we Indian doctors call it "dirty."

The palm of my hand also heals. But it doesn't work just anytime: only when I summon power. If there are people who are sick somewhere, my hands find them. Whenever someone thinks toward me, there on the tip of my middle finger it acts as if shot. If you touch electricity, you'll know what it's like.

Well, so that's my hand power. Now, for my throat power. I used it first for a young woman. I found the pain with my hand and sucked it out. Something like a bubble came up out of my throat. Just as it would if you blew up a big balloon, that's how it came from my mouth. Everyone there saw it. It had become inflated quite a lot when it floated from my mouth, like foaming soap bubbles.

Ever since then I've been sucking out illness. This place right here [pointing to the midpoint of her neck] is where the power enters my throat. The disease acts as fast as a lightning bolt striking a tree. It acts in a flash, shutting off the breath. One doesn't notice how long one holds one's breath. It's like being in what white people call a trance.

While the disease is coming to me, I'm in a trance. It speaks to me firmly saying, "This is the way it is. It is such and such a kind of disease. This is why that person is sick." But when I come out of the trance I no longer remember what the disease told me. So I ask my patients to bring along a friend to re-member what the disease said to me.

Well, so there you have my throat power and my hand power.

Healing, although it is extremely important, is only one part of a shaman's work. To understand how it fits within shamanic tradi-tions, let's take a closer look at how shamans think, what they do, and the wide range of roles they play in cultures around the world. These roles are hardly unfamiliar to us, though in modern society they are performed by many different kinds of specialists: natural scientists, who study the environment and its flora and fauna; astronomers, who plot the movements of the stars and planets;

historians, who chronicle the deeds of our forebears; and politicians and community leaders, who maintain the social order. And, of course, there are doctors, midwives, and psychologists, who attend to our bodies and minds, and priests, who minister to our spiritual needs.

SHAMANIC ROLES AND PERSPECTIVES

Despite the seemingly universal nature of shamanism, different cultures and individuals have elaborated distinctive forms of shamanic practice. Hunter-gatherers in Asia and North America, for example, call on spirit powers that are generally animals. Shamans in these societies must negotiate with them for good luck in hunting and to maintain the health of the group. Shamans in pastoral herding societies, such as the Mongols of Central Asia, tend to rely on ancestor spirits, both male and female. They call on them for healing and to ensure the fertility of humans and domesticated animals.[8]

Shamanism as a practice, however, has rarely become a formal social institution. Almost everywhere, shamanism was in the past and still is today a set of local activities and perspectives, rather than an ethnic or national institution. Thus, it is best to think in terms of shamanic activities and perspectives rather than about "shamanism" as an ideology or institution. Five fundamental features define shamanic perspectives or worldviews.

Shamanic practitioners share the conviction that all entities— animate or otherwise—are imbued with a holistic life force, vital energy, consciousness, soul, spirit, or some other ethereal or immaterial substance that transcends the laws of classical physics. Each member of this wondrous cosmos is a participant in the life energy that holds the world together. The Polynesian *mana*, Lakota *wakanda*, and Chinese Taoist *ch'i* are conceived of as powerful forces that permeate everything.

Shamans believe in a "web of life" in which all things are interdependent and interconnected; there is a cause-and-effect relationship between different dimensions, forces, and entities of the cosmos. In order to heal, Inuit shamans may imaginatively assume the form of a bird that brings celestial messages.

Shamans organize this complex reality by saying that the world is constructed of a series of levels connected by a central axis in the form of a world tree or mountain. Many Siberian tribes speak of three, seven, or nine sky worlds above the earth upon which humans live, all resting on a disc supported by a giant fish. The Buryats of southern Siberia portray a heaven with ninety-nine provinces, each of which consists of physical landscapes that mirror an earthly landscape, with the roof of each one being the floor of the next one. Shamans travel to these worlds moving up or down through these cosmic levels and sometimes sideways into alternative worlds upon the earth.[9]

Societies everywhere designate certain individuals as taking on the role of "shaman" for their group. Such people have the capacity to understand and change events in the ordinary world. They can accomplish this during normal waking consciousness, as female *machi*, or shamans, in Chile do by climbing a cinnamon-tree altar and playing a frame drum. More typically they enter an alternative state of consciousness by fasting, undertaking a vision quest, engaging in lucid dreaming, or ingesting hallucinogens. Huichol shamans in northwestern Mexico eat peyote, a source of *kupüri* or "life energy," in order to divine the future and heal family problems and illnesses.[10]

Shamans recognize extraordinary forces, entities, or beings whose behavior in an alternative reality affects individuals and events in our ordinary world. They understand that actions or rituals performed in ordinary reality can lead to effects in the alternative sphere. To gain information about events in alternative reality and their effects on this world shamans often read signs such as clouds, tea leaves, birds, and animal entrails, as well as abalone, cowry, and other shells. A proper analysis of these events and objects unveils a hidden, deeper, subtler cosmic message invisible to a casual observer.

THE SHAMANIC CALLING

Such gifted individuals may be selected through inspiration or heredity, that is, they may receive a call directly from the spirits or they may learn through family teachings. Through their connections to specific ancestral spirits and family shrines, songs, prayers, rituals, and healing techniques, hereditary shamans often have an authority that inspirational shamans lack. In fact, inspirational shamans deeply respect hereditary shamans and often approach them seeking recognition and consecration. Sometimes the two kinds of callings are combined.[11]

In Guatemala there is an ancient tradition of shamanic knowledge and practice that is passed down within families. But a person cannot be initiated as a shaman unless she or he has also received a spiritual call during dreams, waking visions, or illnesses. In Momostenango, the Mayan community in which I undertook my own training, hereditary shamanism is transmitted through the male line to women and men alike, or ideally to a couple. Thus, Dennis and I, after our selection for training through dreams and illness, were both adopted into the patrilineage of one of our teachers, Don Andrés. As we learned after our consecration, he adopted not only us but all of our family members (both living and dead) into his lineage.

A combination of heredity and inspiration also occurs in the northern and western regions of Mongolia, where many shamans can trace their calling back through their mother's clan in a continuous unbroken line for nine or more generations.[12] One of the most respected of all living Mongolian shamans, Byambadorj Dondog, traces his lineage back to the twelfth-century shamans of Chinggis Khan's mother's clan. In 1999, when I talked with him, he told me that at the time of his birth a strange event portended his entire life: a snake nearly two meters long entered his family's *ger* (circular tent) and came right up to where his mother was sitting, holding the baby in her arms. Later she told him that this was a sign that he was destined to become the clan shaman, since snakes are one of the forms that members of her clan assume during shamanic séances.

In many areas of the world, an animal or spirit that appears in a dream or vision chooses a shaman. Among my grandmother's people, the Ojibwe of Canada, for example, young children are sent into the woods to encounter spirits. They sit all alone "singing in their hearts," humming silently to the spirits to contact them and call them forth. If they are successful, a bird, deer, or other spirit may notice them and teach them natural wisdom, including sacred healing. Eventually tribal elders take these children on as apprentices and share the knowledge they themselves have gathered during a lifetime of careful observation.

At the heart of shamanic practice is the active pursuit of knowledge. This takes many forms: the understanding of animal and human behavior; the identification of medicinal plants and their uses; the hands-on healing knowledge of bone setting, massage, and midwifery; and the empathic knowledge of the human psyche. Through calendrical study, divination, and prophecy shamans seek knowledge of the future, and through recitations of myths, epics, charms, spells, songs, and the genealogies of previous shamans they pass along knowledge of the past and of the spirit world. And since shamans everywhere wish to know more than they have experienced in their everyday waking lives, they may extend their wisdom through dream journeys or psychedelic trips that provide "a thousand years of human living rolled into a single day."[13]

While shamans are primarily concerned with the maintenance or restoration of equilibrium in individuals, no shaman exists without a culture or subculture to interact with. They address the community's needs and often overlap with priests and prophets. In North Asia many shamans take on priestly duties when they make horse sacrifices during public gatherings. In Mesoamerica priest-shamans practice a form of divination with corn kernels or seeds that link their clients to the cosmos by way of a sacred calendar (figure 3).

Compared with their peers, shamans excel in insight, imagination,

3. *Oxomoco and Cipactonal, the first shamans. In Aztec and Mayan mythology the first shamans were an elderly couple. In this scene from a sixteenth-century Aztec book, they are creating time itself. The wife (at left) divines by casting corn kernels, while her husband (at right) holds an incense burner in his right hand and a bloodletting instrument in his left. On their backs they wear gourds filled with tobacco, signifying their status as priests.*

fluency in language, and knowledge of cultural traditions. That knowledge lies at the heart of shamanism is indicated by indigenous terms for shamans from cultures all over the globe. The term *shaman* itself comes from the Evenki language of Siberia and means "the one who knows." Other general words for shaman, such as Finnish *tietäjä,* Japanese *munusu,* Bella Coola *kusiut,* Nahuatl *tlamatiquetl,* and Quichua *yachaj,* all have the same meaning.[14]

Other terms for shamans refer to key characteristics of their public performances, including Yurok *kegey,* "one who sits or meditates as a practice," Sakhá *oyuun,* "to jump, leap, or play," Buryat *khatarkha,* "to dance or trot like a reindeer," and Huichol *mara'akame,* "singer."[15] Because shamans are able to prophesy, to see and know things that ordinary people cannot, in the far north among the Innu and the Inuit they are called *wabinu,* "seeing person," *elik,* "one who has eyes," *tarak'ut inilgit*, "those with eyes that see in the dark," and *an-gakut*, "seeing with closed eyes." In K'iche' Maya *ajq'ij*, "day keeper," refers to their use of the calendar for divination.[16]

THE PRACTICE OF DIVINATION

There are many systems of divination worldwide. Forms such as tarot, astrology, and palm reading are available today on the streets of our largest cities. In all cases the technique aids in decision making by looking at a current, past, or future situation or problem in light of various types of knowledge. Diviners, like shamans (most shamans practice divination, but in some cultures there are diviners who are not also shamans), are recruited by divine election through birth, sickness, and dreams. Their initiation usually involves a marriage to a spirit spouse. They ask questions and transmit and interpret the answers, called oracles, but the way this is done varies greatly between cultures. Divination can be an individual act, for example, when it involves the interpretation of dreams or the observation of omens. More often, however, it involves a dialogue between a diviner and an audience member or client.

Divination in primal cultures takes a number of forms: gazing into water, clouds, and crystals; the casting of lots, or sortilege; the reading of natural omens; the use of hallucinogenic drugs; and the practice of remembering and interpreting dreams. In fact, divination often combines several of these techniques, perhaps starting with the use of a mechanical procedure that is then combined with visualization to ensure the necessary inward shift in understanding.

For example, K'iche' Mayan day keepers, who practice as diviners, begin by placing groups of seeds and crystals in rows that follow the grid of the 260-day Mayan calendar. They interpret the meanings of the days as they go. Throughout this process they listen for *kacha' uk'ik'el*, "the speaking of the blood," which is a manifestation of the connection between individual bodies and the forces of the cosmos. They ask questions of the client based on the calendar and the movement of *koyopa,* or sheet lightning, that they feel in their own bodies.

The voices in which these diviners address their gods and transmit their answers back are thick with figures of speech. By contrast, diviners speak to their clients in mundane tones. They start with simple questions and later offer interpretations that fill gaps in the client's understanding of the past, present, or future. It is said that when both members of a married couple are trained as diviners and each seeks an answer to the client's question, their combined pronouncements shed more light than those of a diviner working alone. I learned this firsthand in our practice of calendrical divination.

Even though we mastered this technique I had my doubts that we could ever acquire the gift of "the speaking of the blood." Strange as it may seem, not only were Dennis and I able to learn to experience and work with this gift during our time in Guatemala, but in the nearly thirty years since our initiations, we have kept this ability and continue to use it wherever we live. We learned that our bodies are microcosms of the natural world, with their own mountains, plains, lakes, and winds. We also learned to feel how sheet lightning moves both outside, in the atmosphere, and inside, in our own bodies. When we had learned how to interpret these internal movements, as well as count out the days of the Mayan calendar, we were able to divine both for ourselves and for our clients.

When diviners talk about their work, they point to the way different kinds of knowing—inductive, intuitive, and interpretative reasoning, for example—all overlap. As they talk to their clients, they filter the reality of everyday life through symbolic prisms of images and actions. Jumbled ideas, metaphors, and symbols suggest various interpretations that slowly give way to an ordered sequence and to more limited possibilities. Finally, through the dialogue of diviner and client these interpretations crystallize into an unambiguous understanding of the causes of the problem and of what is needed to respond to and change it.

After divining, the shaman must address the problems that were uncovered. This is where the shaman may become a trickster.

Through puns and clever jokes, shamans distract their clients, opening them up to participating in the hard work of admitting some responsibility for their problems. If a patient recognizes her part in creating an illness, for example, she can empower herself to relieve it. In shamanism as in other aspects of life, humor heals.

THE NATURE OF SHAMANISM

Shamanism consists of both a healing practice and a religious sensibility, with startling similarities between shamanistic ideas and activities in cultures as far apart as Siberia, the Amazon basin, Southeast Asia, and Nepal. Birth and death provide key actions and metaphors within these shamanic systems, and novice shamans are said "to be born to" or "to die into" the profession. Later, in their subsequent practices, they may assist at actual births and deaths.

In the distant past there probably were purely shamanist communities, but today shamanism is only one spiritual strand mixed together with others, including, in various degrees, Buddhism, Christianity, Islam, Hinduism, and various local folk religions. Because it lacks an institutional framework and a central figure—there is no Dalai Lama or Pope—shamanism appears, disappears, and reappears in varied historical and political settings. Flexible and innovative, shamanic ideas have been adapted in the remotest jungles and deserts on earth, in the courts of Mayan kings and Chinese emperors, among intellectuals in post-Soviet Siberia, and contemporary pagans in Europe, North America, and Australia.

THREE

Handprints on a Cave Wall:

WOMEN SHAMANS IN PREHISTORY

THE ROOTS OF shamanic activity extend deep into the past, and so too do signs that women have been important, active participants. The skeleton found in Dolní Věstonice, described in chapter one, is convincing evidence of prehistoric women shamans, but it is not the only material evidence. In addition to bones and accompanying artifacts, archaeologists have also found talismanic clay figurines and ancient images of shape-shifting women or women in trances painted or engraved on the walls of caves.

In Siberia the oldest graves of shamans thus far excavated date to the Neolithic period, from between 1700 and 1300 BCE. The earliest skeleton found is that of a young woman wearing two anthropomorphic mammoth-bone figures on her apron. These carvings were attached to her clothing where shamans today among the Yakut, Ket, and Chukchi place carved antler and whalebone icons that personify their guardian spirits. Another recently discovered Neolithic woman shaman's grave, located in the Sakhá Republic, in northeast Siberia, contained several bone ornaments consisting of bird-headed individuals, like those painted on nearby rocks and on local shamans' drums.[1]

Another important archaeological discovery, this time near the Bering Strait, in the province of Chukotka, revealed the remains of an ancient woman shaman. Among the nearly one hundred graves perfectly preserved by the permafrost was a single elaborate stone, wood, and whalebone tomb that contained the skeleton of an elderly woman. The anthropologists who made the discovery—Dorian Sergeev, a native archaeologist, and Sergei Arutiunov, a Russian archaeologist—identified many objects in the tomb that were used in women's activities, as well as a death mask and objects related to healing, dancing, and other shamanic rituals. They quickly realized that the female skeleton, together with the shamanic grave goods in the tomb, indicated that she was a shaman. In the report, which they posted on the Web site of the Arctic Studies Center of the Smithsonian's National Museum of Natural History in 2002, they noted that "Siberian shamans were frequently women, who were also known to be very powerful in spiritual life throughout the northern cultures."[2]

These discoveries of female skeletons buried together with shamanic artifacts continue to surprise many Western scholars as well as the general public because it has been assumed for so long that shamanism was primarily a masculine vocation. This misconception has been sustained, in part, by the practice of assigning sex to bones by the shape of the pelvis, the size of the skull, and the weight and dimensions of limb bones. The problem with this method is that there is great variation in size and weight within the population of each sex. Ambiguous bones, including those of strong or robust females, were often designated as male. At some sites as many as 80 percent of all skeletal remains were considered by Western archaeologists to be male, which is an improbable finding that hints at the scale of the bias. If we add this distortion to the old assumption that a shamanic burial would be a masculine one, we can see that a woman shaman with a robust body had little chance of being correctly identified.[3]

In the past, most of the scientists sexing skeletal materials were male, and as a result evolutionary theories about the origins of human culture had a tendency to emphasize males. But thanks to the emergence of new technologies such as chemical analysis of the mitochondrial DNA that comes through the female line (mtDNA), and an increase in the number of women scientists, especially paleo-anthropologists, progress in the proper sexing of bones has begun to occur. Today, many of our new fossil heroes are turning out to be female.[4]

ICE AGE FIGURINES

Among the earliest indications of women's possible shamanic practice are palm-size feminine figurines. Approximately two hundred little statues of nude women with faceless, downturned heads and large hips or buttocks have been discovered all across Eurasia, from the Pyrenees to Siberia. Ivory, antler, clay, and soft stone figurines dating from the Ice Age were found hidden under rocks in caves and rock shelters, as well as in wall niches and pits near hearths. Despite the variations in their appearance, they were all labeled "Venus figurines," after the Roman goddess of love.

Some authors argue that these figurines were intimately connected to "ancient fertility cults." When the Venus of Willendorf (figure 4, left) was found near Krems, Austria, in 1908, her carved limestone body still had traces of red ocher rubbed into the stone. With her woven hat or hairdo, large hips, full buttocks, and voluminous breasts, she was said to send a compelling sexual message to men. "Those areas of her body which are shown in all their rounded perfection are precisely the areas which would be most important in preliminary phases of love-making, that is the belly, buttocks, thighs, breasts, and shoulders; while the lower legs, lower arms, feet, and hands are withered to nothing." Others have described these "Venuses" as the world's first erotica: Pleistocene pinups, or Playboy centerfold girls.[5]

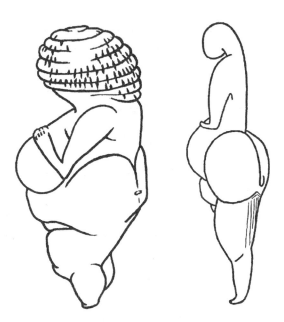

4. *Drawings of the Venus of Willendorf (left) and the Venus of Lespugue (right). Both of these figurines date back to the Upper Paleolithic.*

Descriptions of these figurines as fertility symbols, erotic amulets, or sexual playthings manufactured and used by men reveal the often unconscious biases of previous generations. The assumption is that female bodies were of interest only insofar as they catered to masculine interests, and that women were merely passive spectators in the creative mental life of prehistory. According to this view ancient women had no culture of their own. Instead, they existed primarily for the sexual titillation and reproductive use of males.[6]

Other authors, however, have interpreted these figurines as representations made by women for the use of women. Among those who did so was the Lithuanian archaeologist Marija Gimbutas. She argued that since hundreds of feminine figurines and only a handful of masculine figurines had been found, the primordial deity for our prehistoric ancestors was female.[7]

When I met and talked with her in her office at the University of California in Los Angeles in the early 1980s, Gimbutas was at the height of her career as an archaeologist. Her work had spanned more than thirty years of research, including the excavation and analysis of thousands of artifacts from all over Europe, during which she argued for the existence of a single unified prehistoric religion of the Great Goddess. This religion, she said, reflected a feminine tradition; it emphasized technologies that nourished human lives instead of trying to dominate nature. She refused to label warrior societies as "civilizations," asserting that the generative basis of any civilization lies in its degree of artistic creation, nonmaterial values, and freedom—including a balance of power between the sexes.[8]

Beginning in the 1990s many of her interpretations and theories were sharply criticized by archaeologists, women as well as men, feminists as well as nonfeminists. But her research and publications called attention to pervasive androcentrism—and, at times, even outright sexism—within the field of archaeology. Her work encouraged researchers to pay attention to sex and gender, both within the archaeological record and in the interpretation of material culture. Thanks to her pioneering work, gender has emerged today as an important topic in mainstream archaeology.[9]

Among the nonsexist interpretations of Venus figurines were those of Alexander Marshack. He suggested that naked female statuettes may have been connected to lunar menstrual calendars and that they could also have been used as teaching tools during female coming-of-age rituals. Other scholars, however, noted that since these artifacts are actually rather diverse in shape, pose, and bodily detail, they represent different life stages, such as childhood, the beginning of puberty, and pregnancy.[10]

At the Neolithic site of Kephala, in Greece, female figurines found in graves have been interpreted as territorial markers reinforcing ancestral ties. Those found near hearths in association with spinning and grinding tools were connected with women's work and children's play. Figurines may also have been used as charms to fulfill wishes by magic. This might explain the large number of poorly made and badly damaged figurines found in prehistoric trash mounds. Once a wish had been made, the figurine could have been given to a child as a plaything and discarded after it broke.[11]

Female figurines have recently taken on an important role in European culture. The Venus of Willendorf has even become a national symbol. I learned this firsthand when I was in Austria: whenever she is moved from the Naturhistorisches Museum in Vienna, where she is housed, to another museum for an exhibition she is guarded by tanks!

Yet another interpretation of these Paleolithic figurines is that since many of them are anatomically correct—when considered from the perspective of a woman looking down upon her own naked body—they may have helped women prepare for childbirth (as in our Lamaze classes). They might have also functioned as teaching models, used for instructing young girls, pregnant women, and novice midwives.[12]

I would like to suggest one other theory: these figurines might have belonged to women shamans whose specialized skills included midwifery. As we will see, in many areas of the world midwives are divinely elected; they readily enter into both trance and ecstatic states in order to practice as healers. Consider the Venus of Lespugue (figure 5). This ivory sculpture, just six inches tall, is one of the most elegant Paleolithic figurines ever discovered. She was found in what is now France and is believed to be of late Gravettian manufacture (20,000 BCE).

The many long parallel serrations below her buttocks resemble the string aprons pregnant and menstruating women wore during the prehistoric period. Similar impressions of twined ropes made of plant fiber were pressed into clay figurines found in the woman shaman's grave at Dolní Věstonice. (That was significant for another reason, too: until their discovery it had been assumed that the only Paleolithic weaving had been done with animal sinews, not plant material.) The parallel marks on the Venus of Lespugue also resemble elements of North Asian shamans' clothing dating from the seventeenth through twentieth centuries (chapter four). These engravings show ropes that hang from the shamans' cloaks, twisted with bird feathers and animal fur.[13]

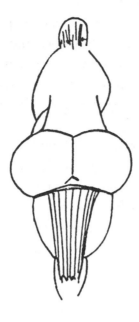

5. *The Venus of Lespugue, with long dangling string ropes resembling those still worn today by many shamans in Siberia and Mongolia.*

PALEOLITHIC CAVE PAINTINGS

On every continent there are caves, rock shelters, and boulders that preserve ancient carvings and paintings with shamanistic associations. Yet while much has been made of a bird-headed masculine figure with an erect penis painted on the walls of the famous cave at Lascaux, France, several clearly feminine shamanic figures from the same time horizon, found in nearby caves in the department of Lot, were simply ignored.[14]

Engraved in the clay ceiling of the cave at Pech-Merle, for example, are drawings of nude female bodies in profile (figure 6). They appear to be pregnant women dancing. The woman on the right seems to be wearing an avian mask, or she may be transforming herself into a bird. Six other figures, similar to these two, were painted in red ocher or hematite on walls in the same cave. Also on the walls and floors near these paintings and engravings were dozens of small

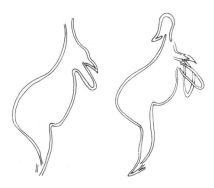

6. *Two of the feminine shamanic engravings found on the walls and ceiling of the cave at Pech-Merle, just east of Cahors in the department of Lot, France. The pregnant woman on the right appears to be undergoing shamanic shape-shifting into a bird.*

handprints and footprints whose shapes identify them as belonging to women and children. Perhaps the nude feminine bodies were painted and engraved by women with their children in tow.

Amusingly, these pregnant figures were originally identified as "bison" by their male discover. Later, André Leroi-Gourhan, a well-known scholar of the Paleolithic, reinterpreted them as interchangeable symbols of bison and women. The bison interpretation was dropped only when similar engravings, found at Gebel Silsilah in Nubia, were interpreted as women.[15]

Of course, it's difficult to understand and appreciate ancient European paintings and engravings without a cultural context. There is, however, some circumstantial evidence that rituals associated with European Paleolithic cave art may have survived until as late as 1458, since Pope Calixtus III forbade Spaniards "to perform rites in the cave with the horse pictures." The connection with horses is important; we know that in an area from Europe to Siberia, horses served as shamans' guardian spirits. And shamanic flight is widely expressed as a horse's gallop, taking the rider on an ecstatic journey to other worlds.[16]

To get at the meanings and uses of ancient engravings I have found it helpful to examine rock art traditions in Africa and Australia that are roughly the same age as those in Europe. These non-European traditions have the advantage of being linked with societies that have known historical connections to the cave art. In some places the practice of rock painting and carving continues to this day.[17]

Ancient African rock art was once thought to have diffused from Paleolithic Europe through North Africa and down the continent to South Africa. However, datable artifacts found in a southern Namibian rock shelter show that the most ancient African rock art extends back more than ten thousand years and was contemporary with some European Paleolithic rock art. Thus the two art forms had independent origins.

In the area of South Africa where Upper Paleolithic murals are located, most of the indigenous people, known as San (or for some years as Bushmen), were forced out nearly a century ago. Fortunately, Wilhelm Bleek, an early explorer and linguist, copied a number of rock paintings in the 1870s. He later talked with his linguistic consultants about the drawings as a way of eliciting words in their language. Their interpretations of the rock art have proven to be invaluable.[18]

In a drawing from the cave at Mangolong (figure 7), we see four people leading a "water cow" along by a rope attached to its nose. Taking it across open country in this way was thought by one of Bleek's San consultants to encourage rain to extend as far as possible. According to another consultant the two figures nearest the animal are "water's medicine men." Each of them carries a tortoiseshell box with dangling strings, filled with aromatic herbs that pacify "angry rain." This consultant also pointed out that there were two women leading the water cow, one of them wearing a cap on her head.[19]

That these four people might have been shamans is indicated by the collective ritual act of leading a rain-bringing animal, which can be harnessed only by shamans, over the parched land. One of the men and one of the women are wearing caps with antelope ears; this indicates their intimate relationship with this power animal. An indigenous woman who discussed the painting with Bleek said that a

7. *African Paleolithic painting from the cave at Mangolong, South Africa, showing four shamans leading a water cow by a rope attached to its nose across open country to bring rain. Two women shamans are in the lead, followed by two men shamans carrying herbs in tortoiseshell boxes.*

springbok would follow her whenever she was wearing her antelope cap. And because rain-bringing animals can be seen only in visions, this painting was very likely made by a shaman. Given the large number of game animals painted on the walls of South African caves, early researchers had assumed that the painters had to be male hunters. The problem with this interpretation is that in hunting and gathering societies, such as the San of South Africa, there are no strongly gendered roles. Trance dances—involving an altered state of consciousness arising during dancing, clapping, and chanting— are communal events that still take place four or more times per month around an open fire. The participants today include most adult family members, both male and female, who are currently gathered near a water hole. Just over one-third of all healing shamans among the San today are women.[20]

According to one woman, "the spirits' hearts will be happy if we women sing passionately, and sickness will be kept away." A well-known San woman shaman, by the name of Wa Na, volunteered that "there are women healers all over, in Chumkwe, in Xaixai, and elsewhere. The women are stronger healers than the men . . . in my case; I was created in a different way, according to my *n/um* [boiling energy]. When I start healing, I first see the thing that is going to kill a person. Then I heal that."[21]

Another elegant mural discovered in Tanzania, East Africa, shows three slender individuals wearing short skirts (figure 8). Paleo-anthropologist Mary Leakey, who was the first European to record this painting, believed "the general appearance and attitudes of these figures is feminine and we assume they are women although they are not shown with breasts."[22] That they are indeed female is again suggested by San trance dances during which women sing and clap their hands while men dance. The figure on the left, holding what appear to be wooden clap sticks, wears the shamanic antelope-ear cap. The woman in the center holds a forked stick in her left hand; it was probably used as a musical instrument, and the three lines coming from her mouth indicate that she may be singing. On the far right the woman appears to be clapping her hands. The proportions of each of these figures suggest a common perception of people in trances, who report feeling as if their bodies were elongated.[23]

A third woman shaman explained that whenever she participates in trance dancing her energy heats up: "it boils." She then leaves the dance, finds an elephant, and is cradled in its tusks. Her companions say she walks away from the other singers, dances around the

8. *Paleolithic cave painting from Tanzania of three women singing and clapping sticks. This activity still takes place today among San women in South Africa.*

campfire, and moves off into the shadows. There she experiences her visionary encounter with the elephant.

It could not be clearer that the encounters with animals that give rise to rock art need not be the work of male hunters, as was once thought. These meetings can occur—for women as well as men—during an altered state of consciousness. Thus healers of either sex may have painted the murals.[24]

FOUR

Summoning Whales, Serpents, and Bears:

WOMEN SHAMANS IN HISTORY

POINT HOPE, ALASKA, is a collection of frame houses at the edge of the Bering Strait, a traditional Iñupiat-speaking village that has been occupied continuously for more than two millennia. Every year at the opening of the bowhead whale-hunting season, an important ritual takes place. A boat captain's wife walks out all alone and lies down on the ice. She points her head toward the village and spreads her legs wide, toward the open sea. The hunters follow right behind her, pulling their whaling boat on a sled. When they reach the ocean, they launch their craft and paddle out into the chilly water.

Suddenly they turn around and race inland toward the woman. Her husband leaps from the boat, runs ashore, and harpoons her, touching her neck through the hood of her parka. After a moment she slowly rises and heads back toward the village. With this act she undergoes a symbolic transformation—from whale as prey to the spirit of whale as honored guest. And during her long walk home, it is said a whale's tail emerges from her mouth. As Edith Turner, an ethnographer at the University of Virginia, put it, "Now she is in a shamanic state of unity with the whale."[1]

Back home the woman sits and listens for the whale to surface. When the men harpoon the animal, she senses it, and she returns to the edge of the ocean. As the catch is landed, she kneels next to the whale, prays silently, and helps to butcher it. Afterward she receives her share: the heart, tail flukes, and flippers. These parts are considered the "essence of whaleness," which she intuitively understands and shares in.

Here as in other hunting cultures, animals are thought to share their spiritual essence with humans. Their heads are severed from their bodies in order to release their inner spirits, or souls, into the wild, where they will be reborn. As part of this process, the hunters return the whale's head to the water, shouting, "Come back!" They say the whale has gone to grow its new parka, to "reflesh" itself so that it can return once more for harvesting.

It is the wife of a hunter who lures and butchers the whale, shares its meat among the people, and releases its soul. Only an animal that was pleased by her past generosity will offer itself up to her husband. The man acknowledges his wife's important role by saying, "I'm not the great hunter, my wife is!"[2]

If prehistoric rock and cave paintings imply that women were involved in animal rituals millennia ago, modern ethnographic accounts such as this one, reported in 1996, and the drawings of women shamans show that women today still perform important shamanic hunting roles in hunter-gatherer cultures (figure 9). Why this has been so difficult to acknowledge will be examined in a later chapter. For now, let's just note that the women who carry out the rituals are as important as the men who hunt. These women truly understand the spiritual unity between humans and animals. With their perception and celebration of the "humanity" of whales and other animals, they, too, are powerful hunting shamans whose job it is to maintain the important relationship between human beings and the extrahuman.

9. *An Inuit couple, both shamans, dance in their spring camp while their sons (at lower right) are out hunting. As they dance they are lifted off the ground by their guardian spirits in the form of flowers. While the man beats his caribou-skin drum, the woman sings. In her song she remembers her first successful hunt many years ago, when she killed a wolf (at upper right) and a bird (in front of her). The people behind the man are spectators.*

HISTORICAL SOURCES FOR WOMEN IN SHAMANISM

As we move into the historical era, we're lucky enough to have written texts chiseled in stone and penned as epics glorifying women religious leaders and healers in ancient societies. Karen Jo Torjesen of Claremont Graduate University has found a great deal of historical evidence that women prophets, priests, and bishops in the early

Christian Church were suppressed by the later Church. Likewise, I have found abundant evidence of powerful women shamanic healers and prophets who were later eclipsed by male shamans. These records also give us some feel for who these women leaders were and what they did, but we must be willing to pay heed to the evidence and cast aside our preconceptions about the kinds of societies they lived in and the extent of their power. There have long been prominent women shamans all over the world; however, in some male-centered societies women have been disadvantaged by a lack of formal initiations. The ethnographer Gilbert Herdt pointed out that in New Guinea, among the Sambia, a number of women managed to become great shamans despite the fact that they were prohibited from performing in all-male religious ceremonies. They were especially skilled in prophecy, diagnosis, catharsis, and healing.[3]

In societies where females enjoyed high social status, women shamans were as powerful as men, sometimes even more so. The sixteenth-century *Jesuit Relations* described a woman shaman among the Montagnais-Naskapi in Canada who took over from a man who could not communicate with the spirits. And in another case a shaman exhorted her people not to be timid in battle. When a Jesuit priest tried to silence her, she drew a knife and threatened to kill him if he interfered. He left immediately.[4]

In many ancient cultures—as is true today—the duties and social position of shamans varied greatly. Some were responsible for calendrical and astronomical observation and knowledge: they foretold eclipses of the sun and moon and indicated favorable and unfavorable days for business transactions or military engagements. In other cultures they were political leaders, spiritual and empirical healers, and prophets, and sometimes they even practiced as priests.[5] Most important, shamans performed these tasks not only in decentralized social and religious organizations, but also in complex, highly centralized states, where rulers were considered sacred.

The earliest written record of a royal woman shaman in the Americas is that of Ix Balam K'ab'al Xook, or Lady of the Jaguar

Shark Lineage. This Mayan noblewoman lived in the ancient city of Yaxchilán, in what is now Chiapas, Mexico. When I first saw her portrait, which was carved into a stone lintel above the central doorway of a temple shortly after her husband's inauguration as king (figure 10), I was struck by the intricacy of the image and its importance. Lady Jaguar Shark is a beautiful woman in Mayan terms, with a large, aristocratic nose, slightly receding chin, and almond eyes. Her gown is brocaded with flowers enclosing small figures of woven mats. The four-petal blossoms represent both feminine blood and

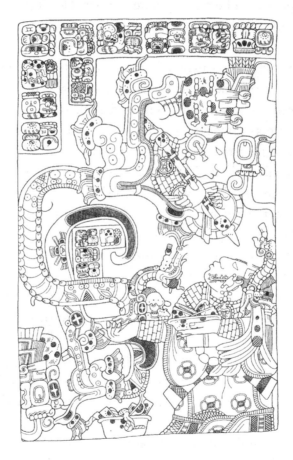

10. *Lady Jaguar Shark and the serpent. From a long and convoluted genealogy (known from other inscriptions at the site) we learn that she was the first wife of Itzamnaaj Balam or "True Magician Jaguar," who ruled Yaxchilán from October 16, 681, until he died on June 13, 742 CE.*

the cave entrance to the watery underworld that shamans visit during their soul journeys. The mat sign at the center of each flower symbolizes royal birth and political authority. The striped sash tied around her waist indicates that she performed bloodletting.[6]

Other evidence indicates that she may also have been an astronomer. However, the role for which she apparently wished to be remembered was that of a shaman who sacrificed blood from her tongue in order to conjure the divine presence of an ancestor. (Just as her husband let blood from his penis, she let blood from her tongue, which symbolizes the clitoris.) This ritual action is visually represented by a bowl containing an open book with jaguar-skin covers, its pages spattered with the blood she drew from her tongue. After bleeding herself she was rewarded with a vision of a celestial being wearing a jaguar-skin headdress and holding a shield and a spear, emerging from the mouth of a two-headed serpent.

The serpent has the markings of a Central American rattlesnake (*Crotalus durissus tzabcan*). For the Maya, snakes embodied the cavernous passages that connect the surface of the earth with the underworld and ultimately with the sky. Since the words for snake and sky are almost the same—*kan* and *kaan* (or *chan* and *chaan,* depending on the Mayan language)—serpents personified the sky. In Lady Jaguar Shark's hieroglyphic text she identifies herself with the Mother of the Gods, who opens the sacred membrane between the heavens and the earth. From her burning blood rises the spirits of ancestors and political power.[7]

Resting on top of her right wrist is a monkey skull combined with a small replica of the snake that rises before her. What exactly is this object? It may be her personal talisman as a shaman, which helps her conjure her warrior-ancestor. Monkey deities were the ancient Mayan patrons of art, writing, and mathematics, so the simian skull is an appropriate symbol for Lady Jaguar Shark's artistic and literary abilities, just as the snake, with its connections to the sky, refers to her ability as an astronomer. However else we interpret this image, it is clearly a powerful representation of this woman's shamanic knowledge.[8]

On the other side of the globe, we also find much evidence of women shamans. The ancient Chinese texts called the "Nine Songs" consist of women's chants to the heavenly spirits. The songs are enticements that use sexual metaphors to invite possession. The opening lines of the chant "To the Mountain Spirit" are as follows:

It seems there is someone over there,
in that fold of the hill,
Clad in creepers, with a belt of mistletoe.
He is gazing at me, his lips parted in a smile.
"Have you taken a fancy to me?
Do I please you with my lovely ways?"
Driving red leopards, followed by stripy civets,
Chariot of magnolia, banners of cassia,
Clad in stone-orchid, with belt of asarum,
I go gathering sweet herbs to give to the one I love.
I live in a dark bamboo grove, where I never see the sky.

The shaman is addressing a male deity when she says, "Have you taken a fancy to me? / Do I please you with my lovely ways?" And the line "I live in a dark bamboo grove" refers to the small bamboo structures in which Chinese women have conducted their séances for centuries.[9]

Shamanism became an official state religion in Korea during the Three Kingdoms period, 57 BCE to 668 CE. And a noble Korean woman was discovered as the major occupant of the largest and most elaborate of the royal tombs constructed during the Old Silla kingdom. Five pairs of gold bracelets, gold earrings, three necklaces, and a gold belt adorned her body. She was wearing one of the most magnificent pure gold crowns ever found. Significantly, it was hung with shamanic symbols: tinkling jade, stylized trees, and deer antlers.[10]

A Japanese figurine dating from sometime between 300 and 600 CE depicts a *miko*, a kind of shamanic priestess, midwife, and oracle who served in shrines. The little earthenware statue shows a woman sitting well back on her chair, bolt upright, with a rapt expression on her serene face (figure 11). Her eyes, despite their unassuming execution, appear as portals of the soul, and her face radiates with life. On her head she wears an unusual headdress: an oblong board with two loops, or ears, on top. (It cannot be traced to any other ancient tradition.) Around her neck, ankles, and wrists are double strings of round beads, and she wears a cloth bandolier across her chest, connected to a long sash around her waist. On her left side, dangling from her sash is a large round mirror ornamented all along its rim with tiny bells.[11]

What is the significance of the mirror? In North Asia mirrors have long been considered vessels for spirits and ancestral souls. The Manchu-Tungusic word for mirror is *panaptu,* which consists of *pana-,* meaning "soul" or "spirit," and *-ptu,* meaning "vessel." In that part of the world, women wear mirrors during their shamanic performances as a way of attracting and holding the spirits. The combination of mirrors and bells helps them to create for their audiences a

11. *This Japanese figurine of a woman shaman dates from 300–600* CE. *It was found by archaeologists together with several others in a royal tomb.*

mystical union of glittering light and shimmering sound. Copper mirrors with bells attached are important items in the shamanic costumes of northern Manchuria. And in Japan, Burma, Vietnam, and Korea shamans also wear mirrors dangling from their necks or tied to their waists for attracting and entrancing spirits.[12]

In the Buryat Republic of southern Russia and in neighboring Mongolia shamans wear large brass discs called *toli* (mirror) around their necks for protection against the spirits. Shamans there also wear cloth headdresses or hats with a braided fringe that covers their faces, so as not to frighten the audience. As one shaman put it, "I am forty, but when a very old spirit enters me, my face changes drastically. When I am being inhabited I change from the inside out—from the bone out. I change totally."[13]

Buryat and Mongolian shamans tie a short stiff whip, resembling a riding crop covered with long braided colorful silk ribbons, to their hands. When they chant and the spirits descend, they use the whips to tap their clients on the back or hands to cleanse and bless them. During healing rituals antlers may be added to their headdresses. A shaman's ceremonial horns, however, do not resemble animal horns but are made from steel (figure 12). As they go through more important rituals, these shamans acquire larger and larger horns; in time each set may have three, nine, or even sixteen sections. This part of the shaman's costume is not considered masculine, since in the animal world female as well as male reindeer have large racks. In fact, as one shaman pointed out to me, female reindeer are generally the leaders of herds roaming the steppes, and they grow the largest racks of all!

Other examples abound of shamans in North Asian states. The Jin (1115–1234), Mongol (1206–1368), and Manchu empires (1644–1911) were all founded by shamans and sustained by their rituals—until aristocrats in each case, put off by shamanism's emphasis on communal harmony, abandoned the practices. Nevertheless, the enthronement ceremonies of Chinese dynasties and even present-day Japanese imperial coronation dress are traceable to shamanic rituals and clothing.[14]

12. *Painting of a Mongolian woman shaman wearing a brass mirror on her chest and beating her drum with a goat-hoof drumstick. She is wearing steel antlers on her shaman's cap, indicating that she is a high-ranking consecrated shaman.*

For a glimpse of the pivotal role women shamans have played in these societies, we can turn to ancient texts. A woman was the heroine of the earliest known shamanic epic, *Wubuxiben Mama,* which began as an oral narrative during the early years of the Jin dynasty (1115–1234 CE). The main character was a famous *khan,* or clan leader, who devoted her life to using her shamanic abilities to protect her family. This twelfth-century epic portrays her as courageously unifying and governing seven hundred tribes in Manchuria and developing trade routes across the Sea of Japan to Kamchatka and the Aleutian Islands. Another famous woman shaman by the name of Teteke was the heroine of a thirteenth-century epic translated into English as *The Tale of the Nishan Shamaness.*[15]

European travelers first encountered shamans in the seventeenth century, and their reactions were fear and disgust. That response flowed from their religious heritage. People who worked with spirits had long been interpreted as "witches," "shamans," "magicians," "sorcerers," and "diviners" in league with the devil. Any person who invoked spirits was calling upon the servants of Satan. Christianity elaborated on this Old Testament heritage: since good spirits such as angels and saints could not be compelled but only supplicated, any spirits that could be compelled were by definition evil, as were the practitioners who commanded them. This profound misunderstanding of shamanic spirituality led to the infamous sixteenth-century European witch hunts that resulted in the deaths of thousands of innocent people, especially women.[16]

It took a long time for Europeans to overcome their prejudices and begin to interact with shamans as human beings. But finally, by the second half of the eighteenth century, travelers with scholarly interests tried to observe, record, and collect shamanic texts and objects with some degree of accuracy and respect. The research conducted in the remote Russian provinces by Johann Gottlieb Georgi, during the 1760s and 1770s, was exemplary. Like many earlier explorers, he singled out the drum and costume as key shamanic attributes and illustrated them (figure 13). Unlike his predecessors, however, Georgi actually talked with the people whose drums and clothing he collected and studied. Realizing the direct connection between shamanism and the origin of the arts, he noted that like the ancient Greek oracles, contemporary shamans spoke in a "flowery unclear language."[17]

His work set a standard later followed by travelers all over Eurasia. Their reports revealed that women actively practiced as shamans and that shamans' gowns were created and sewn by women and eventually were worn not only by women but also by a few men. In some cases, males who learned the practice of shamanism from their mothers, sisters, and wives remained within the feminine tradition. In other cases they went on to develop all-male shamanic cults connected with warfare and political rule.

13. *Eighteenth-century woman shaman from the Krasnoyarsk district in Russia, illustrated by the academic explorer Johann Gottlieb Georgi. She holds her large tambourine drum in her left hand and her drumstick in her right hand. She is wearing a feathered and fringed cap. Ermine skins and long ropes dangle over her heavy cloth robe.*

In Siberia and Mongolia shamans of both sexes wore robes patterned on women's dresses (figure 14). They were covered with icons—circular mirrors and metal rings representing breasts, and a symbolic vulva woven of reindeer hair—that referred to feminine sexuality and the enveloping natural world. By wearing these costumes, shamans showed their integration of animal spirits with feminine generative energy in their own bodies and minds.[18]

Regardless of the clear presence of women shamans, explorers in the Western hemisphere tended to describe them as groups of men. Early colonial explorers in Canada acknowledged that women shamans in aboriginal groups were greatly feared because of their

14. *Woman shaman in eighteenth-century Mongolia. Note the eight large bronze Chinese mirrors on her costume. They served as receptacles for souls and helped both her and her clients to enter trance.*

enormous power. But they used terms such as *fraternity* to describe them. The earl of Southesk wrote in 1859 that among the Ojibwe certain herbs were "known only to the medicine men, who are a sort of Masonic brotherhood, consisting of women as well as men."[19] Although he mentioned the existence of female members of the brotherhood, known locally as the Great Medicine Lodge, he implied that they were merely subsets of, or auxiliaries to, their masculine counterparts. As I learned from my grandmother, this is entirely incorrect. Women *midé*, or members of the Great Medicine Lodge, like their male colleagues, can be initiated into all forms of shamanic knowledge, including herbal pharmacology, known as *mashgigi-waboge,* or "herb brewing." While each *midé* generally practices independently, some of the most powerful shamans work together in small but powerful groups during epidemics, forest fires, and other catastrophes.

In the American Southwest, a nineteenth-century ethnographer by the name of Matilda Coxe Stevenson referred to shamanic organizations as "fraternities." However, she noted that each group had a female leader called the "Great Mother." And in November 1891 she documented an all-night curing séance at Zuni pueblo during which "Beast Gods," including bears and other dangerous wild animals, possessed all of the healers. She identified the human participants as "theurgists," those who channel the energy of the divine.[20]

The female theurgists wear their conventional dress and red-colored, fluffy eagle plumes attached to the forelock; their feet and legs halfway to the knee, and hands and arms midway to the elbow, are painted white. The altar and the floor before it are white with meal, sprinkled by the members of the fraternity, and a line of meal crossed four times extends from the altar to the ladder. The Beast Gods pass over this line to be present, for the time being, in the bodies of the theurgists. The animal fetishes by the altar influence the spiritual presence of the Beast Gods.

When a dozen or more theurgists are on the floor, their bodies thrown forward until they appear like the animals they personate, growling and wrangling with one another, the scene is weird and impressive. As the night wanes and the floor becomes more crowded the scene grows more and more wild and weird and the excitement is intense. The women appear even more excited than the men.

We owe this valuable portrayal of women shamans in action to the fact that Stevenson, like many women of her time, was interested in women's status. Men at that time described women as "wives" and "mothers" of shamans (assuming they noticed women at all), rather than as shamans in their own right. Why was it so easy to erase women from the literature? Well, in part because shamanism generally runs in families and most women shamans were also shamans' wives and mothers.

How valuable, then, is the report of Arctic explorer Knud Rasmussen! In the early years of the twentieth century he recorded an Iglulik séance conducted on the shores of Hudson Bay by a husband-and-wife team. Rasmussen arranged the performance for his own party shortly before a long and dangerous sledge journey. And although he perceived the woman's role as that of "an assistant," helping her husband in his séance, it is clear from the detailed account that this couple was in fact a two-person team. Both parties were equally necessary for the success of the ritual.[21]

All was in darkness; we could only wait for what was to come. For a long time not a sound was heard, but the waiting only increased our anticipations. At last we heard a scraping of heavy claws and a deep growling.

"Here it comes," whispered Tuglik [the shaman's wife and assistant], and all held their breaths.

But nothing happened, except the same scraping and growling mingled with deep, frightened groans; then came a fierce growl, followed by a wild shriek, and at the same moment, Tuglik dashed forward and began talking to the spirits. She spoke in her own particular spirit language.

The spirits spoke now in deep chest notes, now in a high treble. We could hear, in between the words, sounds like those of trickling water, the rushing of wind, a stormy sea, the snuffling of walrus, the growling of bear.

This sitting lasted about an hour, and when all was quiet once more, Tuglik informed us that her husband, in the shape of a fabulous bear, had been out exploring the route we were to follow on our long journey. All obstacles had been swept aside,

accident, sickness, and death were rendered powerless, and we
should all return in safety to our house the following summer.
All this had been communicated in the special language of the
spirits, which Tuglik translated for us.

The bear spirit was announced to the audience through a dramatic enactment during which the male shaman scratched and
growled for some time. At the moment he became fully possessed
by the bear, he groaned, growled, and let out a wild shriek. His wife
rushed forward to interpret for him since now he could speak only
in the esoteric language of the spirits. She shared in his spirit journey, understanding what he said and interpreting it, yet remaining intellectually alert and interactive with both the spirits and the
audience. However, her husband, as a bear-possessed spirit medium,
lost his ability to communicate with the audience.

While many such male-female shamanic teams existed around
the world, so did sexual rivalry within the ranks of shamans. Among
the Abkhazians, who live on the shores of the Black Sea, in the nation of Georgia, women shamans were in the past and still are today
considered more gifted than men. An oral narrative reported in 1972
memorializes the appearance of the first such woman and a subsequent war among shamans.[22]

There once lived a great horseman and warrior by the name of
Achi Zoschan. One night a violent storm with a great deal of
thunder and lightning broke over his camp. When it was over
he found himself transported into the sky talking with Afy, the
God of Thunder and Lightning. It seems that during the storm
he was lifted into the heavens in order to become a mediator
between humans and their gods.

Since he was mortal he chose a young male relative by the

name of Azartl as his successor so that after his own death his people would continue to have an effective mediator between the worlds. However, at this very same time a young female relative was seriously ill. When Afy learned of this he called the chosen one, Azartl, to him and promised to cure the woman if he would resign his right to be a mediator in favor of her. The youth agreed to this.

Soon thereafter a great cattle plague broke out and the young woman prayed to Afy, asking him to let her know the cause of the trouble. He told her, and then gave her the remedy, and the herds were saved. Since this time women shamans have been active.

These women shamans who were subject to the Thunder and Lightning God, however, soon found themselves living in mutual enmity with the male shamans who were subject to the warrior Zoschan.

According to this story, men chose other men as shamans, but women received a call directly from the spirits. Even today, although there are a handful of male practitioners of the shamanic arts among the Abkhazians and other indigenous peoples of the Caucasus, women are generally considered more legitimate—and thus more powerful—than men.

Similar sexual rivalry exists today in northern Mexico, among the Huichol. One myth cycle declares Tatewarí, or Grandfather Fire, the patron deity of the shamans. Another cycle proclaims the original shaman to be the creator goddess Takutsi Nakawé, or Grandmother Growth. After fighting the men who wished to steal her powers, she dived underground, and from the blood of her heart sprang a Brazil tree.[23]

In the mid-1980s a shaman by the name of Ulu Temay, or Arrow Man, told and illustrated a variant of this story: [24]

Takutsi was a powerful woman shaman who created the world with her magical bamboo staff and medicine basket. Long ago she taught my ancestors how to sing and dance and make ceremonies to communicate with the gods and heal the sick.

One day the men became jealous of her and decided to steal her magic. They got her drunk and shot her healing wands and tobacco gourds with arrows. Then they shot her through the chest, but she didn't die—she just fell to the ground, laughing. But when they shot her bamboo staff, where she kept her heart, they finally killed her.

They removed her heart from her staff and planted it in a field, where corn of many colors sprouted. Then they made special shamans' chairs and became the first male shamans.

His narrative, together with his drawing (figure 15), reveals the belief that women were the first shamans, and naturally gifted as such. The only way men could become shamans was to kill the women and steal their paraphernalia and knowledge.

Arrow Man's account suggests something essentially feminine about the shamanic arts. And although it calls into question the very legitimacy of male shamans, large numbers of shamans of both sexes continue to exist among the Huichol. Often they're divided by gender between priestly and healing roles, with males officiating at temple services and females practicing as herbalists, midwives, and diviners. Perhaps the myth reflects the fact that some Huichol men claimed the public ceremonial function for themselves and the women allowed them to do so, while the women maintained their family healing practices. (This division of labor is also found among other Mesoamerican people, including the Aztec and the K'iche' Maya.) [25]

15. *The masculine theft of shamanism. The woman shaman, pictured twice here, is shown sitting in a shaman's woven chair holding a feathered wand and crooked cane with a sacred gourd attached. Just below that we see her feathered wand, shamanic cane of authority, gourd, and chest all shot with arrows by smaller male figures. She was so powerful that merely shooting her would not suffice to kill her; all of her power objects also had to be killed.*

To see how the contest for shamanic power sometimes plays out between men and women, we can look across the Pacific to Taiwan. Indigenous Puyuma people there often claim that a transvestite male named Samguan was the first shaman. There are two problems with that assertion. First, Samguan actually lived; he was twenty-five years old when Japanese invaders arrived in Taiwan in 1895. And second, the islanders' own traditional praise songs tell of a woman ancestor called Udekaw and how she magically traveled to invisible worlds by crossing a bridge and arriving at a faraway beach. She, too, is said to be the first shaman.

How could the identity of the original shaman change from female to transvestite male? The shift apparently took place at the beginning of the Japanese occupation of Taiwan, when shamanic practices were forbidden. The Samguan story says that he was working in his field (women are the farmers in this society) when spirits possessed him. In his ecstasy he saw the special bag women shamans carry as their insignia of office and took it as his own, thus overthrowing Udekaw. Today shamanism is incorporated as a healing modality into the health care system and widely practiced by both women and men in Taiwan.[26]

In the discrepancy between contemporary legends and traditional songs we might discern how, in a moment of political subjection and social disorder, the dominant gender changed. While the ancestral shaman should be remembered as the woman named Udekaw (indeed, she is still sung about in this way), a transvestite man usurped her place in legend and became known as the founder of shamanism.

This is the way one culture nearly erased women shamans from the historical record. But there are many other reasons we have not known about them. Some explanations have their roots in linguistics. For example, the Buryat, Mongolian, and Mayan languages don't have gendered pronouns, such as the *he* and *she* we have in English. When these languages are translated into English there is a tendency to simply use *he* to refer to both women and men.[27] Other reasons that women shamans were erased from history are entwined with theories of evolution and cultural development found in the next chapter.

FIVE

The Disappearing Act:

HOW FEMALE SHAMANISM
WAS ECLIPSED

THE YEAR WAS 1999; the place was northern Mongolia. A small group of shamans, together with their apprentices and helpers, gathered around several piles of boulders on a forested peak outside the capital city of Ulaanbaatar. These were no ordinary boulders; they were ancestral shrines called *ovoos,* and they were crowned by sticks and staves with blue streamers that riffled in the wind.

Each shaman wore a feathered headdress; a cloth mask with a braided fringe; a long dress decorated with tiny bells, twisted ropes, and jingling keys; and high leather boots. Each of them carried a tambourine drum, bronze mirrors, and long strips of silk cloth braided and knotted together into whips known as *gariin ongon,* or "hand icons."[1]

As I watched with a crowd of intent onlookers, the shamans bowed to the four directions and dipped wooden spoons, each marked by nine indentations, into a bowl of fermented mare's milk. They flipped the milk into the air, prayed, and made offerings to the protector spirits of sky, earth, and water. Then they dipped their fingers into shot glasses of vodka and flicked the alcohol in each direction. As the ceremony progressed, they chanted and played mouth harps. A woman shaman named Bayar Odun began to beat her drum, establishing a rhythm that resembled a horse's trotting gait, and soon the others joined her.

Gradually she accelerated into a smooth canter, and then sped it up to a wild, rough gallop. Glowing with energy from this spiritual journey, she played her drum harder, louder, and faster than anyone else. The wooden frame of her "drum horse" was so large that she was able to put her entire head inside the rim and use it as a resonating chamber for her voice. The reindeer-skin drumhead boomed out as Bayar sang and talked with the spirits or scolded them. The sounds she made—a range of birdcalls, whistles, hoots, shrieks, cries, and roars—struck me as eerie and wonderful.

Singing steadily, Bayar raised her drum above her head and twisted her body toward the left, deflecting the spirits she encountered on her flight into the sky. From time to time she took possession of a spiritual being that howled like a wolf or growled like a bear.

Suddenly she shuddered and collapsed backward, her limbs rigid and her back arched. Her family was ready for this moment. They caught her from behind and retrieved her huge wooden drum as it bounced and rolled away. After a couple of minutes an assistant waved some smoldering juniper leaves under her nose in order to revive her. When her husband, who served as her main assistant, picked up and beat her drum, she awoke, shook herself, stood up, and took the drum horse from his hands. Then she resumed her wild journey through the sky.

For me as an observer, the performance was memorable. But it was especially noteworthy because of the way women shamans have been ignored, denigrated, and even erased from the record. Before we examine the reasons for their disappearance, let's note a few points about Bayar and her work.

First, Bayar Odun is a woman and a shaman, one in a long line of shamans in northern Mongolia. Her shamanizing involved animals—reindeer, wolves, and bears—often associated with hunting.

Her husband was her assistant, not the other way around. She practiced both traditional forms of communication with the spirit world: soul flight and spirit possession. Although she sometimes called spiritual beings into her body, she also traveled on a spiritual journey that brought her to another world.

A WILLFUL MISREADING OF THE EVIDENCE

North Asia is generally considered to be the heartland of shamanism, and diaries, memoirs, biographies, and ethnographies from this region show that women have had as great or even greater power as shamans than men. Among the Altayan nomads in Siberia, for example, women were the only shamans from the fourth through the sixth centuries CE. Dressed in elaborate gowns, they represented the spirits of old women who guarded the Road to the Land of the Dead. These ancient crones were believed to be the ancestors of all shamans.[2]

The documentary record picks up again in the eleventh century with fragmentary reports of both female and male shamans among Turkic and Mongolian peoples. More comprehensive information appears in the thirteenth century at the time of the formation of the Mongol empire and the enthronement of Chinggis Khan. By the sixteenth century there were detailed descriptions of shamans' costumes in Yakut, Evenki, and Mongol society. Both sexes dressed in feminine costumes, left their hair long and unbound, and wore women's jewelry and decorations whenever they performed rituals.[3]

In his monumental work on the Tungus, the early-twentieth-century Russian anthropologist Sergei Shirokogoroff noted that women were as common as men among shamans. "In all the Tungus languages the term [shaman] refers to persons of both sexes who have mastered spirits, who at their will can introduce these spirits into themselves and use their power over the spirits in their own interest, particularly helping other people who suffer from the spirits."[4]

Joseph Campbell wrote that "among the circumpolar hunters to this day female shamans are numerous and highly regarded." Early in the twentieth century other anthropologists, including the husband-and-wife team of Maria and Waldemar Jochelson, came to a similar conclusion after they interviewed many Yukaghir, Koryak, Itel'men, and Chukchi individuals in Siberia, including women shamans (figure 16).[5]

One of the most influential writers about shamanism was Mircea Eliade, a historian of religion. His book *Shamanism: Archaic Technique of Ecstasy* (1964) had a worldwide perspective and was consequently widely read; its sweeping synthesis made it the major resource for studying shamanism. However, there are serious limitations to Eliade's work, among them, that he never met a living shaman and thus had to depend on published sources for his information. Even so, given the written historical record of women shamans in Siberia, it is surprising that nearly all of the shamans he

16. *Early-twentieth-century photograph of a Koryak woman shaman with her drum.*

described were men. In fact, he he went out of his way to deny shamanic status to women. He glibly referred to the Mapuche women shamans of Chile as "sorceresses," saying they were evil persons who viciously attacked others by projecting injurious objects into their bodies. The predominance of female shamans in Korea he considered as "deterioration in traditional shamanism." And he said that ancient Chinese women shamans were "possessed persons of a rudimentary type." One of the authors he cited was Jan Jacob Marie de Groot. But de Groot, perhaps the most authoritative source on ancient Chinese religion at the time, had actually noted that women shamans *predominated* in early Chinese shamanism and that they were considered great healers.[6]

Eliade's dismissal of women shamans extended to Japan where he described the rituals practiced by women as merely "techniques of possession by ghosts," making the shamans sound like spiritualists. Yet again, the primary sources he used, together with more recent information, reveal that the earliest and most powerful shamans in Japan were women. Great women shamans *(miko)* who were possessed by heavenly deities had pivotal ritual and political roles in society from the fourth through the tenth century. Only later, under Buddhist influence, did the *miko* lose their political status and become relegated to the "folk" tradition.[7]

Eliade's work on shamanism was so persuasive, even though it was not accurate, because of the times in which he lived and wrote. The book was originally published in French in 1951, when the psychoanalytic movement, with its strongly anti-female bias, was at its high-water mark. His erasure of women from important religious roles was not even remarked upon for forty years.[8]

THE MYTH OF MAN THE HUNTER-SHAMAN

One of the common misconceptions about shamanism is that it is primarily associated with hunting. Anthropologist Piers Vitebsky, for example, insisted that "the classic Siberian idea of the shaman as master of spirits is very much an image of the male hunter or warrior, with his heroic style of journeying across the cosmos and engaging spirits in battle." When you add to this belief the notion that only men have been hunters—whether in prehistoric times or among hunting-gathering people—and that they alone have provided food for helpless mates and children, the result is what I call the myth of man the hunter-shaman.[9]

The argument is closely tied both to theories of evolution and to ideas about gender roles. Anthropologist Michael Ripinsky-Naxon suggested that "shamanistic systems arise from the male-oriented tradition of the Palaeolithic hunters." And other researchers argued that the need to hunt communally led to the first social gathering, the patrilineal or patrilocal band, each consisting of between twenty and two hundred individuals, and each with its own masculine religious healing specialist, the shaman.[10]

Ideas, information, and tools—indeed, the human brain itself—have all been considered products of men's hunting activity. Even language was said to have evolved out of the need for verbal communication by groups of prehistoric men traveling together through tall savanna grasses in search of prey. And what were the women supposed to be doing? Well, evidently they were collecting roots and berries around the campsite or staying in the cave to look after the kids.

This model of prehistoric life appealingly incorporates commonsense ideas about sociality and learning. (The sexual division of labor permitted greater investment in children, allowing cognitive and social skills to develop.) And it draws some support from the archaeological and hominid fossil records. Early stone tools are not often associated with the bones of large animals, but occasionally they are. It is because of those tools that men's hunting and meat-sharing customs became the foundation upon which the entire narrative of human evolution was built.[11]

THE ORIGINAL AFFLUENT SOCIETY

Not everyone agrees, however, that male hunters provided all or even the majority of prehistoric people's daily calories. Researchers working with hunter-gatherers in Botswana have shown that gathering, not hunting, provided most of the tribe's sustenance, and that the combination of the two led to the original affluent society.[12]

In fact, studies in Africa, Asia, Oceania, and the Americas have made it clear that quite a number of "leisure societies" existed. In these cultures people worked at hunting and gathering for only about two days—less than fifteen hours—a week; their social organization could be traced either through women (matrilineal) or through men (patrilineal); and there were bands where women as well as men practiced as shamans.[13]

The technology that women in these societies developed to assist in their gathering activities—digging sticks, hand axes, grinding stones, shell knives, string bags, carrying baskets, and cooking pots—gave rise to science, medicine, and language. In fact, one can argue that the most important tools were not weapons but containers used for gathering, and the baby sling, which allowed women to carry infants while using both hands to hunt or collect plants.[14]

There's no doubt, though, that the glorification of men's hunting techniques has diminished women's tools for collecting and transporting food into mere "sticks" and "containers." And the same mind-set has narrowed our understanding of what is included among hunting techniques.

At Dolní Věstonice, where the earliest known remains of a woman shaman were found, archaeologist Olga Soffer and her colleague James Adovasio discovered plant fibers that had been twined or twisted around each other and then woven. Twining can produce cloth, string, or rope. And cord for making traps, nets, and snares has been found in a number of Upper Paleolithic sites. Could rope traps and snares have been used then? That would explain the small-animal bones found at the site.

About the discoveries, Adovasio remarked, "Mostly men have

done the analysis of Paleolithic sites, and they have in their minds the macho hunter of extinct megafauna. Guys who hunt woolly mammoths are not supposed to be making these." Perhaps they didn't. But traps and nets have silently been declared as uninteresting as the women who made them.[15]

WHY DID IT TAKE SO LONG TO CRITIQUE THE MYTH?

One reason it has taken so long is tied to our view of hunting itself. European and American women over the centuries rarely hunted, and even in the last decade, as women in the United States and Canada have come to embrace the activity, some rather significant distinctions between the attitudes of women hunters and their male counterparts have emerged.

In interviews, women say they're not interested in acquiring trophies, and they often disparage the "stuff-it-and-mount-it school of hunting." Instead, they emphasize the intimate connection with their food and a desire to use every part of the animal they kill. As Jennifer Sells, an Iowa game warden, put it, "I feel more of a connection with my dinner if I hunt it rather than buy it at the store." Another woman hunter in Wyoming turns her kill into elk steaks, burgers, and sausage. She also tans the hides for chaps and gloves. Her attitude toward hunting resembles that of indigenous people worldwide.[16]

As for women hunters in hunter-gatherer societies outside the West, the evidence has rarely even been discussed. An Australian aboriginal rock art drawing, painted during the Upper Paleolithic in what is now the Northern Territory, shows four running women (figure 17). The one in front is carrying a hunting stick, or boomerang, used for millennia to bring down animals. Other nearby rock paintings depict women hunting alone with one-piece multi-barbed spears and hafted stone axes. While some of these images are noted in specialized publications about rock art, they have not yet

17. *Australian Paleolithic cave painting of women hunters. The woman in front is shown throwing the hunting stick known as a boomerang. These red ocher female images, each about nine inches high, were painted in a rock shelter located in the Northern Territory.*

been included in the shamanic literature as evidence for women as hunters.[17]

Archaeological research has also revealed that since the Upper Paleolithic women all over Africa have participated with men in snaring small game, driving larger animals into nets and pit traps, and scavenging game killed by lions. Ethnographic work with the Mbuti in the Congo has demonstrated that large teams of women and men cooperate in net hunting. There, as elsewhere, women who participated in the hunt got a better share of meat and fat than if they remained at home, waiting for the "bacon" to be brought back to them.[18]

In the Philippines, too, researchers have noted that women of the Agta, a hunting-and-gathering people, participated in all of the same subsistence activities as men. They traded with local farmers, fished in streams, collected plant foods, and hunted game animals. In some places women hunted with dogs; in others they were adept with bow and arrows. They killed all of the same prey as men: wild pigs, monkeys, and deer. They were willing to join men in hunting and in helping to carry large game out of the forest, but they also frequently hunted alone. And like men, some women enjoyed hunting more than others and as a result received more meat.[19]

The point is that in many societies there is no form of sexual division of labor when it comes to getting food. If a woman wants to hunt, she is free to do so (figure 18). A man who wishes to gather has the same freedom of choice. Both are worthy, and each person has equal access to shared provisions.[20]

The evidence extends to northern peoples. In Siberia, during the early years of the twentieth century, the best hunter among the Karagas (sometimes called Altai Turk or Tufa) was a woman shaman. And in Alaska, Yukon elder Kitty Smith was so proud of her abilities that she related a number of trapping anecdotes as key episodes in her autobiography. Alaskan women have routinely trapped fur-bearing animals and hunted caribou, moose, reindeer, deer, and bear alone or with relatives.[21]

18. *In this charcoal-and-pencil drawing, done by an Iñupiat student at the end of the nineteenth century, we see a woman with a tattooed chin (indicating she had reached sexual maturity) carrying a reindeer on her back and walking her dog.*

NOTHING BUT WIVES AND ASSISTANTS

The linguistics of translation and common assumptions about the roles of women have obscured the history of women shamans. More than once ethnographers have rendered the word for shaman differently, depending on the gender of the person described.

In Australia, the indigenous term for shaman, *putari*, was translated as "witch doctor" and thought to refer to an older man claiming to have special, usually malevolent powers. Only in the 1980s did Catherine and Robert Berndt discover that women who practiced as midwives were also *putari*. And in the 1990s Diane Bell recognized that female *putari*, like the males, were herbalists and traditional healers with shamanic powers.[22]

In South America, Norman Whitten, an ethnographer working along the Amazon, translated the Quichua word *yachaj* (literally "the one who knows") as "powerful shaman" when he referred to males but as "master potter" when he referred to females. With this seemingly simple act of translation he removed women from a spiritual role and placed them in a secular feminine one.[23]

Ironically, in many shamanic traditions there is a path undertaken primarily by women that bridges artisanship and spirituality. Among the Huichol of west-central Mexico the feminine spiritual discipline focuses on learning to weave, which calls for the ability to access the spirit world in order to create new designs. The path parallels and merges with masculine shamanic practices in such a way that a truly expert woman weaver is also a shaman.[24]

Huichol shamanism runs in families. In the case of Ramón Medina Silva, a well-known Huichol healer, his mother, sister, and wife were all shamans themselves, but they are barely remembered. Ramón's mother taught him history, myth, and animal lore. She passed along song cycles and esoteric details of the spiritual environment. Ramón's wife, Guadalupe de la Cruz Ríos, was also a trained shaman. She helped her husband in his healing practice during his lifetime, and after he was killed in 1971 she became an independent curer, singer, and family leader (figure 19). Ramón's peyote-inspired yarn

19. *Guadalupe de la Cruz Ríos conducts a shamanic ceremony in 1988. Her three-legged log drum has a deerskin head and is carved and painted with spiritual images. This type of drum is considered female and addressed by shamans as "Our Mother the Drum."*

paintings have been widely exhibited and illustrated; Guadalupe's have been generally ignored. Numerous writers have quoted Ramón at length; Guadalupe's verbal wisdom and healing knowledge were never published.[25]

Although there are as many women shamans among the Guaraní of Paraguay and Brazil as men shamans, they, too, have been passed over. When shaman Tupa Nevangayu was recently interviewed for a book with three other male colleagues, he insisted that his wife was also a shamanic healer and that "she has some important things to say." Yet she was allowed only a brief statement instead of a full interview. How was she listed in the published table of contents? She was "a shaman's wife."[26]

Recently an Italian scholar discovered in Nepal that among the Chepang there were many powerful women shamans; all previous studies had denied their existence. One of these women, Krishora, served as the spiritual guide of nine villages. She had the special duty of initiating young men and young women into shamanism. But because her husband and nephew were also shamans, earlier researchers had overlooked her crucial role.[27]

TRANSCENDENCE OR IMMANENCE

The life energy experienced by shamans moves about as freely as smoke or electricity, swirling, gliding, leaping between and entering bodies. The same shaman can therefore experience possession and participate in soul flight. Yet a number of writers persisted in distinguishing between the two, often dividing these abilities by sex. One of them was psychoanalyst Géza Róheim, who strongly influenced Mircea Eliade. In his discussion of the Hungarian shaman, or *táltos,* a term he translated as "male sorcerer," Róheim actually mentioned two women *táltoses,* but he covered this apparent contradiction by saying that they were "witches" who were "just pretending to be healers."[28]

That is highly unlikely: the earliest published observation of Hungarian shamans indicates that *táltoses* were both men and women. And according to local oral tradition, the original shaman, named Rasdi, was a woman. Moreover, archaeologists have found many early female burials with shamanic materials in present-day Hungary.[29]

But those facts do not fit comfortably with Róheim's Freudian theory about the phallic nature of shamanic "ecstatic soul flight." To quote him: "A flying dream is an erection dream, [and] in these dreams the body represents the penis. *Our hypothetical conclusion would be that the flying dream is the nucleus of shamanism*" (italics in the original).[30]

Following Róheim's lead, Eliade limited shamanism to "soul flight"—which he regarded as not only transcendent but also phallic. And he separated it from "possession," which he considered immanent and assigned to women, whom he felt were not really shamans. Women shamans, my grandmother and Essie Parrish among them, would have been shocked by this remarkable dichotomy.

According to Eliade, possession involves a lack of control over the spirits, and shamanism requires control, so possession could not possibly be a legitimate part of shamanism. The lack of control was subsequently described as "feminine in character"—a device women use to gain attention and achieve social prestige. The American anthropologist Michael Harner elaborated on Eliade's ideas when he stated that trance mediumship, or what is now dubbed "channeling," involves a lack of control over the spirits that enter one's body.[31]

Ironically, even some feminist authors have embraced the idea that male shamans engage in ecstatic out-of-body soul flights and female mediums are possessed by alien spirits. Susan Sered, in her otherwise excellent book *Priestess, Mother, Sacred Sister: Religions Dominated by Women* (1994), described soul flight as a masculine adventure. She argued that religious specialists in what she called "female-dominated religions" consistently chose possession rather than ecstatic soul flight. Her ideas presuppose a sexual separation of the ways in which ecstasy is experienced by men and women. According to her essentialist scheme, there is a purely masculine pole that involves leaving one's body, and a purely feminine pole that involves sharing one's body.[32]

The actual situation is far more complex. In Southeast Asia there are traditions in which out-of-body soul flight is considered a feminine action, while possession is considered masculine. In Sumatra, among the Rejang, young fertile women make soul journeys to the spirit world of their ancestors, while young men serve as mediums possessed by spirits. Mature women and men are able to combine soul journeying with spirit possession; over the years of their practice they eventually learn how to imaginatively shape-shift between genders.[33]

Eliade's trivializing approach to women shamans unfortunately influenced many other scholars who, unlike him, actually met living practitioners. Among them was Åke Hultkrantz, a Swedish historian of religion who conducted field research with the Shoshoni during the late 1950s and early 1960s. In reporting on the "medicine men" he met in Wyoming, he remarked casually, "There are also medicine women who have passed the menopause, but they are few, and their powers are not as great as the powers of their male colleagues." He then went on to generalize the statement to other tribes. He wrote that "in Puget Sound (and perhaps elsewhere) female shamans are rare, and their powers are inferior to those of male shamans." And he asserted that "among the Eskimos some women occasionally perform as shamans, but it is testified that only with difficulty do they achieve the same magical effects as their male colleagues." In each of these cases he offered nothing but his own say-so.[34]

When I sought out Hultkrantz's sources, I found that his statements didn't hold up. Other ethnographers working in these areas had discovered an equal proportion of powerful female and male healing shamans: a missionary who lived with indigenous Puget Sound people for many years noted that there were prominent women shamans among the Klallams. He added that all along the Northwest Coast, visionary power is given at birth to women rather than to men.[35]

And we have a stunning material record of Haida women shamans dating all the way back to the seventeenth century. It consists of dozens of shale carvings of women dressed in shamanic clothing and performing in séances. An illustration shows front and back views of a woman wearing a shaman's outfit (figure 20). She has feathers tattooed on her right cheek and a labret, worn by members of important clans, inserted in her lower lip. Her apron and long mantle are painted with the stylized faces of her clan's power animals. In each hand she holds a type of rattle that is filled with pebbles and produces clacking noises when shaken.[36]

Icelandic Arctic explorer and ethnographer Vilhjalmur Stefansson reported that some of the greatest Inuit shamans he knew were women. Other scholars have noted that women shamans performed differently than men but nonetheless enjoyed similar social status, prestige, and power. Danish scholar Therkel Mathiassen observed that all senior Inuit men and women were shamans. And a recent

20. *Wooden sculpture of a Haida woman shaman. The power animals of the shaman's clan adorn her apron and mantle. She holds rattles in each hand.*

study of the published sources reveals "a kind of gender equality" in which "women were equal in their access to the religious sphere."[37]

Nevertheless, Eliade's ideas and attitudes linger on. As recently as 1994 the historian of religion Robert Torrance ignored early studies of women shamans in northern California. He simply decreed that these women's shamanic practices were less important and powerful than those of men. Without carefully reading biographies and ethnographic sketches of women shamans, or undertaking any new field research, he belittled and trivialized this feminine tradition by labeling it "passive shamanism." And he described it as "a static, closed, or repetitive religion" in which a transcendent quest was not even possible.[38] Well, so much for Essie Parrish!

PART TWO

Shamanic Traditions in Action

SIX

The Mystical Union:

EROTICISM, ECSTASY, AND TRANCE

THOSE OF US who have watched shamans go into a trance or take an ecstatic spiritual journey—such as the one I described at the beginning of the last chapter—know how physical and sensual the experience really is. During my own shamanic training among the Maya I discovered the flowing and shimmering of my own bodily vital energy, called *koyopa* or "sheet lightning." Initially these ecstatic feelings seemed strange, and I was frightened that I was becoming possessed by something outside myself. But during my months of shamanic training I eventually learned how to accept and even welcome the movements of sheet lightning since it produced a remarkable bodily-based intuitive form of knowledge called "the speaking of the blood." This gift of accessing bodily intuition has been central to my spiritual understanding and shamanic practice ever since.

In fact, to shamanize is as much a bodily technique as it is a spiritual exercise. Shamans everywhere use combinations of sensory overstimulation and deprivation that electrically and chemically trigger ecstatic consciousness or trance. And we know through scientific studies that the workings of the brain and nervous system both affect and are affected by shamanic activities.

SHAMANIC STATES OF CONSCIOUSNESS

How can we describe the shaman's state of mind during a performance? Some researchers refer to an "altered state of consciousness"; others use "shamanic state of consciousness." I prefer the latter, because shamans combine insights that take place during various altered states—including ecstasy and trance—with insights that take place while they are cognitively aware or lucid.[1]

It is this combination of various mental states and the movement between them that typifies shamanic performance. My Mayan teachers purposely combined cognitive skills such as the rapid counting out of the calendar, backward and forward, together with ecstatic hypnotic skills such as listening to the speaking of the blood and crystal gazing to create a special mental-emotional state of receptivity to all possible information and ideas. Likewise, the Mongolian shaman Bayar Odun combined her strongly cognitive interviewing skills with her remarkable ability to quickly fall into and return from deep trance levels in order to discover novel solutions for her clients' problems.

Ecstasy and *trance* can be used interchangeably, though anthropologists generally use *trance* to refer to both, and historians of religion similarly rely on *ecstasy*. I like to differentiate between the two terms. Trance is a hyperlucid state of sensory overstimulation triggered by music, noises, and odors. The images, auditions, and experiences of trances are generally forgotten afterward. Ecstasy is a state of sensory deprivation and withdrawal. Think of fasting, silence, and darkness. Experiences during ecstasy are not only remembered later but can be revisited again and again. Dreaming, the monitoring of vital energy in the body, and the state produced by psychedelic drugs are ecstatic rather than trance experiences.[2]

Drumming, combined with dancing, singing, and miming, is a

powerful way to bring on a trance. During shamanic performances participants may stamp their feet to one rhythm, clap their hands to a second rhythm, and sing syllables to yet a third. In fact, music that encourages dancing profoundly modifies the structure of our consciousness, changing how we experience both space and time. Musically driven movements enable shamans and their clients to enter into spiritual worlds filled with culturally appropriate cosmic imagery.

In Korea, dancing is central to shamanic performances. Not only does the shaman dance, but the person who requests a séance does so as well. As my colleague Laurel Kendall of the Museum of Natural History in New York City describes it: "A woman sets her money on the drum, is garbed in an appropriate costume, and begins a graceful dance which soon becomes a series of rapid leaps to quickened drumbeats in imitation of the shaman's dance of possession. When the woman has danced to exhaustion, her *momju,* her own personal body-governing god is satisfied." Kendall describes this dancing, which she herself has participated in, as exhilarating, adding that "it refreshes the insides" and creates a sense of excitement and joy, which ends in a "dreamy euphoria" that rises up in waves from the belly to the chest.[3]

She is not imagining things. Dancing encourages hyperventilation, increases the production of adrenaline, and causes a sharp decrease in levels of blood glucose. These physiological responses stimulate the brain to release endorphins, groups of proteins with potent analgesic properties that create painkilling compounds resembling opiates. Thus, trance-inducing techniques trigger a chemically induced euphoria, even in the absence of mind-altering drugs.[4]

Throughout the world drums are the main generators of the trances in which shamans journey back and forth between the upper, middle, and lower realms. During her séances, the famous Sakhá shaman Maria Andrianovna Suzdalova flaps her arms and hops about like a bird, making warbling sounds. Then, sitting astride her drum, she snorts like a reindeer as she drums herself into a trance (figure 21).[5]

There's an excellent scientific reason for the percussion's effect.

21. *Skipping reindeer dance of a Sakhá woman shaman.*

Neurophysiologists have discovered that rhythmic sounds can significantly alter brain wave patterns and induce trances. More specifically, when we're awake, one hemisphere of the brain dominates the other in an asynchronous pattern of brain waves. (Typically the right hemisphere generates alpha waves, vibrating at seven to fourteen cycles per second, while the left hemisphere generates beta waves, vibrating at fourteen to twenty-one cycles per second.) Through a process called "entrainment," one of these rhythms draws the other into harmonic resonance.

Percussion—whether from drums, rattles, gongs, or clappers—changes asynchronous brain-wave patterns into synchronous ones. Because we *hear* the stimulus, neurophysiologists call this process "sonic driving," and it may result in visual sensations of color, pattern, and movement. Practitioners also report unexpectedly loud roaring sounds and even full-blown hallucinations.[6]

These intense sensory experiences—so difficult to describe in words—are also related to a combination of brain symmetry and chemistry. During ecstatic mystical experiences the image-based right hemisphere of the brain comes to dominate the left hemisphere, where most language processing takes place. Mystical states, like dreams, are fundamentally nonlinear, nonlinguistic, and distorted beyond recognition when put into words or conveyed to others.

This is why many people are reticent when asked to describe their visions and why many others prefer to draw, paint, or weave key images from these experiences rather than attempt to directly talk about them.[7]

VITAL ENERGY

When shamans perform, they often turn their eyes inward as they monitor their life force, or vital energy, either to reach another state of consciousness or to heal others. For a shaman, energy is an expression of spirit transforming into matter. Vital energy is the form of electricity that enables us to heal, though only recently have neuroscientists begun to develop instruments sensitive enough to detect and measure it.[8]

Recognizing and controlling vital energy is crucial to shamanic healing traditions. Dela Keats is a noted Alaskan shaman who has received honorary doctorates for her work from the University of Alaska, the University of California at San Francisco, and the College of Osteopathic Medicine of the Pacific. In a recent interview she said that for sixty-two years she has used her bodily energy to heal people: "I have no books, nothing for curing; just my hands. I find the places where energy is stopped up and release it."[9]

Keats was trained in traditional Iñupiat healing by her relatives. She learned to locate the internal organs in her own abdomen and became aware of how each one felt. Then she trained her fingers to note minute changes within the organ. When she worked with her patients, she asked questions, cajoled, teased, and laughed until they relaxed enough to enable her to explore and massage the area of their discomfort.

In South Africa, among the San, a young woman learns to recognize and use vital energy by means of a psychoactive plant known as *gwa*. A mother feeds her daughter small quantities of the plant and helps her deal with the energy—a rhythmical trembling that the San describe as *tara,* or "the action of lightning"—that courses through her body. Later in life, group dancing, singing, and clapping will be enough to activate this energy. [10]

Nisa, a middle-aged San woman, beautifully expressed the sensation: "It feels like there is a hole going through your body. You tremble in rhythm, even your crotch trembles. If you reach !aia [trance], you call out for water, because you are hot inside. Even if you don't know the songs, you can !aia. The n/um [energy] itself tells you how to sing and dance."[11]

Once they're in a trance, San healers are able to see into their own or others' bodies. Like spontaneous touch healers in other parts of the world, they lay on hands or vibrate them close to the skin's surface to remove sickness. During their healing trances they take the sickness into themselves and then forcibly expel it by shaking their hands and bodies. As the San describe it, they shake the beads off their skin aprons.

The physical movements of trembling are significant for shamans in other parts of the world. The Diné, or Navajo, of the American Southwest identify potential shamans by the uncontrollable trembling that seizes them. That's a sign of possession by the spirit of the Gila monster, a poisonous lizard. A ceremony helps transform the trembling into a manageable experience that can be used to diagnose illness.[12]

Walking Thunder, a medicine woman practicing within this tradition, explained the trembling as follows: "We believe that tiny lightning can enter your body and cause you to move. When medicine people feel the lightning, they'll get a chill or a body twitch. This is how lightning works in our healing. When lightning moves inside your body, that's the Thunder way with the Wind. This is behind the twitching of a holy person [shamanic healer]."[13]

A similar kind of bodily possession carries with it shamanic knowledge among the Inuit of Canada. A Netsilik woman by the name of Uvavnuk described how one winter evening, when the moon was not visible, she went outside. A glowing ball of fire suddenly dropped from the sky to the earth, hitting her. A split second before it entered her body she perceived that one side of the meteor was a bear and the other side was a human being with the fangs of a bear. When the ball of fire actually struck, she was filled with flaming light. Once she had recovered, she ran home singing:[14]

> *The great sea moves me, sets me adrift.*
> *It moves me like algae on stones in running brook water.*
> *The vault of heaven moves me.*
> *Mighty weather storms through my soul.*
> *It carries me with it.*
> *Trembling with joy.*

After this initial experience with vital energy Uvavnuk felt that nothing was hidden from her and immediately began to shamanize. Whenever she sang, everybody who heard her felt their minds cleansed of evil thoughts, releasing them into joy.

The Chinese tradition of Taoism describes vital energy as a circulation of *ch'i yün,* meaning "rhythmic vitality." *Ch'i* is an elusive term whose meanings include vitality, life force, and bioelectricity. But the significance of *ch'i* is perhaps best suggested by its literal meaning—"breath." The pronunciation of the written character *ch'i,* as it is articulated in all known Chinese dialects, centers on exhaling the breath. In Taoist tradition everything in existence contains *ch'i:* heaven and earth, sun and moon, day and night, months, hours, the air we breathe, and the food we eat. Thus, while *ch'i* may partly be understood as breath or wind, it also includes essence, soul, energy, and universal vital force.[15]

Closely related to *ch'i* are two other energy forms. The first, *jing,* or "sexual energy," doubles when it interacts with the second, *shen,* or "spiritual energy." Merged together, they become the basic healing energy of *ch'i.* The ancient practice of sitting in meditation helped practitioners to both experience and create visual maps of energy flows in their bodies. These maps were eventually codified and used for the healing technique known as acupuncture. In time the nature of *ch'i* as an electromagnetic current was recognized, and practitioners learned how to increase its quantity and intensity by using special breathing exercises and other bodily techniques such as t'ai ch'i chuan and ch'i kung.[16]

Some Taoist practitioners describe their work as an internal alchemy in which women and men, working together or separately, turn their aroused sexual energy inward and upward, transforming it into a combined feminine-masculine healing power. For example, the modern Thai practitioners Mantak and Maneewan Chia conceptualize the exercise of healing love as a mixing of the energies of sexuality, spirituality, and the life force.

At the moment of sexual orgasm, lovers experience their bodies melting into a highly charged center of energy (figure 22). By moving this energy through the body—from the genitals to the navel, solar plexus, heart, throat, third eye, and crown—they change it into spirit. In so doing they amplify weak or missing energies in their partner. Practitioners encourage such erotic sensitivity as a way of experiencing the interconnectedness of inner and outer worlds.[17]

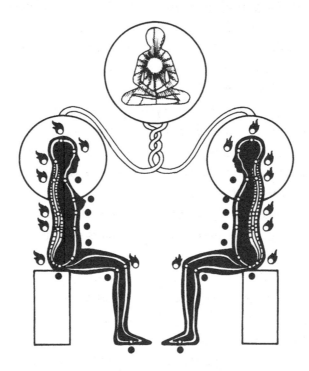

22. Taoist practice of healing love.

EROTIC ECSTASY

Erotic energy is an essential component of many shamanic traditions, which often characterize it as a monster's roar, brilliant flashes of light, or lightning thunderbolts. For the Classic Maya the erotic energy of the trance state was portrayed as the roar of an earth monster or jaguar (figure 23). Fire flickering in the eyes is a favorite image in North Asia, while images of flowers lit by lightning occur in East Asia and Central America. In East Asian traditions the connection between a lotus blossom and lightning symbolizes the sexual union of female with male. And in the Central American Mayan tradition, in which I was trained, the erotic flower is an opalescent orchid touched by lightning. It quivers orgasmically in the same way that sheet lightning trembles on a distant horizon. In all these independent shamanic traditions symbolic forms of sexual intercourse represent a coming

23. *Ancient Mayan carved shell of woman in ecstatic trance. She stands at a cave entrance, which is portrayed as the mouth of the earth monster. Arching over her head is the monster's upper jaw, and above her tied-back hair is its huge eye. Crouched on top of the jaw is an iguana. Carved shell with red paint rubbed into the grooves, the Late Classic period (600–900 CE).*

together of intuitive insight about the nature of ultimate reality with the practical knowledge of everyday life.

Abstinence is used in many traditions as a way of manipulating sexual energy. In the Mayan tradition I was trained in there were many "permission days" when neither our teachers nor my husband and I could enjoy sexual contact. On these special days we were told not even to think about sex. As a result of reducing sexual contact to only certain days, we found that we stored up reserves of vital energy that helped us to concentrate, walk long distances, and eventually to heal clients.

Sexually ecstatic states are celebrated literally as well as symbolically in tantric and kundalini yoga, both of which evolved out of North Asian shamanic practices. The Sanskrit word *tantra* comes from the root *tan*, meaning "to stretch" or "to weave." Tantra is the art of weaving together the spiritual and material worlds. It is a way of realizing the divine essence through bodily experience, especially the creative force of sexuality. The Sanskrit term *kundalini*, meaning "serpent power," designates divine sexual energy.[18]

Practitioners of tantric yoga feel erotic energy as a sensation of heat, which they describe as liquid fire, near the base of the spine. As this fiery energy moves up channels on each side of the spinal column, slowly rising like a snake, opening one energy center after another, the practitioner rhythmically shudders in response. The person hears strange buzzing or roaring sounds and sees rainbow-colored lights that fade into a brilliant white light. At the top of the head, primordial sound is transformed into a vision of a crescent moon rising from a thousand-petaled white lotus. As this occurs, all separation between self and the world dissolves into orgasmic bliss.

In tantric and kundalini yoga the so-called right-handed schools practice symbolic sexual intercourse. The left-handed schools actually engage in intercourse, and for those believers, at the moment when what each lover wants most is what the other wants most to give, it is impossible to say whether the experience of sexual climax is physical or spiritual.[19]

The blending of sacred eroticism with ecstatic visionary experience is hardly confined to Asia; it once had an important role in Christianity. St. Teresa refers to being "a bride of Christ," a phrase still used today when a nun takes her final vows, and Carmelite nuns have described erotic experiences that frequently occur to them during prayer. The hostility of Roman Catholic theologians toward altered states of consciousness has led them to explain away the openly erotic and deeply ecstatic language of Christian mystics. This is ironic, since Roman Catholics share a sacramental understanding of God's existence in the act of love itself. When God is present in the lovers, the sex act manifests God to each partner.[20]

THE PHYSIOLOGICAL EXPLANATION

Many of us know the experience of being swept away in a passionate torrent of desire; it takes us out of our inhibitions and conventional behaviors. A person in love feels caught by a force that seems to come from outside the self. During orgasm lovers often appear as if possessed by spirits, shuddering and quivering, groaning and crying out, momentarily blind and deaf to all that surrounds them. Scientists point to a strong neurological connection between sexuality, particularly female sexuality, and going into a trance.[21]

A powerful electrical connection across women's brain hemispheres contributes to their heightened ability to experience ecstasy. The sheer number and the density of neurons in women's brains are significantly greater than in men. Moreover, neurons course between the left and right sides of the brain within the corpus callosum, a connective passageway that is larger in women than in men. Another neural pathway linking the two hemispheres—known as the anterior commissure—is notably larger and denser in women than in men. And a third band of fibers connecting the thalami of the two sides of the brain—the massa intermedia—is present more often in females than in males.[22]

Some women feel orgasms so intensely that they enter an altered state of consciousness. And it is this ability that leads to women's extraordinary skills in shamanic practice. Indeed, the word for orgasm is the same as the word for trance in a number of languages.

SYMBOLIC SEXUAL RELATIONS

It's impossible to deny the physically sexual component of shamanic activity. Yet in many traditions there's an added dimension: shamans, by harnessing either masculine or feminine energies, may also engage in metaphorical sexual relations with a spirit helper of the opposite sex. They may even take on the sexual identity of this spirit. Female shamans generally accept male spirit helpers as guides, while male shamans accept female spirit helpers. The energy from a source of one sex may help cure a patient of the opposite sex; for example, a shaman may tap the sexual energy of a female birch tree in order to cure a male human being.[23]

Zoia Duranova, a renowned Sakhá physician and shaman living today in the Russian Republic, revealed in a recent newspaper interview that her shamanic powers and healing abilities take the form of a spirit animal, which appears as a white stallion. Her double transformation from female human to male animal reveals Duranova's skills in changing boundaries and symbols.[24]

The bond between a shamanic candidate and a guardian spirit is often sexual; in many traditions it's a kind of marriage. In Siberia ancestral spirits—both male and female—hold down or "ride" the candidate in his or her dreams. The person awakens feeling cold, exhausted, even paralyzed, but this terrifying, ecstatic experience is interpreted as either a metaphorical marriage to the spirit or a serious illness that must be healed by another shaman.[25]

Clothing can heighten or shape the experience. In Korea a woman shaman may put on men's garments during her performance so as to receive a masculine spirit into her body. When the trance reaches its peak, a mystical union occurs: the female shaman and the male spirit embodied in her clothing become one. Such mystical unions are modeled on local wedding patterns. In Japan, a woman at the end of her seven-year shamanic apprenticeship dons a wedding dress and holds a rice pot and a pan in her hands—the same implements that a bride brings to her new home. Symbolic intercourse with her spirit husband emotionally connects the masculine and feminine worlds as well as the spiritual and earthly realms. She is both a woman related to human society through an earthly spouse, and a spirit tied to the spiritual world through a spirit husband.[26]

In an ethnographic report by my colleague Melford Spiro of the University of California at San Diego we learn that in Myanmar (formerly Burma) a young woman dreamed repeatedly of a spirit suitor. She was encouraged by her friends to symbolically wed him, in a ceremony that culminated in shamanic initiation. As an orchestra played she performed a special dance, and then she entered a screened-off area where a group of female shamans waited. One of them moved a mirror back and forth in front of the "bride's" face, hypnotizing her, while pressing another mirror against her back. A second shaman attached strings of cotton to her ankles and wrists, placed a longer cord diagonally across her shoulders, and pierced her hair knot with a needle to which a cotton string was attached. When the young woman drifted into sleep, she became both the wife of the spirit and an initiated shaman. The ritual ended with a dance during which she entered trance. From this point on not only would she be in love with and loved by her spiritual spouse, but she would also be able to transform herself into him through appropriate dress and dance gestures.[27]

Scientific analysis and ethnographic accounts can give us an understanding of the way sexuality, trance, and the healing use of vital energy all merge in a shaman's activities. Yet such stories and explanations pale before the experience of actually watching a powerful shaman in action. Bayar Odun is just such a shaman, and in the next chapter we see these elements come together in her life and work.

SEVEN

Riding the Wind Horse:

A SHAMANIC PERFORMANCE

IN THE LATE SUMMER of 1999, I traveled with my husband, Dennis, to Ulaanbaatar, the capital city of Mongolia, where we witnessed the public rebirth of shamanism. On the banks of the Tuul River, below rocky cliffs and near scattered boulders covered by ancient paintings and engravings, I watched as Bayar Odun joined a small group of other shamans, both women and men, to perform ceremonies at the shrine called Great Sky (figure 24). They raised their shaman's bundles to the heavens and chanted to their ancestral spirits: "Great ancestors of my family tree listen to me, hear me well...."

Since the early years of the twentieth century, under Communist rule, it had been unsafe to worship like this in such a public place. Shamans who dared to shamanize in public had been rounded up and sent to gulags or killed. Their children had quickly learned that if they wanted to preserve any of their ancestral knowledge, they needed to attend medical school so that they could practice at least some of their family's healing arts.

By now the Soviet Union had broken apart, the Russian army

24. *Mongolian woman shamans holding up their bundles. The bundles are filled with bronze mirrors and other equipment and are held toward the sacred cliffs. This is the first time these shamanic bundles were shown in public since the Soviet takeover of Mongolia in the early 1920s.*

had abandoned its local bases, and the Mongolian government was encouraging national identity by placing Chinggis Khan's face on the paper money. The time had clearly come to reopen the shamanic shrines where Chinggis Khan and his followers had worshiped.

For some seventy years Bayar's family, together with others in the Khöwsgöl district of northern Mongolia, had secretly kept their traditions alive by shamanizing indoors at night, without drums, and only with people they knew and trusted. Now they could once again practice their art during the day and outdoors, even with total strangers present.

The reopening of the Great Sky shrine was timed to coincide with the Fifth Conference of the International Society for Shamanistic Research. The delegates included scholars from many nations, together with practicing shamans from all over Mongolia and nearby parts of Russia and China. They presented papers on topics that ranged from the healing power of storytelling to the dedication ceremony for a new shaman. The most important event, though, was the way theory turned to practice at the Great Sky ceremony, part of which I described in chapter five.[1]

A SHAMAN AT HOME

After the public event, Bayar invited a few of the conference delegates to an evening séance at her family's compound on the outskirts of Ulaanbaatar. A high wooden fence enclosed the two large rectangular concrete houses and a *ger* (yurt), or circular tent consisting of a wooden frame covered with felt. The séance took place in the larger house, where a dozen guests sat on benches along the walls or settled down on the linoleum floor, which had been laid over packed earth.

Hanging on the wall, over the red, blue, and gold painted wood chest that served as an altar, was a rectangular bag with silk strips attached to its rim (figure 25). My interpreter, a local Soviet-trained psychologist, whispered to me that this was a sacred childbirth bag. Inside, dangling upside down from a red thread, was a small felt doll, an icon that encourages a fetus to stay inside its human dwelling place until it is summoned by a shaman to be born. This special bag was a sign that Bayar knew how to help women with fertility and childbirth.[2] It also contained the *ongon,* or deified souls of deceased shamans in Bayar's lineage, who served as her protective spirits. On the altar, propped against the wall directly below the sacred talisman, there was a photograph of Bayar's late mother, who had trained and initiated her.

Bayar was the tenth generation of her family's shamans. Her twenty-three-year-old daughter, Baljir, was taking the shamanic path as well. And Bayar had recently designated her three-year-old grandson as the official hereditary shaman for the twelfth generation.

She entered the room wearing an owl-feathered headdress with a red half mask and a fringe of string. She was resplendent in her blue silk shaman's gown, which had flying-squirrel-fur cuffs and collar, tufts of eagle feathers along the arms, rows of rattling iron keys attached across the back, and multicolored silk ribbons knotted and

25. *The Mongolian shaman Bayar Odun and the author (left) hold children in their laps. They are sitting before a long wooden altar under the spirit bag.*

braided together into "snakes."[3] A long leather train reaching from neck to ankle was embroidered with images of bears, wolves, deer, horses, and camels.

Bowing to the four directions and to the *ongon,* she picked up her drum with its nine (the Mongolian sacred number) iron rings inside and sang to Changkilang Xatan, her celestial female protector spirit. Then Bayar, for the second time that day, began to ride her drum horse (figure 26) wildly into the sky.

More than once she tumbled off her mount, falling unconscious for a few minutes. Eventually she sat down cross-legged on the floor. She held her huge drum vertically between her legs and pounded it, causing the rings to make crackling sounds. Chanting loudly, she bounced up and down, riding her drum horse back to the sky. From time to time she whistled, and several times more she fell off her

26. *Drum horse, pen-and-ink drawing of the spirit of a shaman's drum. It is sometimes painted on a drumhead, but it can also be painted on a sheet of paper tacked above a shaman's altar.*

horse, but each time she was revived by her husband and continued on her journey.

She was following an ancient path whose secrets had been handed down from generation to generation. Together with her protective spirits, she galloped along on her spiritual horse; its movements were visible in the bouncing of her body. Suddenly, as her spirit horse fused with her mind and body, sparks of fire flickered through her eyes. At that instant her horse was transformed into the subtle energy known in Mongolian as *hiimori,* or "wind horse" (figure 27). It raced through her mind, blood, and flesh, causing her to twitch and tremble.

Bayar's husband served as her main assistant; his help was needed whenever she crossed into the spirit world. His job was to recognize the spirits she contacted, jump up to greet them, and interpret what they said for the audience. Bayar herself could only express the spirits' desires with gestures, laughter, whistling, and a single word repeated over and over: "*Ikra! Ikra! Ikra!* I need! I need! I need!"

27. *Pen-and-ink drawing of the Mongolian wind horse, a visualization of the spiritual energy known as* hiimori. *This magical winged horse wears the* syombo, *consisting of a crescent moon with its horns pointing upward and holding a sun disk, topped by the three flames of time: past, present, and future. Chinggis Khan's battle standard, and nearly every Mongolian flag afterward, included these important shamanic icons.*

When she closed her eyes and began to shake her head violently from side to side her husband removed her earrings and metal hair ornaments. Then he circulated among us, looking for eyeglasses and metal earrings or barrettes. He gently asked us to take them off, explaining that the ancestral spirits were from a much earlier time, long before glass and metal were made. Since these spirits were unaccustomed to flashes of light bouncing off shiny surfaces, they might become confused.

For more than two hours Bayar alternated between drumming, singing, and praying. From time to time she was suddenly possessed by a spirit and fell down, letting her drum roll across the floor. Her husband gave her juniper smoke to revive her and helped her to stand up. After each possession she immediately started drumming, singing, and praying rapidly in a low voice. Then she stopped, removed her feathered headdress, and stepped out of her gown. She placed the garment on Baljir's shoulders, thus transferring the essence of her own spiritual guardians into her daughter's body. The young woman bowed to each of the four directions and to the sacred child-birth bag, then took hold of the drum and began to ride it herself. As she did so, her mother spoke loudly and sang, all the while jerking on a long hide rope (the horse's rein) tied to the inside of the drum. In this way she led her daughter along the shamanic path.

THE HEALING AUDIENCE

Thirty minutes later Bayar removed the gown from Baljir and tied the girl's hair up in a purple and blue flowered silk bandanna. Then mother and daughter sat down on the floor in front of their altar and received their clients. Each person seeking healing or advice presented a clean paper bill face up, with the top of Chinggis Khan's head pointing toward the shaman, who kissed the money, placed it on her forehead, and prayed.

Several times Bayar accurately described the nature and precise location of clients' illnesses before they even opened their mouths to speak. In one instance, she informed a middle-aged woman that her energy was blocked just below her navel; that meant she had stomach problems—an ulcer or perhaps cancer. Bayar firmly instructed her to see a physician. Then, cutting a length of red cotton string, she handed it to the woman and told her to tie it around her waist as protection until she received medical treatment.

One of the guests was a cinematographer from Paris who had come to attend the conference. Bayar proclaimed that he had been running around for years filming shamans, not out of respect for their healing traditions but out of curiosity. He had been in Russia, she said, and he was hoping to return there. But that was a dangerous plan, she warned, so dangerous, in fact, that he would have a fatal accident within seven days.

Clearly shaken by this sudden pronouncement, the Frenchman admitted that he had been filming shamans throughout North Asia. He was planning to leave in a few days for a shoot in Ulan-Ude, a town in the Buryat Republic just over the Russian border. Bayar promised to conduct a healing ceremony for him and ordered him out of the house to purchase vodka and vanilla cookies.

As he left she giggled and quietly asked the remaining clients what they wished to tell her about themselves or wanted to know about their future. One old woman presented her arthritic fingers. Bayar placed her *toli*, or bronze mirror, on the woman's shaking hands, then pulled it off quickly. Like a magnet, the mirror would draw the illness out, she told me later.

Another case developed into a therapeutic discussion between a husband and wife about the causes of their many miscarriages. Bayar encouraged them to open their hearts, minds, and bodies in order to heal their relationship. They should come back in a few days, she said, so that she could help them make an appropriate birth icon for their home altar.

Finally, a painfully thin woman described her problems: sore eyes and a headache. Bayar massaged and blew on the affected areas, then asked her guests if they knew any good eye doctors. A Japanese couple ventured the name of a surgeon in Tokyo but noted that the airline ticket was expensive. Turning back to the client, Bayar told her that she needed to see an eye specialist in town as soon as possible.

When the filmmaker returned from the store, Bayar accepted his gifts. To the vodka and cookies he added snapshots of himself standing at the open door of his home outside Paris. She blessed him by pouring shots of vodka over his head, then exorcised him with several flicks of her silken whip on his back (figure 28).

When everyone else had made their requests, I tentatively approached Bayar on my knees, holding out a ten-thousand-tugrug note (worth approximately ten dollars) in the proper manner. The shaman shook her head and whispered that I should come again the following afternoon with a bottle of vodka, some vanilla sweets, and my husband. Then she looked around at her audience and announced out loud that she had asked Great Sky to give us many blessings and good luck in everything we did. It was nearly dawn when her husband told us that it was time to leave.

28. *Bayar Odun is holding up her knotted whip.*

VODKA AND KISSES

When Dennis and I returned with our translator the next day Bayar was napping in her altar room. As we quietly entered, she rolled toward us, cracked open her eyes, smiled, and invited us over.

She sat up on the edge of her double bed and insisted that I sit down next to her, light a cigarette, take a drag, and hand it to her. She stroked my hair, then braided and unbraided it, and as she did so she instructed me to pour and drink a shot of vodka, and to serve her a shot, too. After tossing down the drink, Bayar looked at me closely. She stared deeply into my eyes and remarked, "I don't know, but you must know something about shamanism." Then she added in a booming masculine voice, "I have never accepted foreigners before. I never thought it possible. But now I do."

At that point she wriggled out of bed, walked over to her altar, picked up her silken whip, and sat down on the floor. She took her mouth harp out of its carved wooden box and played a sad tune. Swaying from side to side she hummed, talked, and laughed with her spirit familiars. My interpreter whispered to me that Bayar seemed to be in a state of mind called *yavgan böölo*, "alert shamanizing." This was quite different from the deeper trance, the *unaatai böölo* or "mounted shamanizing," we had witnessed the night before. I wished I had brought along a pencil and a pad of paper, but writing notes seemed inappropriate, so I simply concentrated on memorizing everything she said.

Turning back to us, she smiled, touched my hand, and kissed me on both cheeks, then hugged and kissed Dennis as well (figure 29).

29. *Bayar Odun is coaxing the author's husband to drink another shot of vodka. Bayar's husband sits behind them. A pack of cigarettes and a bottle of vodka can be seen at lower left.*

She giggled and insisted that I photograph the two of them sharing cigarettes and vodka. Since Dennis doesn't smoke it was clearly a test for him to accept drags from her cigarette. Shrieking with laughter, she pulled in deeply on her cigarette, blew smoke in his face, and then poured liquor on his head. Finally she exuberantly kissed his cheeks again and again.

She beckoned me to sit down on the other side of her, then turned and suddenly kissed me on the lips, long and hard, playfully sticking her tongue deep inside my mouth. Her kisses were so intense—and the energy she transmitted to me was so strong—that I became light-headed and nearly fainted.

As I sat there on the floor in front of her altar, feeling the effects of the kisses and the vodka, I thought about how long Mongolian shamans had been waiting for the opportunity to shed their secrecy. Then it was time for Bayar to turn her attention to her clients, who were already forming a line that stretched from her door down the street.

EIGHT

Crossroads Between Worlds:

THE POWER OF DREAMING

RESEARCHERS HAVE LARGELY ignored the healing that arises from shamanic dream training. Timothy White, the editor of the popular magazine *Shaman's Drum,* noted that over the sixteen-year history of the journal he has published very few articles focused on shamanic dream work traditions. He explained this neglect by observing that dreams are so integral to shamanic cultures that it is easy to take them for granted. Excited by trance ceremonies, observers have emphasized the outwardly exotic elements of shamanism— flashy costumes, hypnotic drumming, and monotonous chanting. They entirely missed the fact that shamans listen to and amplify an inner expression of the psyche.[1]

Dreaming is a universal experience, one that we may attempt to induce or avoid, remember or forget. It can occur while we are awake or asleep. The waking path consists of guided fantasies known as omens, waking dreams, and visions. On the sleeping side are personal dreams (based on everyday events or wishes of the soul), prophetic dreams, archetypal dreams, nightmares, and lucid dreams.[2]

People who grow up within shamanic traditions regard their

dreams and visions as valuable sources of knowledge and develop techniques for dreaming that may be different for men and women. By using the word *dreaming* here I mean the entire process of inducing a dream state by undertaking dream incubation or a vision quest, the dream itself, and sharing the dream. From the earliest times the sharing and interpretation of dreams and visions have been of interest to humankind. They can be shared through representation by drawing, painting, and describing a dream. Dreams and visions can also be shared through presentation by reenacting the images and narratives in poetry, song, and dance. Shamans everywhere use both these techniques to engage with the image-filled dreaming world.

Even as a young child, I was aware of my own dreams. The earliest ones, like those of most children, centered on animals, and I shared them with my grandmother, who helped me to understand how the animals I dreamed of related to my spiritual development. Her interpretation of my spotted turtle dream helped me to understand and accept my slowness in all things. I later realized that this dream was also a prophetic dream since it foreshadowed the time I would spend inside an iron lung. The beaded turtle amulet she made for me helped me to visualize, know, accept, and value my turtleness. By taking my inner dream and giving it an outer shape, she encouraged me in the knowledge that I am truly Turtle.

My dream on the night my grandmother died took me on a classic shamanic journey through the night sky; thus it was archetypal, imaginative, and mythic. When we arrived at the nest filled with serpent bones she gave me a shimmering egg designating me as a shaman. One year later, on the anniversary of her death, she visited and spoke to me directly, charging me "to not allow the wisdom of old Indian women to die out." Only now, by writing this book, am I beginning to fulfill her prophecy.

My experience has convinced me that one can unconsciously slip into a dream state or consciously learn to enter it. Dreaming is a crossroads location, halfway between the world of the senses and the world of intuitive understanding. At that point it is possible to leave the normal waking state, in which one perceives only through the senses, without leaving physical reality. This practice, known among the Maya as "completing the dreaming," closely resembles the Jungian method of "active imagination." Jungian dream analysis regards all of one's dream images as aspects of the self; the symbols within a dream are "translated" into words upon waking or during an analytic session. One brings out and elaborates the metaphor in the original experience, amplifying it through rhyme or wordplay.[3]

Mayan shamans do something similar, but they do it when they are still asleep in a dream state. During my apprenticeship I was taught to interact with each dream symbol as it appeared to me, in order to learn what it was trying to teach me. As I did so I was simultaneously aware of being asleep, removed from the external world, and of being awake, receptive to the inner world. This was possible because sleep and wakefulness are what neuroscientists have called "mixed states," in which several neural systems overlap at different brain stem levels. As a result, conscious and unconscious components blend together.[4]

LUCID DREAMING

Have you ever decided to wake up from a dream? Your awareness of being in a dream state while asleep is called "lucid dreaming." But what if you held on to that awareness and decided not to wake up? It is possible to learn to do just that, since lucid dreaming is open to various dream-training techniques. The maximum development of lucid dreaming leads to subjectively powerful dream images and enhanced self-awareness, similar to peak experiences and to the form of meditative awareness found in Eastern philosophies.[5]

Within shamanic traditions, the key moment of lucidity occurs during an interior dialogue between different parts of the self or psyche. The dreamer is simultaneously aware of being asleep and removed from the external world and of being awake and receptive to the inner world. In that paradoxical space between sleeping and waking, as the lucid dream takes shape out of dreaming consciousness there exist complex sensory crossovers, or synesthesias, that are visual, auditory, and tactile. These interrupt the narrative flow of a dream and fuse dreamer to imagery in such a way that the dream is experienced as simultaneously fearful and joyful. Because of the mix of emotion and thought, a lucid dream leaves the dreamer with an expansive thrill or numinous feeling.[6]

For many years philosophers dismissed lucidity as merely a mental awakening during sleep. Not until laboratory research demonstrated that lucidity was actually accompanied by the same normal rapid eye movement (REM) that occurs during dreaming—and subjects were trained to signal their awareness of their dream state by making exaggerated eye movements—did researchers suggest that lucidity was a legitimate part of dreaming. This very special consciousness ranges from a quasi-lucid state in which one is aware of dreaming but unable to control the content of one's dreams to being able to enter the dream space and affect the dream's outcome.[7]

The lucid dream state can also occur during vision quests when persons who are not asleep unexpectedly recognize that they are blending exterior waking images with interior dreamscapes. Teemiartissaq, an Inuit woman living in Greenland who was undergoing shamanic training (figure 30), described to the Arctic explorer William Thalbitzer a terrifying moment of visionary lucidity.[8]

One day when I went into the mountains I saw a spirit that I had never seen before. It was hanging onto a mountain ledge, swinging back and forth with his hair waving wildly.

Then all of a sudden another spirit bobbed up from a grave. It was a whistling spirit, for it was blood red all over the face. I wanted to flee, but it was impossible. For such a spirit creeps inside us and licks us all over.

30. *Teemiartissaq, an Inuit woman shaman and dreamer who lived in the early twentieth century.*

That grave, oh that sinister grave. As I was about to approach it, I saw that the flat top-stone on the grave was rocking violently. I stopped in terror. Then I awoke a little bit and thought: "Why should I fear it? Am I continually, for the present, not to reach it?"

Then the fear left me as I drew nearer the grave. When I came close to it the stone opened and the spirit known as Qila arose. But because he was turned sidewise toward my shoulders, I was not fully conscious of him. I first became aware of him as he moved across my thighs.

Qila said to me: "I am strongly bound. The former human being, whom they had bound, I carry about with me."

I replied: "Yes, yes, in a little while you shall become more pliable." He then turned away from me. And at the same

moment, of its own accord, the top-stone fell with a crash and
lay in its place, rocking.

Lucidity protects one against nightmares like this one, but it also demonstrates one's shamanic ability to produce, guide, and control one's dreaming. Since Teemiartissaq was just beginning her shamanic training she could not yet turn her quasi-lucid nightmare into a lucid dream.

Several methods for achieving lucidity are described in the autobiography of Ruby Modesto, a well-known Cahuilla shaman who died at the age of sixty-seven in 1980. This remarkable woman spent her adult life near Palm Springs as an herbalist, spiritual healer, and midwife. Controlling the course of dreaming—a process she called "Real Dreaming"—was at the center of her healing practice.

Her uncle taught her to "set up dreaming" by giving herself directions concerning what she wanted to explore. Then she was able to remain within the dreaming state long enough to manipulate the outcome of the dream. In a similar way, she eventually learned how to explore the spiritual dimension of everyday waking reality.[9]

The way you do Real Dreaming is by remembering to tell yourself to go to sleep in your first-level ordinary dream. You consciously tell yourself to lie down and go to sleep. Then you dream a second dream. This is the second level and the prerequisite for Real Dreaming.

Uncle Charlie [her shamanic teacher] called this process "setting up dreaming." You can tell yourself ahead of time where you want to go, or what you want to see, or what you want to learn. On the third level you learn and see unusual things, not of this world. The hills and terrain are different.

On both the second and third dream levels you can talk to people and ask questions about what you want to know.

Real Dreaming resembles Hindu "dream witnessing" and Tibetan Buddhist "dream yoga." Both these traditions evolved out of shamanism in the first through the seventh centuries, when city-states arose and state religions evolved. At this time loud drumming was looked down upon, because it was considered earthly, and therefore bad. In response, shamans developed silent, undetectable methods of changing their consciousness by looking into cloudy brass mirrors and engaging in special breathing techniques. They also perfected ways of enhancing dreaming as a form of meditation naturally available during sleep.[10]

My Mongolian friend, Bayar Odun, told me that when she was first training as a shaman she dreamed repeatedly about mirrors. Her grandmother appeared standing before her holding a large mirror in her right hand and a set of three smaller mirrors tied together with a red string in her left hand. As she studied these mirrors her grandmother smiled, then laughed, and both she and the mirrors disappeared. A few weeks later, when Bayar was tending her reindeer herd, she noticed a young animal circling a thin spot in the snow. She went over and dug up the snow and even removed some of the mud underneath. There, about six inches below the surface, were the four mirrors from her dream!

Today she keeps them on her altar and uses them to find and pull out illness from below her patients' skin. When I was talking with Bayar about her mirror dream, she suddenly handed the four mirrors to me. They were warm and tingly, as though an electric current ran through them. On their backs were Chinese characters that she said represented good luck and happiness. Bayar also told me the largest brass mirror absorbed and gave off very powerful energy and brought clear, prophetic dreams. I found that out for myself that very evening, when I dreamed of seeing such a mirror in an antique shop. The following morning I went to a local shop, found the mirror in a display case, and purchased it. For the remainder of my stay in Mongolia, I experienced many more lucid dreams than ever before in my life.

A key characteristic of lucid dreaming is that the experience is so vivid that it verges on wakefulness. A Tzotzil Mayan weaver and flower vendor named Tonik Nibak reported the following dream.[11]

I was washing my hair and it all fell out. But then I thought, "Why would my hair fall out like that? Well, that's fine! It always has so many lice in it. Never mind, I'll cover myself with an old blanket."

Then picking up a rag, I wrapped it around my head, covered myself with a shawl, and went outside to gather firewood. I found a pine stump, dug up all its roots, stripped off the rotten parts, bound them together, and carried them home. There I climbed over the fence and put my bundle down next to a live oak tree and flew off.

When I landed far away I was asked by someone there why I had left my wood in a heap and flown off. I became concerned and flew back to get it. But I wasn't flying anymore and woke up.

It seemed to me as if it was already light and as if I was on the earth's surface. It didn't seem as if I were in my dream. My wood arrived safely. I sat down at home with my load. I made a tiny log corral. I stacked the logs and looked at them. Then, I woke up.

Although gathering firewood is an everyday activity for the Tzotzil, dreaming of it indicates that the dreamer (or a close relative) will die. The opening image of the dreamer's hair falling out also prophesied her death, but she rejected this interpretation. Remaining within the dream, she shifted her consciousness into a lucid dream state and retrieved the firewood. In so doing she symbolically reversed the prophecy, thereby hoping to outwit death.

Tonik's feeling of flying is a universal marker of lucidity. It signifies that one's soul (the part of the self that flies) is knowledgeable, a prerequisite for shamanic training. The opposite experience, a heightened bodily or kinesthetic awareness that often comes during waking dreams or vision quests, is another ingredient of shamanic dreaming.

WAKING DREAMS AND VISIONS

Young people in many cultures are taught to pay attention to any animal that appears during a waking dreamlike state. The animal may "talk" with the person, using movements or cries, to foretell an upcoming event. If the dreamer pays attention and honors this being, it may then become a lifelong guardian spirit, dream helper, or ally.

A well-known Crow medicine woman, Pretty Shield, related a story about her grandmother, Seven Stars. One day in the mid-1850s, the woman was sewing a buffalo robe. As she worked, a chickadee suddenly appeared before her.[12]

At first it did not talk. It just picked up bits of the fat in the fleshings lying on the robe. Then my grandmother talked to the little bird.

Finally after its belly was full the chickadee said, "Leave your work for a while, and follow me. I wish to talk to you over by that creek. Get somebody to take care of your little girl, and meet me at the creek."

My grandmother ran to her lodge and got a woman friend to care for the little girl. She then took a sweatbath, put on her finest clothes, and went to the creek.

At first grandmother did not see the chickadee. She could hear the bird talking and laughing to itself, but could not see it until it came to sit on a willow twig right above her head. "Look," the chickadee said, going up into the air, flying higher and higher. Straight up it went, growing larger and larger and larger, until it was as big as a golden eagle.

"See," it called down to my grandmother, "there is great power in little things." And my grandmother saw that the bird held a buffalo calf in each of its taloned feet.

"I am a woman, as you are. Like you I have to work, and make the best of this life. I am your friend, and yet to help you I must first hurt you. You, however, will have three sons, but will lose two of them. One will live to be a good man. Your family must never eat eggs, never," said the bird.

For the rest of her life Seven Stars and one of her sons ate no eggs. Her husband and two other sons, however, paid no attention to her vision and continued to eat the forbidden food. Not long after, an enemy tribe killed the three men. Seven Stars, however, who followed the chickadee's teaching, became a wise woman with a guardian spirit and the knowledge of medicine. The remaining son, who observed the food taboo, also became a shaman.

There's another lesson in Seven Stars' adherence to her dream message, in contrast to the disregard of her male relatives: under colonialism, men were encouraged to abandon their native cultures as inferior. Women instead tended to reject the new ways of life and upheld traditional practices. Seven Stars' story suggests that the masculine path of skepticism is the path of death, while the feminine path of belief is the path of life.

VISION QUESTING

Though the practice has diminished since the mid-1850s, vision quests were once undertaken by all North American Indian youths upon reaching puberty. At this very special threshold in their lives, they were encouraged by their elders to communicate directly with spirits and deities through dreams and visions.

Boys were sent out alone to mountaintops, while girls were sequestered in nearby gardens or small lodges. The adolescents fasted and prayed until a spirit manifested itself and magically took them far away to another mountaintop, garden, or lodge. If they were lucky, they became entranced and talked with animal and ancestral spirits who granted them many gifts—long life, fertility, knowledge of herbal medicines, clairvoyance, and telepathy.[13]

In the mid-1920s a young Mandan woman named Stays Yellow fasted for a vision in a lodge her mother had built for her in the woods. She stayed awake all night and in the predawn light drifted off to sleep and dreamed that relatives of hers, an old couple, were doctoring a woman through a difficult childbirth. They cut up and boiled strange-looking black roots. Then the old woman chewed the roots and sprayed their juice over a group of dead water snakes. Every time she did this, a snake came alive and slithered away. The last of the snakes, though, was slow to revive, for she was pregnant. Each time the woman blew on her she gave birth. The couple then told Stays Yellow that from that day forth she would have the power to help women who had difficulty with childbirth. Indeed, she trained as a midwife and herbalist and went on to teach her art to other young women.[14]

Tela Star Hawk Lake, a northern California spiritual healer, recalled her own initial vision quest, which took place in the early 1970s.[15]

One night a strange thing occurred. I was singing and praying with my eyes closed and I heard the scream of my Hawk. Then

I heard a ringing noise in my ears. As I looked up into the sky searching for Hawk, I found it, and suddenly saw my favorite Star. I cried from the power and humility. Hawk flew higher and higher out of sight, straight toward Star as darkness began to take over the day.

It was evening and I felt that Hawk was carrying my prayers with it, but a strange feeling came over me. I could feel it pulling my soul out of my body and my whole body began to tremble violently. My soul was now in the Hawk. It was merged with the spirit and power of the Hawk. I was now Hawk.

It flew directly into the night sky, out of sight, as the stars became brighter. Then suddenly, as the ringing noise got louder in my ears, and my body continued to tremble with power surging through it, I could see the Star shoot straight out of the sky, directly into me, and a large flash of light surrounded my entire body. I was knocked unconscious by the experience and was in a coma for several days.

After several other vision quests, during which she learned both lucid dreaming and shape-shifting, Tela Star Hawk Lake became a powerful healer (figure 31). Together with Robert Medicine Grizzly-bear Lake, she now has a large multicultural healing practice in the western United States.[16]

DREAM INCUBATION

People who have lost a living connection with their elders and their culture of dreaming may try to strengthen their spiritual bonds through dream incubation: they make a pilgrimage to a place where people have experienced special dreams in the past. There they spend

31. *Tela Star Hawk Lake is a twentieth-century California shaman of Yurok, Karuk, Hupa, Chilula, and Irish-American heritage. She is standing before a traditional plank house wearing a woven hat and holding a rattle in her left hand and a healing wand in her right hand.*

the night, or several nights, in the hopes of having an important dream.

A contemporary Cree artist, Shirley Cheechoo, undertook several such pilgrimages to a magical place known as Dreamer's Rock, on the Whitefish Reserve in Ontario. On one journey she and two women friends went to the rock in the hopes of incubating a dream. They prayed, burned tobacco and sweetgrass, and slept. At dawn a hole appeared in the sky, gradually opening into a large circle. From the center a sunbeam streamed down upon them. As Shirley described her experience: "I could see the sparkles of light all around me. I knew the spirits were there. I knew I had touched another level of existence."[17]

Others may draw or sculpt images of the spirits they wish to encounter. An Abenake husband-and-wife team from Quebec,

Canada, carves and paints their elders' spirit guides, Spider Woman and Caribou Man, to accomplish that end. In a catalogue for the 1992 exhibit of their sculptures at the San Diego Museum of Man they shared one of their favorite stories about lucid dreaming.[18]

One day my father told me, "In my dream last night I awakened, and then I turned over and saw the morning sun shining through a dew-covered spider web. So beautiful it was! It was filled with sparkling color, a million tiny lights in a hand's breadth.

"A black and yellow spider was busy repairing a tear in the web from an insect that got away. The spider stopped weaving and said in a tiny little voice, 'This is a Dream Net; it only lets good dreams through. This hole was left by the dream you are dreaming now!' " That's what my father said.

Native Americans have long associated spiderwebs with protective and healing powers. Orb webs were placed directly on top of a puncture wound to stop the flow of blood. A web painted on a shield was thought to be protective, like an actual spider's web, whose sticky spiral strands and long radiating support lines cannot easily be destroyed by arrows or bullets, which pass through, leaving only tiny holes.

Similarly, protective web designs are sewn and painted on baby hoods and cradles to stop bad dreams from penetrating a baby's open fontanel. And throughout North America today small nets known as "dream catchers" are made by cutting a supple willow or red dogwood branch, bending it into a circle, and weaving plant materials or sinew into a spiraling orb within the circle. Several tiny glass beads or semiprecious stones—garnet, turquoise, rose quartz, or malachite—are attached to the "web." Finally a larger bead and a feather from a wild turkey, cardinal, or bluebird are tied in the center (figure 32). These represent the head and body of a garden spider hanging head downward from the center of the web.[19]

The dream catcher is lashed to the top of an infant's cradleboard to filter all dreams. Only the good ones that flow through the opening at the center of the net are allowed into the baby's dreaming consciousness. Today, Native American artists all over the country create dream nets as amulets for adults as well as for children. Sold at intertribal powwows, they are used as a way of attracting good images and keeping bad ones away from our nightly dreamscapes.

In November 2001, Governor Gary Johnson of New Mexico purchased ten thousand dream catchers made by Native American craftspeople and brought them to the state capitol in Santa Fe. There, at the Round House, they were blessed by an intertribal group of medicine women and men, flown to New York City, and

32. *Contemporary Southwestern dream catcher. This dream catcher is made of buckskin rawhide and fishing line with a painted feather hanging from a ceramic bead.*

given to the families of victims of the collapsed World Trade Center towers. Many of these family members were suffering from a chronic inability to dream, nodding off during the day, or enduring nightmarish images of destruction and terror. The hope was that the Native American dream catchers would promote the good dreams necessary for healthy minds and would bring some healing for these victims.

Dreaming is a powerful force. It allows us access to the past and helps with autonomy for the future. Dreams are the closest thing to shamanic journeys that all of us experience; indeed, "spirit messages," or prophecies, can manifest themselves to anyone who pays attention to their dreams. If we learn to be more mentally aware in our dreaming, we can become more open to healing images. As we do so, we move beyond a perception of dreams as static entities, mythic texts, or landscapes and toward an understanding of dreaming as a spiritual process of transformation within the poetic landscape of the human soul.

NINE

The Dolphin Wore Diamonds:

FOLLOWING THE PATH OF DREAMS

EARLY IN OUR shamanic training among the Maya one of our teachers, Don Andrés, asked Dennis and me what we had dreamed the previous night. Although I did not expect this question, I jumped right in: "I dreamed that I was standing on a grassy knoll looking down into a beautiful valley filled with wildflowers of every color. There directly below me was a white convertible with its top down. Inside were four couples, totally naked, making love and—"

Andrés blurted out, "Oh, my!" Then he covered his face with his hands.

I was embarrassed but continued. "Just a little closer to me, on the side of this same hill, I saw a cardboard box jumping all around. Finally it burst open. Inside, in each corner, was a white rabbit— four pure white rabbits with tiny pink noses and black dot eyes. So beautiful!"

He instantly replied, "This is an announcement of your work here with us. Your cardboard box is a small wooden shrine we call the *mebil*. The box has many little animals inside—birds, rabbits, and deer. But they aren't exactly animals. You will soon encounter this treasure."

"But what about the couples making love in the car?" I asked, trying to focus some attention on the first half of my dream.

Taking a swallow of coffee, he replied, "The four pairs are the four of us, together with our divining bundles, our seeds, and crystals. We are four pairs."

"Are the divining bundles male or female?" Dennis asked.

"Yours is a woman, and Barbara's is a man," Andrés replied in a matter-of-fact tone.

"What about the two other pairs?" I asked.

"We and our divining bundles are the other two. We were all four together in your dream. And we are all four together in the work that we are doing," said Doña Talín, who was sitting nearby.

"When she woke up, she was laughing and laughing over those little rabbits," Dennis said.

"Yes, when the hour comes to encounter the shrine, one is pleased. By means of this small box, little by little, things will abound. You will see soon enough."

"The rabbits were white, pure white!" I repeated with excitement.

"Yes, they weren't stained, so they are somewhat new," Talín replied calmly.

"And the people were pure white also; they weren't really people, they were—"

She cut me off in midsentence. "Like dolls?" she asked.

"Yes. But white like this china cup, not like white skin color," I replied, pointing to my coffee cup.

"This means that the divining bundles are new. You will enter this dream again and move it along, complete it," she said, carrying the cups away to her cookhouse.

Andrés stood up, stretched, cleared his throat, and walked off in a leisurely manner toward the turkey pens below the house.

Dennis and I were suddenly alone on the front porch, not knowing what to do. I felt as though I'd embarrassed our teachers with my sexy-couples-in-the-convertible dream. But that was what I had dreamed. Maybe, I thought, we North Americans are oversexed, even in our dreaming. After all, we are constantly bombarded by sexual images in advertising and movies. Or maybe I had so much of a puritanical overlay on my own sexuality that I could not easily talk about such things without feeling shame.

Andrés soon reappeared with a smile on his lips and two turkey eggs in his hands, one for each of us. Sitting down on the bench directly across from us, he held out the eggs on his open palms and said, "Now you will have dreams, each one of you, in which you will marry someone else. Do not be ashamed of these dreams, for you are not directly marrying another person. Your divining bundles will become your spouses in the world of the spirits. There you will learn how sexual energy feeds you, gives you strength. How it travels throughout your entire body and develops in your heart and mind."

As he gently transferred the eggs into our hands, he continued, "Sometimes I dream that I am marrying someone else, that I have a second spouse. I wake up right away and tell Talín the dream. This is a good dream, a lucky dream for us, since it means that we will soon receive a blessing. So do not be embarrassed to tell us these sexual dreams. They are very lucky.

"Last night Talín also dreamed. She woke me up about midnight because she dreamed of marrying someone else, a dark man. We sat up together the rest of the night and talked about her dream. The dark man was the Holy Earth. The Earth was very pleased with her and wanted to marry her.

"The women are beginning to dream together," he went on, "which means that our work together will come out well. Women's sexual dreams are very good. So it seems we four will continue."

When Talín returned, she took my hands in hers and said, "The images in your dreams move your thoughts, and your mind moves these images. You must learn to understand what the four couples and the four rabbits mean in your dreams. What your body thinks. What your heart wants."

I found myself mystified by her statement but decided to try to wake up a little during my dreaming. If I could accomplish that, then perhaps I could also learn how to change, amplify, or complete my dreams.

THE DOLPHIN APPEARS

Several nights later I dreamed that I was scuba diving for abalone in the Pacific Ocean off Santa Catalina Island. In fact, I was sound asleep in our adobe house on the west coast of Guatemala. But I clearly recognized the spot; I had dived there for abalone many times during my undergraduate years.

Swimming languidly through the kelp forests with my crowbar in my right hand and my game pouch tied to my weight belt, I began flipping over rocks. As I passed through a narrow place, filled with clumps of tangled dark plants, I came upon a cave. It frightened me at first, but as I approached the opening a beam of light shot down through the milky water, illuminating the cave floor. There was a miniature village inside, built out of opalescent abalone and bright pink conch shells. Staring at a strange shell house lodged in a wall, I saw a woman inside, about my own age, weaving kelp leaves into a basket.

Suddenly, a large fish darted out of the mouth of the cave. Fearing that it was a shark, I woke up inside my dreaming and carefully examined my bare outstretched hands. No blood; she hadn't attacked. Then I looked back at the huge grayish white fish. It was now a gentle bottle-nosed dolphin. But she was wearing a diamond necklace!

Moving her head from side to side and up and down, this elegant dolphin inspected me from mask to tank to flipper. Smiling and bowing in my direction, she held out her flipper, as though to touch me, or perhaps to shake my hand. However, her friendliness scared me. (Afterward I remembered that in some cultures dolphins, the swiftest of all sea animals, transport the souls of the dead to the next life.)

I suddenly became aware that the oxygen in my tank was low, and I began my ascent to the surface. Slowly, very slowly, to avoid getting the bends, I ascended. And although I didn't look back, I was keenly aware that the dolphin was following right behind me. When we burst through the surface of the water, breaching together like whales, I awoke with a start.

As I related the dream to my teachers, Doña Talín began counting the days of the Mayan calendar on her fingers. Then she fell silent and looked down at her legs. After a while she said, "It seems this has to do with the family, your family."

"Yes, it's the women's side of the family," added Andrés, pointing to his own left thigh. "The lightning moved, and the blood spoke here, on the back of my thigh," he whispered, lifting his left pant leg and pointing to the very center of his thigh. He was referring to "the speaking of the blood," caused by rapid movements of subtle energy. Andrés and Talín had said these bodily sensations felt like an icy wind within their arteries and veins. They also reiterated that the left side of each of our bodies was female and the right side was male.

"It is inside the family, your family," Talín said, lightly touching my sweater. "This is your ancestor. She is the one who is giving you this sign that the work you are accomplishing here with us, and the permissions we are asking for you, are going to come out into the light of day."

My dream had occurred on the night that Eight Deer became Nine Yellow on the Mayan calendar. I knew from our training that the numbers eight and nine were strongly shamanic. My dream therefore concerned my future as a shaman.

That morning Talín and Andrés had gone together to their family shrine on a local hilltop. There they had laid out pine boughs and dozens of multicolored flowers. They burned yellow tallow and white wax candles, followed by a large pile of dark copal incense. With these offerings and their prayers, they asked permission of their ancestors to train and initiate us as shamans.

Could this dream be an answer to the question of whether the ancestors would give their consent? What did it mean? Was I acceptable to them or not?

Since the speaking of the blood experienced by Andrés was under his left, female thigh, it indicated that a deceased woman relative of mine was the one who needed to give her permission. If she did not approve of my training and upcoming initiation, my teachers would learn of it either within their bodies or in their dreams. They would abruptly stop the apprenticeship.

Still worried about the meaning of the dream, I asked hesitantly, "And the shark that became a dolphin, what does that mean?"

"It was a woman who has already died, who came to give you this news, this sign. Dreams are signs, but I'm not sure just what this one wanted to communicate," he replied.

"But you woke up a little in your dream so that you could learn something new, something important. That's good," said Talín. "The dolphin came out to the surface of the water with you, which means that your training will come out well. You will complete it. If the dolphin had dived deep into the ocean, it would have meant that your training would fail. You would drown."

"You said the light came down into the water?" Andrés asked in a serious tone.

"Yes, but the dolphin came up when I came up."

"Ah, then there is some danger. But in the end the work is going to marry up with you, come out into the light," he said with a chuckle. "But I don't know if it was your mother or your grandmother who emerged from the cave to give you this sign."

"Perhaps it was both of them," suggested Talín. "One after the other they came: first the shark and then the dolphin. We will have to study this. With these two women there is some danger, but there's also some good, a favor perhaps. In time you will come to know the true nature of these two women, these two female animals, to know their *naguals,* their spirits."

"You'll need to think about it, to picture it, to visit again with these fish in order to learn from them," added Andrés.

"In the future you will dream this dream again so that you can complete it properly. When it comes back, you must enter the dream. Only in this way will you begin to complete your dreaming," continued Talín.

"What about the cave in my dream?" I asked. "Is that important? Does it mean anything in particular? Should I think about it?"

"It seems that the cave is the tomb of a woman who has already died. Is your mother still living?" asked Talín.

"Yes, but both of my grandmothers are dead."

"Then it's one of your grandmothers who came out of the cave toward you. She represented herself to you in dolphin form. Was either one of your grandmothers a healer?"

"Yes, my mother's mother was a midwife, an herbalist, a prophet. But how did you know?"

"It was the necklace. In your dream you saw clear stones around her neck. They must have been crystals. She wore her divining crystals, her healing and medicine knowledge, so that you could recognize her in the dark. Maybe she was thinking that you might want to follow her and learn her healing ways."

"What about the shells on the cave floor?" I asked. "The colors were so intense; they were more beautiful than any shells I'd ever seen in my entire life. What about them?"

"The shells, well, the shells are not really shells, of course," Andrés replied hesitantly. "All kinds were found there?"

"Yes."

"Then perhaps these are the seeds, the crystals—"

"Maybe it was your divining bundle that you found there in that cave," interrupted Talín. "But then again, maybe not—it may be something altogether different, something we have not spoken about yet. There is more here that we do not know about. Later you must return to this dream and complete it."

"What do the dark plants symbolize?" I asked, thinking that every item in the dream would have a meaning, like the entries found in dream dictionaries and myth encyclopedias.

"Well, you could say that the plants are like the shade," Andrés replied kindly. "When one is in the shade, the ground seems dark.

When one comes out into the sun, then everything is clear. Now the important thing is, you did wake up a little in your dream, right?"

I nodded, and he continued, "You will need to work on doing this more in the future, so that you can complete your dreaming."

COMPLETING THE DREAM

I tried hard for many nights to complete my dolphin dream, but it eluded me, and as the weeks passed, I began to believe it would never reappear and to worry that if I failed to complete this dream they might not initiate me. Finally, 260 days later, when Eight Deer once again became Nine Yellow on the Mayan calendar, I suddenly found myself in a three-story house, underwater. Three dolphins were circling near the windows outside peering in at me. They were swimming round and round rapidly, counterclockwise.

There were swellings in the center of their heads between their wide-spaced eyes, near the blowhole. From these bumps shone lights—brilliant, piercing lights. Whenever a dolphin passed by a window it looked in at me and cast its light over me. It was so dazzling I was frightened and looked for a place to hide from the glare.

The dolphins circled and circled past the windows on all three stories, one after another, again and again. Then they began broadcasting whistling sounds: squeaks, squawks, and blats that turned into clacking and yelping. They were clearly trying to advise me of something, something important. But try as I might, I could not understand them.

THE DOLPHINS' MESSAGE

I awoke feeling happy with the return visit and pleased that I had managed to get the dolphins to converse with me. But I was baffled and anxious, since I could not understand their message and thus had only partially completed my dreaming.

Talín looked at me kindly and said, "The water is good. It is life. These dolphins are your guardians and your guides: the ones who carry you wherever you want to go. You ride them deep down into the ocean, and then the door opens to the left. To the feminine—"

Andrés interrupted excitedly, "Dolphins are the ones that will bring you the news from now on. They are your *nagual,* the face of your day, your destiny. Dolphins give light, the knowledge of crystals. Inside the divining bundle the seeds and crystals provide the illumination for whatever one wants to know, for wherever one wants to go. This pulsating light is good; it is knowledge, crystal knowledge.

"Now, as I have told you already, *no'jonik* means 'to know' or 'to meditate.' This is the face of your day, your character. You cannot turn away from it. You will live with this day forever."

He had already divined my Mayan birth date as Belejib' No'j, or Nine Thought, a day that symbolized creative thinking and knowledge of all sorts. Since dolphins are famous for their ability to navigate through the ocean by using sonar, emitting sounds and receiving back echoes, they seemed to be an auspicious symbol for my future practice of dream interpretation and divination.

Just as dolphins pilot by using echolocation for sensing underwater objects and creatures, so diviners pilot by bouncing their messages off the minds and bodies of their clients and patients. In many cultures shamans send out, and receive back, vital energy (heat or electricity) and sounds (singing or drumming) that enable them to locate and communicate with the psyches of their clients.

But there was another detail I felt compelled to ask my teachers about. "Why was I looking for a place to hide?"

Andrés answered immediately, "Because these customs, these traditions, give a strong light, strong knowledge. It could put out your eyes. So you must be careful, very careful."

Talín added, "The dolphins are your guides, your shrines. And the three-level house in your dream is a sign of the three shrines: Large Declaration Place and Small Declaration Place are the two upper floors. They are located on the hills above here. They are very powerful. And the basement in your dream is the Water Place in the canyon next to the stream. It is a low place, a cool place, a place of healing."

"What does it mean that everything outside the windows looked like it was underwater?" I asked.

"A dream that one can see into the water is a clear dream," replied Talín. "It is good. One wants it. One wants something important, powerful. But one isn't able to grab hold of it, to grasp it directly, to understand it. But you will."

"It will take a little time yet," said Andrés. "You are not yet complete. You are not yet ready to divine, to interpret the dreams of others, to heal. But soon, when you have lost your fear, you will have many people coming to you. They will ask for your help. And as I told you, once you are ready you cannot turn them away."

"You must try to help each one of them to understand their dreams, to learn to complete them, to know their destiny and heal themselves. This is your calling, your destiny. You cannot escape," Talín said firmly.

Our teachers then reminded us that we all dream many times each night—and for that matter, during the day also. When we do not remember our dreams and thus do not complete our dreaming, we are "being dragged down into muddy water." One must struggle hard not to allow this to happen.

This practice of dream completion encourages one to focus in on key symbols and then to amplify, move, or change them in some way during one's dreaming. A dream clarification process is also central to many other shamanic and psychological systems found worldwide.

Following the path of dreams turned out to be an important doorway between my inner self and my outer world. Completing my dreams is a crucial skill that I still practice to this day.

TEN

Song of the Coneflower:

HERBALISM AND PLANT POWER

THE SUMMER BEFORE I turned nine years old my grand-mother took me to her log cabin in Saskatchewan. The first thing she did was to give me a string of nine cowry shells as a bracelet. Each tiny pear-shaped shell had an iridescent purple interior with powerful female energy. "You will be a woman soon," she said. "Your mind and body will change, and you will bleed each new moon. When this happens you must go into the woods and listen for wisdom. You will be entering a wonderful new stage in your life, a time when the plants, animals, and birds will teach you what you need to know."

She opened her pie cabinet and took out a soft woven basket filled with dried roots, seeds, nuts, moss, leaves, berries, bulbs, and fruits. Sticking her hand inside, she pulled out a root she called blue cohosh and said it was good for menstrual cramps. Reaching in again, she grabbed a fistful of dried raspberries with their leaves and some chamomile flowers. Humming softly to herself, she carefully laid out four dried leaves, four berries, and four flowers on the red and white checked oilcloth that covered her table.

As I studied the herbs, she explained how they worked together to strengthen the muscles of the womb.[1] Each summer I was to gather, dry, and store them for a healing brew for my menstrual bleeding. I took out a school notebook, drew the leaves and berries, and wrote out her instructions. She checked my work, nodded, then reached up and took down a battered Maxwell House coffee can from the top of her cupboard. Removing a pinch of dried black corn smut from inside the can, she mixed it with a small amount of fresh springwater in a clamshell and said, "This is for birthing; it increases contractions. Write it down."

When I had done so, she reached over and pressed hard with the heels of her thumbs on my stomach, just below the belly button. "Inside, here, is where the womb is. This is the place where one pushes to expel the bloody sack the baby grows in, the placenta. You must deliver it soon after the baby is born. Give the woman a drink of red baneberry right away to purge her of the afterbirth. If it stays inside too long, she may get blood poisoning and die. If it doesn't want to come out, tie a stone to it so it won't jump back up toward the chest. Then use your thumbs to push it out, and cut the umbilical cord to release the baby."

She continued with her lessons. To prevent the mother from having a blood clot, I was to make her a bitter tea of skunk currant and red raspberry. To help her milk flow, I should steep dandelion root and give it to her to drink. The following day I was to take her to the sweat lodge for a healing massage, then cook her a meal of dandelion greens with pork or venison and maple sap vinegar.

As I listened to my grandmother's instructions I realized, with some trepidation, that what had begun as a simple lesson about herbs had somehow become a midwife's teaching. I knew she had practiced as an herbalist and midwife for many years, but I could not believe she thought of me as her apprentice.

"Remember to give the umbilical cord to the husband's mother to dry and keep as an amulet. Later she can grind it up, mix it with hot water, and give it to the grown child to improve fertility."

She went on to explain that if a birth took place during the day,

I had to take the afterbirth outside and bury it under a tree. But if the baby was born at night, I was to throw the placenta into the fire. It was important to remember to do that immediately, because if it was not returned to nature the mother might never be given another child. "We must always return what we have used to Mother Earth," she taught me.

The newborn had to be washed in water in which wormwood and reindeer moss had been boiled. Within a month of the birth I should be able to tell if the infant was a "new being" or an "old being." If the couple had previously lost a baby and they dreamed about it during the pregnancy, then it was possible that the child wanted to come back "to be done again." If that was so, distinctive birthmarks would appear, indicating that the baby was an old being, a reincarnation of a deceased family member.

"Such babies are powerful," she warned. "They are born of death and know the crossing between the worlds. During their lives they serve their people as midwives and warriors. You, Barbara, were such a baby."

I nearly fainted. Perhaps I was too young to absorb such powerful teaching. I quickly closed my notebook and tried to forget everything she had told me. For the next several summers I refused to visit her.

THE ENERGY OF PLANTS

Not until I was fourteen did I again spend an entire summer in the north. That year at school I had a wonderful experience with a woman biology teacher who suggested that it might be a good summer project for me to learn from my grandmother how to recognize, gather, and store herbs. So when I went to Canada, I took two pieces of plywood, a tablet of drawing paper, and a ball of string in order to press plant samples the way we did for our school assignments.

When I arrived with my plant press tucked under my arm, my

grandmother was horrified. "Why do you want to own plants?" she asked in a stern voice. "Have you no shame?" Any plant we picked had to be handled in such a way that it was not hurt and could be used in the future. It was not to be owned or stored away in some musty museum. My plant press was quickly abandoned.

Each day our lessons began early in the morning. My grandmother started with the fragrant sweet ferns *(Comptonia peregrina)* that were growing all around her cabin. Picking up a fistful of fronds, she said they were used to sprinkle water on hot coals during a steam bath. Fresh fronds also made a tea to reduce fevers, a mouthwash to treat gum sores, and a compress to relieve the rash caused by poison ivy. They were good for lining blueberry buckets and covering the harvested berries to protect them from fruit flies and bright sunlight. I carefully drew a single frond and wrote all the information in my notebook.

The next plant she identified was Canadian wild ginger *(Asarum canadense)*. I already knew this aromatic root, since she cooked it with virtually all the foods we ate. She told me that it cleansed the blood and aided in digestion. Combined with other medicinal herbs, it sped up and strengthened their action. My grandmother also used chopped ginger as a poultice for my left leg, which was still stiff after my bout with polio.

She made another salve for my leg from the flowers of pearly everlasting *(Anaphalis margaritacea)*. Placing the blossoms on the hot rocks in her sweat lodge, she sat me down to inhale their odor. Then she added small branches and twigs from southern red cedar *(Juniperus virginiana)* and Canada yew *(Taxus canadensis)*. The odor of the burning flowers and evergreen pitch both relaxed and invigorated me as she thoroughly massaged the flower ointment into my leg. For hours afterward my limb felt soft and pliable.

Over the summer she taught me that plant species possess different characteristics and even different chemistries, depending on the time of day and season of the year they are picked. Certain herbs should be gathered only in the early morning before the dew is off the leaves; others should be collected during the light of the full moon. When I wished to harvest a plant, I was to dress in clean clothes, tell the plant why I was pulling it out of the ground, and ask its permission to do so.

The next step was to dig a small hole in the earth and sprinkle in *kinnikinnick,* a mixture of tobacco, herbs, and various peeled, toasted, and shredded twig barks. As I dropped in the offering, I was to tell the plants my name and let them know I intended to use the herb for healing. At this point I might be able to sense the plants' permission; a breeze might come up, or one of the plants might begin to sing. I was not to pick the one that was singing but another one growing nearby. If it resisted when I went to pull it, then I could not take it.

Through these lessons I gradually became aware that each species, and indeed each plant, possessed an energy or life essence of its own. Not only were the plants living beings, but they could also communicate with me. Many had special songs.

One day when I was alone in the woods I heard a soft, sweet voice singing. As I looked around I saw several purple coneflowers swaying gracefully in the breeze. The song was clearly coming from one of them. I sat down and listened carefully. When I had learned the song, I dug up one of the coneflowers and put a tiny bit of the root in my mouth. Immediately I experienced a curious numbing sensation. My grandmother had taught me that roots that numb the tongue are strong medicine—good for helping the body recover from colds and flu.

When I mentioned this incident to my grandmother, she smiled and said that the ability to hear plants sing and to converse with them is what defines a *midé*—a shaman, a person of spiritual power who heals with sacred plants.

Next I had to learn how to prepare and use plants for healing. My grandmother's herbal recipes were similar to her dinner recipes. She mixed her ingredients intuitively, by sight, odor, and taste. She never measured things out with teaspoons and cups but instead put in pinches and handfuls of flowers, leaves, and roots.

Gradually, she taught me to make infusions, tinctures, and salves.

An infusion was the result of immersing an herb—usually its buds, flowers, or leaves—in hot or cold springwater and letting it sit for several hours. Immersing a plant in a mixture of alcohol and water, leaving it in a cool place for a couple of weeks, and then decanting it created a tincture. A salve was the result of covering an herb with olive oil or petroleum jelly, placing it in the sun for two weeks or so, then pressing it through a cloth and decanting the oil.

As important as these healing recipes were, I soon realized that my grandmother's basic theory of healing was far more significant. She seemed uninterested in the causes of particular illnesses. She always admonished me to remember that an illness is located not in a specific organ but in the context of a person's entire life. She observed the patterns of events that led to bodily and emotional disharmony in her patients. Once she knew this, she could intervene and bring about harmony and renewed balance.

She believed that even though a healthy equilibrium was the norm, our balance is fragile and regularly disrupted. That is the reason for the sicknesses in the world. She searched for malfunctioning or displaced organs, fractured limbs, and sprained muscles and manipulated them back into place. Then she tied them with plant fibers, set them with wood splints, and made a salve to heal the area. And she warned me that learning the proper plants to use was a slow process that could take an entire lifetime.

ANIMAL GUIDES

Most herbalists, like other shamans, have animal guides that help them find particular plants for their practice. As a trained and initiated *midé*, my grandmother followed the bear path; she received many of her best remedies during dreams and waking visions in which she encountered a female bear who became her teacher.

Bears serve as guides to midwives and herbalists wherever the animals are found. The animals' habits help explain the connection:

they give birth unaided during hibernation and use herbs to heal themselves. Bears locate the plants they want, sometimes going long distances to find them, and dig them out of the ground with their claws. Like humans, bears eat roots as well as nuts, berries, and cherries. It was no coincidence that most of my grandmother's medicinal remedies contained a combination of roots, berries, and fruits.

Bear shamanism is a powerful healing tradition throughout native North America. Fallen from the Sky (Mary Sdipp-shin-mah), a member of the Flathead Nation, was taught to be an herbalist and midwife by a female grizzly bear spirit when she was six years old. As she recounted the story to the folklorist Ella Clark, her mother had taken her up into the Sierras to pick huckleberries. They arrived on a ridgetop, got off their horses, and started gathering the fruit. After a while the woman told her daughter that she had an errand to do and asked her to stay there. She could pick and eat as many berries as she wished.[2]

I picked some berries and then I sat down and ate them. The sun set, but Mother did not come back. . . . I cried and cried and cried. Then I walked farther up the ridge, crying and crying. . . . I slept for a while and then I climbed a little higher, still crying.

When the sun came up, I was very tired and sat down facing a gulch thick with forest. I heard something down there. It was the voice of a human being. Then I saw something coming toward me, coming where the trees were not thick.

A woman and two children were coming. I felt pretty good, now that I knew people were nearby. The three turned into the brush, out of sight, but I could still hear them. . . . Soon the three of them came right up to me, and the mother said, "Well, little girl, what are you doing here? You must be lost. We heard you crying, and so we came up here to help you."

The mother was a middle-aged woman, well dressed in buckskin. Around her shoulders the buckskin was painted red, and she wore trinkets. The little boy and the little girl were also dressed in buckskin in the way we used to dress.

"Don't cry any more, little girl," the mother said gently. "Come along with us."

I jumped up and went with them. When we got to the bottom of the gulch where the bank was not steep, we stopped to get a drink. . . . When I finished and sat up, I was alone again. I cried until I heard the mother's voice say, "Don't cry, little girl. Come up here."

They were sitting on a bank, and I climbed up to them. Then the mother said, "Now we are going to take you back to your people. When you grow up, you will be a good medicine woman. I give you power over all kinds of sickness. I give you power to heal people. I give you special power to help women give birth." . . .

I glanced away and when I looked back, they were gone. Instead, a grizzly bear with two little cubs sat there beside me!

The little girl's waking vision gave her some of Grizzly Bear Woman's herbal and birthing knowledge. She later trained with an experienced medicine woman and after many years of apprenticeship became a well-known herbalist and midwife.

In the Himalayas bears are also considered teachers and guides. Called *balu*, or "harvest giver," in several languages, bears are the shamans' most important guardians and protectors. The animals reveal many medicinal plants, including such psychedelic herbs as high-altitude bamboo *(Arundinaria maling)*, which contains DMT, an extremely potent hallucinogen. Shamans in Nepal commonly use bear paws, claws, and teeth in their healing ceremonies, especially in curing chest problems.[3]

HERBALISTS AND SHAMANS

For the past thirty years I have studied sacred plant medicine experientially, through conversations with indigenous healers, and by reading scientific articles and books. The extent of the tradition can be mind-boggling. For example, indigenous healers in the Americas use more than fifteen hundred plants for hypoglycemic and antidiabetic properties alone—including American barberry, Canada fleabane, alum root, bilberry, goat's rue, fenugreek, nopal cactus, bitter melon, garlic, mulberry leaves, olive leaves, wild ginger, and ginseng.[4]

Moreover, in their identification, collection, preparation, and use of these and other herbs for health and healing, herbalists go beyond the rational intelligence that is based on everyday experience and teaching. They also rely on inspirational knowledge; in their worldview, reality is revealed during dreaming, trancing, and other alternative forms of consciousness.

For indigenous peoples it is wisdom rather than knowledge per se that is the goal. Knowledge consists of empirical information passed on from teacher to pupil. Wisdom adds to that an intuitive grasp of the complex connections and forms of consciousness in the natural world. Herbalists insist that in order to choose the proper medicine for any situation, a healer must "come to know plants" as living beings. It is not the plant alone that cures; the healing comes from the greater power that exists within the spirits of the plant, the healer, the patient, and the culture. To pay attention only to the so-called active ingredients of a medicinal herb—as many scientific ethnobotanists have been trained to do—is to lose sight of its significance in the wider context of the living world.

While there are herbalists in many societies who are not trained as shamans—they do not enter a trance or experience ecstasy—all shamans know the plant realm well. And in most cultures herbal healing, like midwifery, is a strongly feminine specialty. In Java and Bali, for example, women shamans are both midwives and herbalists. In Chile most of the Mapuche shamans are women. They train with knowledgeable herbalists, but they also dream herbal remedies during their shamanic training. On the day of their initiation, they lie on a bed of herbal remedies and are massaged with cinnamon and laurel leaves. This heals them from any traces of the illnesses that revealed they were to be trained as shamans.[5]

The Mapuche shaman Machi Tomasa recounted how she dreamed that a mermaid gave her shamanic power in the form of horses, fish, and herbs.[6]

One night during my training a mermaid saw me, but I did not see her. I felt her in my body. It was so strong that I could not move. The zumpall *is a very beautiful type of mermaid, she has her face painted, and she likes to dance in water. My shamanic power comes from the lake.*

Another night two mermaids brought me two saddled horses and they gave me fish. The mermaids told me what herbs to use with my patients. They named the herbs and they showed them to me.

These were the herbs that her teacher gathered for her shamanic bed during the initiation ritual.

Wherever herbal healing is highly developed, shamans consult psychoactive plants—what are called "traveling herbs" in the Himalayas—to learn which ones are to be used as herbal remedies and which are to be taken to travel into alternate realities. Such psychoactive plants are fundamentally connected to shamanism, and shamans in many traditions invoke them each by name before they attempt to enter a trance.[7]

In Nepal, a Kirati woman shaman named Parvati Rai uses fly agaric (*Amanita muscaria*) as an herbal remedy in her shamanic practice.

She warms the mushroom and applies it to the skin of her patients to heal their cuts and abrasions. She presses the mushroom cap directly on the wound, which quickly heals. This mushroom also makes good curry pickles, she says. Anyone who eats them is greatly strengthened by the vital energy these mushrooms possess.[8]

Since shamanic initiation everywhere involves healing and strengthening the novice, many healing herbs, including powerful hallucinogenic plants, are frequently used for these rituals. Young women of the Shangana-Tsonga people, who live along the Mozambique–South Africa border, are given bush datura *(Datura fastuosa)* during their coming-of-age ceremonies. The initiate rests on a mat, preparing for her "journey of fantasy." Older women dance around her and sing about crossing the river to adulthood. Then they present her with a large shell containing datura juice and chant as they drink it: "One digs up the medicinal plants. Take the medicine of which you have heard so much." As the young woman is rubbed with datura branches, she's told to look for the snakes of feminine wisdom and listen for the voice of the goddess of fertility. The sound of drumming helps lead her into a trance, and the initiate perceives bluish green patterns belonging to the spirit world of her ancestors.[9]

In Colombia, Ecuador, and Peru, several species of tree datura have been cultivated for thousands of years, and women there brew the hallucinogenic leaves, roots, and showy flowers into a tea for use during menstrual and initiation rituals. Under the influence of this drug, the women can look backward and forward in time, and Mother Earth appears to them—both in daytime visions and nighttime dreams—in an iridescent black dress. When the women awake, they pass along their newfound knowledge through myths, songs, and pottery designs.[10]

A Guambiano woman shaman from the southern Andes of Colombia, who uses datura blossoms and seeds in her own healing practice, pictured herself under a tree covered with datura flowers (figure 33), while an eagle hovered above.[11]

33. *This Guambiano woman shaman from the Andes of Colombia pictures herself at the foot of a datura tree. She is experiencing her spirit joining with the body of an eagle as she begins her shamanic flight.*

We are all part of a living world in which plants feed and heal us. However, most of us have lost any sense of our unity with the biosphere. It is all the more valuable, therefore, that despite centuries of ridicule and repression, herbal healing has managed to survive and even flourish. In fact, these healing practices are enjoying a remarkable resurgence worldwide.[12] Today with the frantic search for new drugs to treat cancer and AIDS the field of pharmacognosy has shifted its emphasis from random sampling to the targeting of specific vegetation for testing based on indigenous medicinal and botanical knowledge. This radical change in approach is based on the hypothesis that broadly held knowledge of the use of a particular plant species over many generations provides an indication of its efficacy. It is now well known that indigenous healers have not only passed down an ancient and valuable heritage but continue to discover new herbal tonics and blends for strengthening the immune system.[13] As we will see in the following chapter, however, the use of psychedelic plants for healing and self-knowledge continues to be feared, maligned, and prosecuted.

ELEVEN

The Flowery Dream:

THE SHAMANIC USE OF PSYCHEDELICS

W E   S A T   I N   our house in the village of Tepoztlán, about an hour's drive south of Mexico City, listening to a Mexican couple of Aztec heritage chanting as they clapped their hands against their thighs. The year was 1976. There had been a major earthquake in Guatemala, and now Dennis and I would not be allowed to enter the country for some weeks. So a friend found us a short-term rental, and we settled in to wait. We were very worried about what had happened to the Mayas we knew, and whether they were dead or alive. Since there was no way to get in touch with them, we arranged for a local healing ceremony.

That evening, as the shamans led us through the ritual, we each ate ten honey-cured psilocybin mushrooms. Even though they were dripping in sweet honey, they still tasted bitter. I noticed that the caps of this particular variety *(Psilocybe mexicana)* were bluish, and the hollow stipe was yellowish pink on top, changing into red-brown at the base. As I studied the mushrooms still in the jar, the ones I had eaten slowly began to take effect. At first I felt warm and tingly all over, and I wanted to get up and dance.

But when I looked around, my friends were shrinking into tiny cartoon figures with purplish auras. Then everything else in the room, including the chairs and tables, began shrinking, too. I felt that I was a giant with feet the size of pickup trucks. I couldn't dance, I realized. Somehow I had entered a miniature world filled with song and color, and I didn't want to trample it underfoot. Multicolored arabesques suddenly whirled around the room. I reached out playfully to catch one, but it eluded me.

When I concentrated on the fate of my Mayan friends in Guatemala I suddenly became aware that I had to urinate. I shakily stood up and walked into the bathroom. An old woman stared back at me from the mirror over the sink. My hair was all white, and my brow was furrowed; there were crow's feet around the corners of my eyes, and my face and neck were as wrinkled as those of a ninety-year-old crone. As I stared at my image, the skin melted off my face to reveal my skull. Each eye socket was surrounded by tiny white twinkles of light. When I went to wash my hands, in place of arms I saw only tendons covered with spidery yellow-white webs of light. *So this is what happens when one dies,* I thought. *Are my friends dead?*

On the way back to the main room I heard a booming sound, something like an explosion deep in a mine, and with my heart pounding I quickly sat down. The shamans had counseled us that the mushrooms would help us truly see ourselves now and in the future, but somehow, even though I had had such experiences before, I was not ready for this eerie spiritual adventure.

As I calmed down, a strange joy suffused me. Now I could accept the fact that I myself had aged and that my friends might have died. I felt ready to learn how to live each day more fully. At this moment of realization the kaleidoscopic hallucinations returned. I was once again in a world of riotous color and blaring sound. But now the chanting had become a full orchestra, and I was far away, at some fantastic medieval ball in Europe. Men in powdered wigs, tight pants, and high-topped shoes were dancing with women who suddenly turned into cats!

Famished, I wandered into the kitchen to find something to eat. There was cheese—cheddar and Swiss. I tasted a chunk of each, but they were exactly alike, not at all cheeselike, merely bland and fatty. *How strange!* I thought. The variation in their colors was just dye. The products were the same; only advertising had convinced us they were somehow different.

By now it was dawn and everyone had left. In the main room I curled up with a sofa pillow and floated away. When I awoke, I tried to capture some of the beauty and horror of the experience by painting with watercolors. Then I turned to my daybook and wrote about the mushrooms and what they had shown me about the end of life. While it was terrifying, I learned that it was possible to bear it.

HALLUCINOGENS AND SHAMANISM

There are more than two hundred plants that shamans around the world use to alter their consciousness so they can communicate with the natural and spiritual world, achieve artistic inspiration and self-knowledge, know the future and the hidden past, and perform purification and healing. These drugs blur the distinction between everyday reality and the world of dreams. They often create a subtle joy that blends with a feeling of timelessness, unity, and cosmic consciousness. Frightening illusions such as the experience of rapid aging and even dying also appear, and the ego must be resilient enough to accommodate them or else become terrified and fall ill.

Unlike such psychotropic substances as caffeine, alcohol, tranquilizers, or the addictive drugs heroin and cocaine, all of which act on the central nervous system to calm or stimulate, hallucinogens act directly on the brain to produce sights and sounds without visual or auditory stimuli. Hallucinogens accomplish this without causing physical addiction, craving, or lasting psychological disturbances. As anyone who has ever tried psychedelics can attest, they often bring about an eerie dreamlike state marked by a change in the perception of self in space and time.[1]

The Aztecs of central Mexico call this experience *temixoch*, "the flowery dream," and say that psychedelic plants release the consumer's *tonalli*, "spiritual essence" or "soul." Once the soul leaves the body, it takes a magical flight into mythic time and space, where it talks with the gods. This epic journey is clearly an instance of shamanic soul flight.[2]

Psychedelics also create a mental state filled with synesthetic imagery. This means that input through one sense—sight, for example—is experienced through another sense, such as hearing. Thus, a person who eats peyote may "hear" the sun come up with a roar. Each hallucinogen has its own set of effects. Ayahuasca, a mixture containing the bark of a South American vine and leaves of other forest plants, breaks up the visual field into kaleidoscopic images of yellow, red, purple, or blue. Psilocybin mushrooms, while they also break up the visual field into geometrical forms, can promote a feeling of enlargement or shrinking as well as flying through the air and of being spoken to by the voices of ancestors, animals, or the sacred plant itself.

Hallucinogens do more than create strange sounds and cartoons in the head; taken in an appropriate setting with a shamanic attitude or sacramental intention, these plants serve as catalysts for deeper levels of self-knowledge. In 1979 Gordon Wasson, one of the most famous students of plant hallucinogens, coined the word *entheogen*, meaning "god generated within," for psychedelics. He was not implying that the plant substances themselves were gods, or even that the god within was merely a chemical effect. Rather, he argued that these drugs, taken in the appropriate place with the right mental and psychological set, can awaken us, if only for a few hours, to the presence of a god within ourselves.[3]

It would be impossible to discuss all psychedelic drugs in this chapter, but I shall focus on three important kinds—mushrooms, peyote, and San Pedro cactus—because, beyond their widespread shamanic use, they have religious, medical, and legal implications. These hallucinogens also help point out how men and women shamans differ in their approaches to healing.

MAGIC MUSHROOMS

The custom of eating hallucinogenic mushrooms dates back millennia. The earliest evidence for it comes from the central Sahara region of southern Algeria, where Neolithic rock art from the Tassili Plateau shows images of grazing animals together with pictures of humans whose fingers, heads, and torsos are outlined with mushrooms, as though they were turning into the plants or had them growing out of their bodies. Despite the record from Africa, however, hallucinogenic mushrooms more commonly grow and are used in Eurasia and Mesoamerica.

Rock art paintings discovered on the Chukotka Peninsula of Siberia suggest that the scarlet-capped, white-flecked mushroom known as fly agaric *(Amanita muscaria)* has been consumed by shamans there since the beginning of the Bronze Age. Large boulders scattered along the Pegtymel River are etched with drawings of mushrooms and small female figures. Like the "fly-agaric girls" reportedly seen by intoxicated persons, each girl has a mushroom either floating above her head or emerging out of it (figure 34).[4]

Some researchers believe that juice from this mushroom was the principal ingredient in soma, the sacred drink of the Aryans of North India, as well as in the ambrosia of the Greeks. Bronze Age

34. *These petroglyphs are from the Chukotka Peninsula, Siberia. The mushroom at the upper left is a fly agaric* (Amanita muscaria).

Scandinavians and Saami nomads in Lapland also used fly agaric for healing and spiritual purposes, since it alters perceptions, creating a translucent, shimmering, and timeless world. Another effect of eating the mushroom includes strange distortions in the perceived size and shape of objects; they appear much smaller or much larger. Lewis Carroll seems to have had this characteristic in mind when he wrote *Alice in Wonderland*, since Alice shrinks or stretches, depending on which side of the mushroom she nibbles, or whether she eats from the stem or the cap.[5]

Fly agaric grows in the expansive birch, fir, and pine forests of North Asia, and Russian explorers of the sixteenth, seventeenth, and eighteenth centuries encountered a number of tribes there who used the mushrooms to help them communicate with spirits. Mansi, Saami, and Chukchi shamans ate fly agaric to travel to the Land of the Dead, so they could learn the causes of illness. Later ethnographers reported that some shamans got their mushrooms from Koryak herders, who gathered the mushrooms, dried them, and traded the plants to healers from their own and other tribes. And in the early twentieth century the use of fly agaric was recorded among the Siberian Nenets, though in that tribe only shamans who knew precisely where the plant grew could see its spirit in trance. Today Koryak, Nenets, and Khanty shamans continue to use fly agaric.[6]

When a group of mycologists traveled to the Kamchatka Peninsula in 1996 in search of the mushrooms, they met a woman shaman who gathered the plants for her healing rituals. They videotaped Tatiana Urkachan and recorded her practices in *The Song of Mukhomor*. One memorable scene shows this strikingly handsome woman wearing a red and white polka-dot dress that exactly matches the two red-and-white-capped mushrooms she holds in her left hand. As she sits quietly rocking in her seat she talks, sings, and prays to the mushrooms, asking them to bless and heal all those at her séance.[7]

Fly agaric also grows in the birch, pine, and cedar forests of North America, and its shamanic use has been well documented among Native Americans in northwestern Canada and the Great Lakes region

of the United States. A nine-year-old Ojibwe girl named Keewaydinoqua spent two years, 1925 and 1926, with a famous woman
herbalist and midwife. During this time she learned how to prepare
various hallucinogenic and nonhallucinogenic mushrooms for healing. She was trained in the first three levels of the Great Medicine
Lodge, or, as she put it, "I was medicined three times." At her initiation, she was given a single large cowry shell tied on a leather string,
to wear under her shirt around her neck. She was also shown a picto-
graphic birch-bark scroll that recounted the origin story of fly agaric,
known as *miskwedo* in Ojibwe and considered the spiritual child of
Grandmother Cedar and Grandfather Birch. Ojibwe shamans at
that time prepared this mushroom by mixing it with a kind of blueberry juice, which strengthens its overall hallucinogenic effects.[8]

In Mesoamerica, stone figures of women and mushrooms from
the early Pre-Classic Period (1000–500 BCE) have been discovered
all along the Pacific coast of Guatemala. Even today, when the Mixtec, Mazatec, and Zapotec peoples of Oaxaca grind mushrooms for
use in all-night healing rituals, they do so with stone rollers on stone
tables shown in ancient carvings (figure 35).[9]

The Aztecs recognized and employed a number of hallucinogenic

35. *A Pre-Classic mushroom effigy stone found in Guatemala. It shows a
bare-breasted woman emerging from the mushroom stipe holding a grinding stone.*

mushrooms. In the sixteenth-century work known as the *Florentine Codex,* Aztec informants noted that there were "mushrooms growing under the hay, in the fields or on the plains; they are round and have a somewhat tall, thin, rounded base. They are used as medicines for fevers and gout; it takes no more than two or three, and those who eat them see visions." And painted manuscripts from Oaxaca depict several Mixtec goddesses with mushrooms emerging from their heads. In the Mixtec *Codex Vindobonensis,* a healing goddess holds up a pair of mushrooms that she appears to be about to ingest (figure 36). These mushrooms are taken in male-female pairs that make a married couple, an important cosmological symbol of sexual union and psychological completion.[10]

Today, psilocybin mushrooms play an important role in healing and divinatory ceremonies in several Aztec communities in Mexico, as I myself discovered. Shamanic healers and their clients eat the mushrooms—either ground into a fine powder or whole—as a way of communicating with the deities, understanding past or future events, and divining the causes of illness and misfortune.[11]

For the Mazatec of northeastern Oaxaca, Mexico, these psychedelics are directly associated with the curing of illness. Because there is a biochemical effect as well as a cultural one, anyone is free to eat mushrooms and may do so in order to heal themselves. However, for the shaman the eating and administering of mushrooms is a

36. *Lady One Eagle in the* Codex Vindobonensis *holding up a male-female pair of mushrooms.*

vocation. The mushrooms "speak," say the Mazatec, and it is the job of shamans to transmit their message in the form of a chant or a song. These songs and chants give structure to their own visions and to those of their intoxicated participants, evoking particular sounds and images and activating symbols of healing. Shamans are seers, oracles, and oral poets, and their artistic language creates a healing path for their patients.[12]

In the mid-1960s an Australian named Henry Munn married into a family of Mazatec shamans and documented mushroom use in the village of Huautla de Jiménez. Mothers, fathers, aunts, uncles, grandparents, and grandchildren all gathered to eat hallucinogenic mushrooms whenever they had physical illnesses, mental troubles, family disputes, or ethical problems to resolve. Munn's wife helped him tape-record and translate the chanting of a talented husband-and-wife shaman team, Irene Pineda de Figueroa and Román Estrada. In the several hundred pages of poetry that resulted, differences of gender between these consults clearly emerged. Irene and Román conducted séances together several nights a week, during which both they and their patients came under the influence of mushrooms. At one séance, shortly after Irene had eaten four mushrooms, she began chanting softly, asking the plants to help her determine the cause of the client's illness.[13]

> *We are going to search and question*
> *Untie and disentangle.*
> *Let us go searching for the path*
> *The tracks of her feet*
> *The tracks of her nails*
> *From the right side to the left side*
> *Let us look!*

As she continued chanting, she subtly changed from including herself in the second person, *us,* to referring to herself in the third person, as *she.*

Woman of medicines and cures
Who walks with her appearance and her soul.
She is the woman of remedy and medicine.
A woman who speaks
A woman who puts everything together
Doctor woman
Woman of words
Wise woman of problems.

Without even moving from the spot where she was sitting, Irene was on her shamanic journey. Her consciousness roamed through space, searching for the internal psychological causes of the illness and releasing them. Emphasizing birth and agricultural growth, she sang of medicine, sweetness, and goodwill. She frequently repeated the words *freshness, tenderness,* and *happiness.*

Román also ate the mushrooms, but his chant affirmed his sacred role as a mediator between the human and elemental powers that determine a person's future. To underline his own independence, he used the pronoun *I* and identified himself with the crackle of electricity as his words flashed with the powerful force of bolt lightning. As he confronted danger and promised to vanquish it by allying himself with the forces of nature he did battle with external political and social causes of illness, using bold, aggressive words such as *danger* and *fear.*[14]

I am he who speaks with Father Mountain
He who speaks with danger.
I sweep in mountains of fear
Mountains of nerves.
I am dry lightning.
I am comet lightning.
I am dangerous lightning.
I am big lightning.
I am the lightning of rocky places.

His wife, on the other hand, talked about searching, questioning, releasing, untying, and disentangling. Instead of calling upon a masculine deity or a meteorological force for help in her divining, Irene spoke directly to the hallucinogenic mushrooms, requesting their aid in the cure of the sickness.

María Sabina, the most famous Mazatec shaman of the mid-twentieth century, was able to combine both feminine and masculine practices (figure 37). Growing up in poverty in rural Mexico, she and her younger sister Ana played in the forest. One day they found some handsome mushrooms and, because they were hungry, ate them raw. As María remembered it, "We felt dizzy, as if we were drunk. We began to cry. But then this dizziness passed, and we became very content. Later we felt good. It was like a new hope in our lives."[15]

When their mother discovered what they had done, she told them never to eat the mushrooms again. It was twenty years before María Sabina broke that command, and she did so in order to heal her sister. She gathered twelve mushrooms from the forest, gave six to her

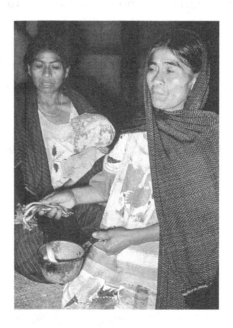

37. *Mazatec shaman María Sabina incensing mushrooms.*

sister, and ate the other six herself. Though María was illiterate, during her visions she heard herself reading and singing from a book handed to her by a total stranger. Becoming a "wise one," she felt an ecstatic sense of her own shamanic destiny. When her sister recovered, the news of the cure spread throughout the mountain villages. Soon people were making pilgrimages to María for healing.

In 1954 Gordon Wasson recorded María Sabina as she performed a nightlong healing séance for a seventeen-year-old boy. She began by addressing her patient in a soft, feminine voice.[16]

"Am I all right?" asked the boy.
"Your spirit is all right. I am with you," she replied kindly.
"But you are in a tough spot."
"I think so," he answered.

As she said this, María already knew that the boy would die; she was comforting his spirit. Then she shifted into a hard, masculine voice and asked the mushrooms to help her. And in yet a third voice, she spoke in the person of the sacred mushrooms themselves.

As the session proceeded and the effects of the mushrooms increased, she began chanting. Poetically describing herself to the mushrooms and listing all the things she was seeing in her vision, she opened with her most feminine of voices.[17]

Woman who waits am I
Woman who divines am I
Woman of justice am I
Woman of law am I
Woman of the Southern Cross am I
Woman of the first star am I.
For I go up into the sky.

Then she quickly shifted into the stronger and more powerful masculine-sounding voice:

> *Lawyer woman am I.*
> *Woman of transactions am I.*
> *Mexican woman am I.*
> *Woman like a clock am I.*
> *Woman like an eagle am I.*
> *Woman like an opossum am I.*
> *Woman like a hunting dog am I.*
> *Woman like a wolf am I.*
> *I'll show my power!*
> *He isn't sick because of an illness.*
> *It is a blow of fortune that hit him.*
> *His body went to sleep.*
> *He hasn't got an ordinary sickness.*
> *Now our son has died because a puma has eaten him up.*
> *It has eaten up his animal double.*
> *The puma has eaten him up!*

Mazatecs believe that a person's spiritual essence takes the form of an animal double, which is both an ordinary animal and an external spirit or soul called a *nagual.* The person and the *nagual* lead parallel lives: when one dies, the other one also dies.

The mushrooms told María that a puma had devoured the boy's *nagual,* so she knew that it could not be retrieved and consequently he would die. She repeated the mushroom's warning over and over again until the boy finally realized that there was no hope for him. Even though the other participants in the séance urged the boy to fight death, he turned pale and collapsed. Six weeks later, he died.

PEYOTE

Although it is a small, slow-growing cactus without spines, peyote *(Lophophora williamsii)* has a deep taproot that encourages new growth, creating plants with multiple heads that can be harvested again and again. It grows in the Chihuahua Desert, from north-central Mexico into southern Texas, and many peoples of that area have told the story of its sacred origin. The story usually goes something like this:[18]

One afternoon a pregnant woman became lost from her band and gave birth unaided to a baby girl. She cut the navel cord with a stone knife from her pouch and lay back helpless under a low leafy mescal bush watching a flock of buzzards gathering overhead.

She watched in terror as they swooped and soared lower with each downward beat of their great black wings. They must have sensed that she was about to die. Then she suddenly heard a voice speaking directly to her. "Eat the plant that is growing beside you," it said. "That is life and blessing for you and all your people."

Weakly, she turned her head and the only plant in sight was a small cactus. It was without thorns, and its head was divided into lobes. She reached for the plant and pulled it up, root and all, and ate the head.

Strength returned to her immediately. She sat up and looked all around. It was nearly dawn; the sun was just starting to rise. She lifted her infant to her filling breasts and fed her. Then, gathering up as many cactus plants as she could find and carry, she rose and walked on. By evening she reached her people.

Ever since then peyote has been used in religion and medicine—to relieve pain, to increase the flow of milk in a new mother's breasts, to foster energy and endurance, and as a poultice for wounds. Peyote is also a powerful psychedelic, containing more than fifty-five alkaloids (hallucinogenic chemicals), though its potency varies from season to season, from soil to soil, and from clump to clump. It's a bitter, metallic-tasting plant and usually produces queasiness and vomiting. To avoid these side effects shamans may grind it into a powder and drink it as an infusion, or else use it as an enema.[19]

Peyote's hallucinogenic effects—created through the interaction of several alkaloids, including mescaline—last for eight to ten hours. At first familiar objects look different. Colors and sounds intensify, and it seems as though the inner meaning of all things material and spiritual becomes clear. Opening or closing the eyes can change the visual experience, producing vivid afterimages and halos or a constantly changing kaleidoscopic display. After about four hours the effects lessen, leading to a stage of peaceful introspection. After ten hours, when most of the effects have ceased, the overwhelming bodily tiredness can only be relieved by sleep.[20]

Scientists have studied the visual effects of peyote and other psychedelic drugs and discovered that the earlier images are entirely different from later ones. Visions in the first stage originate in the neural network connecting the retina of the eye with the brain. These luminous flickering images, known as phosphenes (from the Greek *phos,* "light," and *phainein,* "to show"), can also be produced by outside stimulation, such as pressure on the eyeballs, or during sexual intercourse.[21]

Laboratory experiments have defined a number of distinct phosphenes produced by the human brain. They vary from tiny pulsating dots to wiggly lines, hexagons, glowing circles, curlicues, and star-, flower-, or diamond-shaped elements (figure 38). They come in hues of green, blue, purple, orange, and yellow and are sometimes interpreted as clusters of fruits, flowers, and feathery leaves.[22]

In the second, more symbolic stage of hallucination such geometrical perceptions recede or disappear. Now the participant may feel that she understands unsuspected or long-forgotten memories,

38. *These types of diamonds, hexagons, stars, flowers, arabesques, wiggly lines, and rows of dots are the most common phosphene patterns observed by people the world over during the early stages of hallucinogenic intoxication.*

not only of her infancy but also of the creation of the world. The shapes may seem to be mythical scenes filled with spirits, ancestors, and deities. Eventually these images, too, disappear, and the subject enters a state of bliss filled with soft music and fluffy clouds.

HUICHOL PEYOTE USE

In the past many Mexican peoples used peyote for divination, to achieve ecstatic states, and to heal. Today the twenty-five thousand Huichol Indians living in the states of Jalisco and Nayarit—who call themselves Wixárika, meaning "healers" or "prophets"—are the sole bearers of a large range of peyote beliefs, customs, and practices. In fact, peyote, known as *hikuli* in the Huichol language, is still the focus of much of their religious life today.[23]

During peyote ceremonies individuals consume as many of the fresh or dried "buttons" as they desire. At first participants feel a sudden chill; a powerful tremor shakes their body, followed by a sensation of rushing winds and then sleepiness. Luminous flashes streak across their visual field. These phosphene images, called *nearika*, are considered mirrors or portals to other worlds, allowing participants to visit Wirikuta, the womb of creation, to be healed and reborn.

Some *nearika* take the form of pulsating mandalas that represent gods and goddesses of sun, water, and fire. Women consider these patterns to be gifts from the deities and feel that it is their duty to record them in their weaving and embroidery. Failure to share these sacred messages with their family and community may result in hardship and illness. Stacey Schaefer, an ethnographer friend who teaches at the University of California at Chico, has been an active participant in dozens of peyote pilgrimages. In her essay "The Crossing of the Souls: Peyote, Perception, and Meaning among the Huichol Indians," published in her volume edited with Peter Furst, *People of the Peyote,* she quotes this report from a Huichol woman:[24]

I saw a large plant where we had left our offerings for the Mother of Peyote. Rays of light like ribbons were coming from this plant. On one side there was a lit candle. This same candle had roots. There was a deer where the peyote was. The deer acted like it was drunk. Then white foam started to come from its mouth, the kind of foam that comes from grinding peyote. It was coming out of its mouth. The foam looked like soap, like when peyote is ritually killed. That's how it was pouring out. But the deer was talking to me. I didn't hear her very well until she saw me, and we looked each other right in the eye.

The mescaline in the peyote can also bring on smells, tastes, sounds, and other physical sensations. Schaefer noted, "On one occasion, during the wee hours of the morning, I awoke to hear a woman break into a spontaneous song. She sang on and off for close to an hour. Later, I asked my *comadre* [godmother] about this, and she said it was the peyote that brought her the songs." Another woman who recalled her deep peyote experience said:[25]

Wind Person came to visit me. He spoke to me and told me I had to remember his song. He began to sing it and repeated the song over and over until I knew it well. In the morning I sang the song for the temple group, and it is now a part of me forever.

A Huichol baby is introduced to peyote while inside her mother's womb and later through her milk. Infants who have had even the tiniest amount of peyote become very calm, smile often, and occasionally grab at what they believe must be objects. At about age five or six, children are given pieces of the sacred cactus to chew. Peyote provides them with the psychedelic insights that are central to their learning sacred mythology and healing rituals. As young adults they will communicate the exquisite colors, shapes, and subject matter of their peyote-induced visions in colored drawings, yarn paintings, beadwork, embroidery, and weaving.[26]

Women and men describe and enact their hallucinogenic experiences in distinct ways. Men represent their visions in figurative multicolored drawings and yarn paintings. Women are more likely to include geometrical representations of peyote buttons and subtle hints of images from their visions in weavings. During peyote intoxication men may break into song, which they accompany with violin playing and dancing; women tend to remain seated, wrapped in blankets. Throughout the night they sing messages from the ancestors intended for specific family members. Over time some women may simply be able to hold a peyote button or even merely be in its presence and break into a healing song.

Since 1994 Huichols have been legally free to collect peyote within the ecological reserve of Wirikuta, located in the state of San Luis Potosí, many miles from their home territory, and transport it to their communities. Nevertheless, in 1998 Mexican authorities seized a large amount of peyote and arrested seven Huichol pilgrims, including two women and a child, for drug trafficking. Though the pilgrims were not charged with possession of peyote, they were nonetheless harassed and kept in jail for sixty-two hours.[27]

THE NATIVE AMERICAN CHURCH

Although the earliest record of peyote use in what is now the United States dates from 1760 in Texas, it really didn't take hold until the 1890s, when it became a key part of the Ghost Dance movement on the Great Plains. Members of the peyote cult incorporated themselves in Oklahoma in 1918 as the "Native American Church," with peyote as its religious sacrament. They developed a religious ideology known as the "Peyote Road" that rapidly spread into southern Canada. The organization is now known as the "Native American Church of North America."[28] Although there is still occasional harassment of peyotists under the Drug Abuse Prevention and Control Act—cactus is included among prohibited narcotics—the church and its more than 250,000 active members are protected by law. Today, in several Western states the peyote religion is open to all worshipers, regardless of race.

Members of the peyote religion in North America, like the Huichol of Mexico, have developed their own special art, music, legends, and rituals. The handles of their ceremonial rattles and fans are intricately inlaid with fine beadwork. Peyotists also make and wear silver and beaded jewelry with water bird designs that indicate their affiliation with the church. Women peyotists weave belts, earrings, pins, and hair ornaments and decorate them with beaded birds and rainbows, which represent the visions and feelings of flight during a peyote ceremony.

The peyote ritual usually takes place around a fire in a ceremonial tipi with an earthen altar. During the all-night rite, the shamans and their patients eat the cactus, then sit in a circle while patients pray, confess their wrongdoings, and talk about their problems. They sing peyote songs, accompanied by the sounds of gourd rattles and the rapid beating of a water drum. A painting by Ernest Spybuck, a well-known artist who was a leader of the peyote religion among the Shawnee, shows men and women praying and singing together around a fire built on a crescent-moon earthen altar (figure 39). They wave eagle feathers and shake gourd rattles.[29]

Some tribes have added Christian symbols to their peyote rituals and embraced the idea that women, because they menstruate and give birth, are polluting influences. As a result, a few Native American peyote groups bar women until after menopause, but this is not generally true. In other tribes, including the Delaware and Comanche, women of all ages are allowed to participate in peyote healing ceremonies. This may be because many women shamans joined the peyote cult rather than opposing it.[30]

A Comanche woman named Sanapia, born in Fort Sill, Oklahoma, in the spring of 1895, was both the leading eagle shaman of her generation and a well-known peyotist. In difficult cases she concluded her eagle doctoring with a peyote ceremony. Whenever she did this she invited a peyote leader, or "road man," to open the ceremonial. Then she picked up the peyote button from the altar and talked to it as she transferred it from one hand to the other. Drawing its essence into her palms, she began to tremble uncontrollably as the power entered her. As she later explained to her adopted son, my colleague David Jones of the University of Central Florida, "When

39. *Peyote ceremony in a tent showing women together with men sitting around a crescent moon altar. The insert at the bottom right shows the final healing ritual held early the next morning.*

I pray like that . . . Well, that power just comes over me, comes down and gives me the chills and I start shaking all at once and pretty soon it goes away and then I start. Sometimes I can't hardly touch them, the way my hand be shaking. It makes me feel like that power wants to make me get them well right now."[31]

When Sanapia regained her composure, she took a segment of white root, chewed it to a moist pulp, and spewed the juice over her patient's head and arms. Then she removed the pulp from her mouth, rolled it between her palms, and rubbed it over the patient's body. Finally she deposited the partially chewed root in the patient's mouth and told him to swallow it. Then she fanned him with an eagle feather as she sang a peyote song until spirits entered her body. At this point in the ceremony she stood up, walked out of the tipi, and sang alone in the dark. Eventually she perceived two tiny lights burning on the crest of a nearby hill. They slowly approached, and when they stood before her she identified them as her deceased mother and uncle, both famous eagle shamans.

Sanapia told her dead relatives that she was all alone and totally helpless. She had no one besides them to whom she could turn for help. Then she stood absolutely motionless, waiting for her eagle to appear. As she explained, "I see that eagle . . . big, big . . . shining so pretty on its feathers. And I guess I am being silly because I start crying some more just like some old woman. But I hear it in my mind, you know, say, 'Go ahead, get him well. You can do it.' "[32] She returned to her patient and used her eagle power to cure him.

Among traditional Diné, or Navajo, of Arizona, Walking Thunder is a well-known contemporary medicine woman and peyotist whose mother first introduced her to the cactus. That first evening, when she was only six, she ate just a tiny bit, and her body tingled all over. At nine, she attended her first full peyote meeting. When the road man's beaded staff came around to her position, she startled everyone by reaching out and grabbing it, instead of just passing it on to a nearby adult. And although she did not know any peyote songs at that time, one came to her immediately. The peyote leader smiled and prophesied that she would one day become a powerful medicine woman. At another meeting this same medicine man gave her a spoonful of peyote every thirty minutes until she could take no more.[33]

I was flying high, as you would say in the white man's way. The medicine was really working on me and gave me visions. I told the medicine man that it was getting scary because I started seeing graveyards where people were buried. I saw the bodies lying there and the marks on the coffins. The medicine man said that my sickness had to do with the Ghostway. It involved people who had died.

When the peyote medicine started doctoring me, I felt puffy.

I felt like I was sitting high in the sky. It made me feel the people around me but I could only see their feet. The medicine fixed me up inside and my body hurt from it. I heard my heartbeat and my liver move. I heard my insides moving and saw my own fat. I was able to see myself in a true way.

Even after the meeting was over and the medicine man went away, the medicine continued to work on me for another week and a half. People came to my house asking for help because they believed I was under the influence of holy spiritual ways. I went and helped them. From that point on, many patients came to me.

SAN PEDRO CACTUS

Many of the alkaloids that are present in psilocybin mushrooms and peyote also exist in the night-blooming cactus known as San Pedro cactus *(Trichocereus pachanoi)*. A bite of the cactus produces warmth combined with a sudden awareness of the practitioner's own electrical field. Sounds seem to shift, and pulsating chains of light fill the visual field, revolving themselves into thousands of geometrical designs, patterns that are influenced by cultural background as well as the gender and the emotional makeup of the person.[34]

This cactus has been used in shamanic healing for more than three thousand years by Andean peoples in Ecuador, Bolivia, and Peru. Ceramics from the Mochica culture (from 100 BCE to about 700 CE) show rituals very much like those still undertaken on the north coast of Peru. The vessels depict shamans practicing massage, sucking, and surgery; others show individuals transformed into their animal familiars. One vase from the Lambayeque tradition—which flourished along the north coast of Peru from about 700 to 1475 CE—portrays a woman shaman holding a piece of San Pedro cactus (figure 40). The woman's lips are thrust forward as if she is throwing

40. *A one-thousand-year-old Peruvian ceramic vessel of a veiled female shaman holding a piece of San Pedro cactus in her left hand and a curved knife in her right hand. Her lips are thrust forward as though she were sucking out an illness or blowing a kiss.*

a kiss or sucking out an illness, ancient gestures of reverence and healing that are still characteristic of the Quechua and Aymara peoples. Today women shamans and herbalists gather and use the cactus for healing and sell it in open-air marketplaces.[35]

During nightlong séances, shamans drink a hallucinogenic brew, called *achuma* in Quechua, made from the San Pedro cactus. They arrange their ritual objects as an altar on the ground and perform healing rites for strangers, family, and friends on a fee-for-service basis. While the overall outline of their shamanic practice is similar for women and men, the differences in their healing philosophies and therapeutic strategies are especially telling.[36]

The male shamans of Peru, Bolivia, and Ecuador, together with females trained and initiated by male relatives, transcend illness by fighting unseen enemies and ordering them away. Women shamans together with men trained within a more feminine tradition focus on healing inner emotional and physical imbalances; they insist on a patient's self-awareness, purification, acceptance, and surrender.

Eduardo Calderon, a well-known Peruvian shaman who practiced a strongly masculine ritual, described the left side of his altar as representing darkness and the right side light. On this divided terrain, the tensions of cosmological and human opposites played out. To his left he arranged fragments of ancient Peruvian ceramics, stones, a bottle of cane alcohol, and a deer hoof. To his right he placed crystals, shells, saints' images, rattles, holy water, perfumes, a columnar piece of San Pedro cactus, sweet lime, and black tobacco. The central area he called "the commanding authority" and "the needle in the balance between good and evil." There he placed a large tin can filled with hallucinogenic cactus water surrounded by rows of upright canes and other objects, including a late-nineteenth-century cavalry officer's sword. His altar objects embodied the forces of the universe involved in causing and curing illness. When he manipulated and dominated the powers within the objects, he was metaphorically acting upon the forces responsible for the patient's suffering. As he put it, "the altar is nothing more than a control panel by which one is able to calibrate the infinity of accesses into each person."[37]

Eduardo opened his séances by picking up his deer hoof, which symbolized curiosity, swiftness, and elusiveness, and held it out to detect and exorcise attacking spirits. One by one he lifted his various staffs, swords, and daggers and swung them over his patient's head in dramatic mock battle to vanquish spiritual enemies. Later he vigorously massaged his clients and therapeutically popped their joints. He was not unique. Other masculine shamans within the same tradition also brandish swords, sometimes even taking them outside, flashing them around, and stabbing them into the ground. Several have other weapons—including pistols, bronze knives, and stone mace heads—that they use to parry the blows of unseen foes. They say their weapons are necessary in order to fight fire with fire. They share the belief that life entails endless battles with those who cause harm; this adversarial quality is apparent in their physical behavior and therapeutic philosophies. Their rituals embrace confrontation and conflict rather than compromise or conciliation. To cure illness they contact and use powerful forces from outside themselves.[38]

Women shamans in this same tradition, like the men, consume San Pedro cactus to journey to an alternative reality. They also lay out complex altars where they conduct their healing ceremonies. But the objects on their altars and the way they use them depend on whether the pieces were originally collected by a woman or a man. A woman may inherit her father's altar along with the doctrine of good versus evil and life-giving versus life-taking. But in her spiritual cleansings she disperses the authority of the wooden staffs and other power objects such as guns, knives, and swords in order to "see" the cause of affliction and help "draw out" the illness. She allows her patients and their family members to touch the power objects and even use them to remove the sickness themselves.[39]

While women's altars may contain weapons, these are usually not arranged in a straight military row that separates healer and client. Instead, women pair each male object with a female object. During séances the pairs of objects work together. Even single objects are imbued with a combination of masculine and feminine healing powers. The pairing extends to the participants at the séance. The woman healer sits before her altar at the center of the assembled group and arranges an equal number of women and men on either side of her. If there are an odd number of participants, she simply reassigns the extra female to be a male, or the extra male to be a female, for the duration of her healing ceremony.

After a woman inherits her father's altar, she may modify his healing rituals. A contemporary healer named Clorinda was apprenticed to her father at age five; she assisted him until his death, when she

41. *Clorinda, a Peruvian woman shaman is sitting before the* mesa *or healing altar she inherited from her father. Standing against the wall are a number of wooden staves and antique guns.*

was twenty-two (figure 41). She then inherited his altar with its staffs and weapons. But instead of fighting evil spirits with these objects, she gently rubs the staffs over her patient's body and asks her client to entrust all evil to the weapons, saying, "I am raising myself up. I am throwing away all envy, all obstacles, all prejudice, all misfortune, all blindfolds."[40]

When a woman shaman follows the feminine path, the overall composition and arrangement of her altar is quite different. An altar owned by Mama Juana Simbaña, a well-known Quichua shaman who practices out of her home near Quito, Ecuador, includes ancient artifacts, seashells, large breastlike stones, a glass crucifix, and a Japanese geisha doll in a glass case (figure 42). While she uses all of these icons in treating women's ailments, she reserves her geisha for healing the emotional illnesses and venereal diseases of prostitutes.[41]

Whenever Mama Juana begins a healing ceremony, she drinks

42. *Mama Juana Simbaña's healing altar. Among the objects on the altar are dozens of marbles and breast-shaped stones, an ancient hand axe, a top from a glass decanter, and a Japanese geisha doll.*

the San Pedro cactus brew and sings to her breast-shaped stones. Then she fumigates them with tobacco smoke and sprays them with a mixture of flower juice, anise liqueur, and cane alcohol. She uses candles rather than wooden canes or weapons for diagnosis and healing. Praying with candles in her hands, she rubs them over her patient's body and lights the wicks. Gazing into the candle flame, she sees her patient's double. After a while she announces what she has learned about the person's psychological or interpersonal problems. At this point she sucks toxins from the patient's body (figure 43), then finishes the session by spraying the person with a combination of flowers, anise liqueur, and cane alcohol.

The thread that connects these shamans on the feminine path is the powerful idea of women as compassionate healers and nurturers. Their use of psychedelic plants is not something they do only to or for others. Instead, it is an interactive process that takes place through

43. *Mama Juana is healing a woman client at her home in Ecuador by sucking out the illness.*

an intimate healer-patient-plant relationship. The foundations are spiritual and interpersonal rather than heroic and individual. Women in these traditions establish bonds that are life-giving and life-enriching both for themselves and for their patients.

PART THREE

The Female Cycle: Menstruation, Birth, and Creation

TWELVE

Butterflies in the Moonlight:

BLOOD MAGIC

WITHIN THE DARK fluids of menstrual and birthing blood resides the vital essence of the most feminine form of spiritual energy. Concentrated and deeply mysterious, this force touches every woman and links her to a formidable shamanic tradition. Understanding that energy—and the rich web of myths and symbols that surround it—will help us to more clearly see women in their transcendent roles.

Female hormones play a central role in women's shamanic abilities. Just before and during menstruation women experience their strongest healing and oracular powers. Mood swings and heightened sensitivity at this time of the month—which in the West have been labeled premenstrual syndrome (PMS) and treated as an illness—are actually manifestations of an altered state of consciousness made possible by female biology. Along with a receptiveness to trance and ecstasy there's another advantage: as serum estrogen levels rise in a woman's body, the levels of key neurotransmitters also rise, increasing the amount of adrenaline available for strenuous all-night healing sessions.[1]

Women shamans are keenly aware of their monthly renewal of energy. The Mongolian shaman Bayar Odun commented to me that her recent shamanizing had been particularly strong since she had just begun her period. She laughed and whispered to me, with a twinkle in her eye, "When we get our periods, we women take over as the leaders in the public ceremonies. I suppose you noticed that when I was drumming, my wind horse filled with blood. My drumming became very powerful, and the men could only sit and wonder at my strength."

FLOWERS AS FEMININE LIFE FORCE

The positive energies of feminine blood are celebrated in a complex visual and literary symbolism that embraces images of flowers and is tied to the phases of the moon. Feminine blood is honored in many places as the "flower" of the womb. In the botanical world the purpose of flowers is to make fruits and bring about new plants of their own species. By analogy, just as flowers contain future fruits, so uterine blood contains the essence of future generations. In the Bible menstrual blood is called the "flower that precedes the fruit of the womb" (Leviticus 15:24). And when a girl first menstruates, she may be said to have "borne the flower." In French *les fleurs,* or "the flowers," is the name for a young girl's first menstrual flow.[2]

In Côte d'Ivoire in West Africa, a Beng elder gave a similar explanation to my colleague Alma Gottlieb, an anthropologist at the University of Illinois. She said that women's blood is very special because it contains a living being. "It works like a tree. Before bearing fruit, a tree must first bear flowers. Menstrual blood is like the flower: it must emerge before the fruit—the baby—can be born."[3] And in my own research among the Maya of Belize and Guatemala I have found that the word for flower is a metaphor for the placenta.

In India the red lotus represents female reproductive organs, and tribal people there still celebrate the fertility of a young woman who has reached menarche with songs that describe her as a budding coconut flower. Thereafter, whenever she feels a quickening of her energy during her menstrual period, the blood may be mixed with wine and consumed as a special ritual drink by the female members of her extended family. In the Andaman Islands of the Bay of Bengal a young woman took the name of a flower after her first menstruation. At that point she was said to be "in blossom." When she was pregnant, her body ripened to its "full fruit," and she was considered a complete woman.[4]

Flower symbolism in Mexico goes back to its myths. An illustration from an ancient Aztec painted manuscript depicts the reproductive organs and menstrual blood of Xochiquetzal, or Flowery Quetzal Feather, as a single long-stemmed flower (figure 44). According to Aztec mythology, this goddess of the moon and love first menstruated when she was bitten on her genitals by a bat that sprang from the semen of Quetzalcoatl, or Quetzal-Feathered Serpent. She bled fragrant flowers and in so doing introduced sexual pleasure into the world.[5]

In central Mexico flowers remain symbols for the feminine life force and all sensual delights, including sexual love, art, music, weaving, embroidery, silversmithing, sculpting, singing, and dancing. In the contemporary lore of the region, a red siren is said to live inside

44. *Xochiquetzal, the Aztec goddess of love and the moon. This illustration is from the* Codex Vaticanus B. *Her menstrual blood is represented by a single flower emerging from between her legs.*

the moon and is responsible for menstruation. In Nahuatl (the language of the Aztecs) the womb was called "flowerpot," which was also the name given to the patroness of midwives.[6]

The Huichol believe a goddess, Grandmother Growth, made flowers from her bloody undergarments and threw them into a spring in the desert near the place where the sacred peyote cactus now grows. From these cactus flowers her daughter, the goddess of childbirth, was created. Every year families make pilgrimages to the daughter's home, which is a shrine at the edge of the spring. They sing, dance, and pray for fertility, leaving offerings of beaded bowls, crossed sticks entwined with yarn known as "god eyes," and woven bamboo-and-cotton mats.[7]

Similar flower imagery—sometimes linked with watery places that symbolize the birth canal—exists throughout Asia. In China's southern provinces of Guangdong and Fujian, every woman is said to possess a flower that represents her femininity. Each of her children has a double growing in a flowerpot planted in a heavenly garden. In order to be born, the fetus must cross the "hundred-flower bridge," the place of transformation and reincarnation linking sky and earth. During this dangerous passage a flower deity known as Lady of the Waterside protects both the pregnant woman and her child. In Korea the first shaman was a woman who maintained a mountain village filled with blossoming azaleas and lotuses. Since these flowers can revive the dead they came to be thought of as creating an imaginal world located across a river from the sensual world.[8]

Artists in many cultures use flowers as both magical and sexual symbols in song, poetry, and paintings. The visual relationship between the clitoris and a half-opened flower, for example, is a frequent motif, in part because flower petals unfold to reveal the pistil and stamen at its reproductive center. Many of Georgia O'Keeffe's flowers represent the female body even though she herself refused to make that statement, since she did not wish to be labeled as a "female artist." Nevertheless, she did essentially admit the connection when she told her biographer, "I am trying with all my skill to do a painting that is all of woman, as well as all of me." More recently, artist Suzanne Santoro was franker about the meaning of her images. When asked about her *Flower and Clitoris* painting, she said that she had deliberately "placed the flower next to the clitoris as a means of understanding the structure of the female genitals."[9]

ENTERING THE FLOW OF TIME

The phases of the moon have always been used to mark the passage of time. Each month the moon waxes, becomes full, wanes, and then disappears for three nights before being reborn as the "new moon." Thus the moon's disappearance is never final, and its recurring cycle connects it with the rhythms of life: conception, birth, death, and rebirth. In culture after culture, the moon symbolizes renewal, immortality, and eternity. The waxing and waning of the moon also have been thought to control both ocean tides and menstrual blood. Thus, the word for moon in Greek—*mene,* meaning "measure of time"—serves as the root in the word *menstruate.*[10]

The crescent moon, in the form of an ox horn, was carved at the entrance of an Upper Paleolithic rock shelter in the Dordogne region of France. A limestone slab there shows a naked woman with pendulous breasts and a pregnant belly. In her left hand she holds the horn, which is engraved with thirteen lines. Researchers believe these notations indicate that people at that time linked a woman's menstrual cycle to an annual thirteen-moon cycle and in so doing created the first calendar.[11]

Approximately three thousand years ago, Indian, Chinese, and Mayan women used their observations of the moon to develop calendars that are still in active use. In India the twenty-eight-day lunar calendar was divided into two fourteen-day periods—the dark half and the bright half of the moon. Together these mark both the menstrual and lunar cycles, with the full moon as the cosmic symbol for pregnancy. Within the Chinese cosmological system the full moon represents the conjunction of yin and yang, where darkness, femininity, and the stillness of the earth combine with the movements of the constellations and other heavenly bodies. Women's pregnancy due dates were reckoned by carefully noting twenty-eight stellar positions, known as "mansions," through which the moon passed.[12]

In Central America Mayan midwives observed that when a woman skipped her menstrual period she delivered her baby about 260 days later. In order to keep track of the elapsed time, they noted the full moon closest to the day she first realized she was pregnant and then counted nine full moons to arrive at the approximate due date. This practice gave rise to a lunar calendar that provided the basis for all other Mayan calendars, and it is still used by midwives.[13]

The moon is portrayed as an amorous goddess in Chinese and Mayan mythology. An ancient Chinese story says the moon goddess quarreled with her husband because he was jealous of her ability to menstruate. He accused her of keeping this "elixir of immortality" to herself. She was so angered by his unfounded accusation that she abandoned him and went to live forever in the house of the moon. When she did so, she forbade all men to attend her annual harvest full moon festival. Both the Chinese and Mayan moon goddesses are said to have intercourse as frequently as rabbits; their fecundity directly affects the plant world, causing seeds to germinate and plants to flourish. The pre-Columbian Mayan moon goddess even appears on pottery as a young woman sitting on the crescent of the Maya glyph for moon, holding a large rabbit in her lap (figure 45). The rabbit is said to reflect the patterns visible on the surface of the full moon.[14]

MENSTRUAL SYNCHRONY AND SECLUSION

Scientific studies indicate that women who live together in small communities tend to harmonize their menstrual periods. This occurs both because they know the timing of each other's bleeding and because they experience similar patterns of nocturnal light. (In the absence of other forms of light at night ovulation is triggered by the full moon.)[15]

45. *The moon goddess sitting on the crescent moon glyph painted on a Classic Mayan vessel. She is holding a rabbit, a symbol of fecundity, in her lap.*

In Australia, among the Yolngu, a girl's first menses was considered so beneficial and powerful that older women saved some of the blood to use later during rituals marking her maturity. At each subsequent period, until a girl was fully grown, these women massaged this blood into her shoulders to stimulate her development. In order to do this they gathered together in menstrual camps every month during the full moon. Women who were not menstruating—and were neither pregnant nor postmenopausal—were encouraged to menstruate by narrating the story of the first feminine bleeding, which was illustrated with the help of string figures.[16]

Long ago there lived two little girls known as the Djanggawul Sisters. They were out walking one afternoon with their brother on a long journey. As they traveled together across the earth, springs gushed from the ground and trees sprang up covered with leaves and birds.

When they got tired they sat down. But when they got up they left their sacred dillybags [string pouches] on the ground and their brother stole them. They realized that although he had taken their pouches the power of these emblems remained because they still had their wombs.

They sat back down with their feet out and legs apart. And as they looked at one another they began to bleed. Then each one made a loop of the other's menstrual blood and put it around her neck. This is the way they created the first string figures.

A popular figure made during these gatherings is called "blood of three women" (figure 46). The design—a single string interwoven in three segments held by the thumb, index finger, and baby finger of each hand—represents the close connections among young women bleeding together at the same time of the month.

In Polynesia females have traditionally gathered once a month in women's houses to talk and learn from one another. Hawaiian women to this day also withdraw to their *hale pe'a* or menstrual house. While they spend time together sharing information and

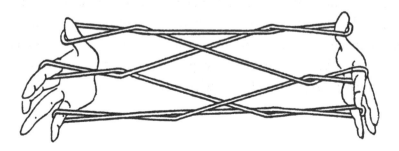

46. *Yolngu string figure. The "blood of three women," a string figure created each month by indigenous Australian women during their menstrual gatherings.*

making bark mats, their food is prepared and brought to them by their husbands and sons. Similarly, on Mogmog Island, in the Pacific atoll of Ulithi, many women retire to a large house each month during their menses. They bring their young children with them and spend time together weaving and talking.[17]

PUBERTY RITUALS

Puberty rituals for young women help them experience the power of their new adult status first through the inward path of meditation, then by a joyous communal ritual. Menarche provides an important gateway on their path to discovering their sexuality. For a Diné girl the blood she sheds, called *chooyin* or "sacred power," signifies her reproductive energy. A woman herbalist told me, "This first blood from your period is life blood. So you have a special ceremony called *kinaalda*, or 'first menstruation.' The girl's family looks for a woman who lives up to the ideals of womanhood—good health, ambition, and knowledge of tradition—to guide their daughter through the rituals."

On the morning of the first day the young woman is dressed in the image of the goddess called Changing Woman or Spider Woman, the deity whose weaving creates and repairs the universe. The girl wears a deep red velveteen blouse and gathered satin skirt, a woven red and black woolen sash, moccasins with deerskin leggings, long turquoise earrings, silver concho belt, turquoise necklaces, and cast silver bracelets and rings. Family members and close friends loan much of the jewelry to her so that it will be revitalized and blessed by her coming-of-age ritual.

Once she is fully dressed, the girl kneels, facing east; her hair is washed in yucca root suds and combed with a grass brush. It is tied back at the nape of her neck and held in place with a special thong cut from mountain lion skin. Then she stands in the center of the room while her relatives spread out blankets and other textiles. She will lie on these and be massaged. As one participant explained,

"When you have your Kinaalda, you are back in your infancy stage of life. Your body is in a stage of softness. You are thought of as a newborn baby. And you feel like that. That is why your body is molded to create strength and durability in your limbs and body."[18]

Her sponsor massages her with a flat, smooth object. If she wants the girl to become an excellent weaver, she will use a weaving batten. To make her a distinguished scholar, she uses a textbook. Beginning with the young woman's feet and legs, the sponsor moves up the girl's body toward her head. As she massages, she calls out positive characteristics. While stroking her feet she says, "Let her be swift and graceful as a deer." When massaging her legs, she says, "Let her have strength." If she wants the young woman to excel at weaving, she kneads her hands and arms, saying, "Let her be a good weaver."

At this point the young woman stands up and steps to the center of the room, where all of the children line up. One by one they approach her as the living embodiment of Spider Woman. She places her palms on the sides of their heads and stretches them upward so that they will grow tall. As one mother put it, "It is like a healing ceremony. She conducts healing with her Kinaalda, on the children. Everyone participating is blessed."[19]

Farther north, the Lakota of the pre-reservation period marked a girl's first feminine bleeding in a different way. She went with her mother to the women's lodge in order to seek a vision. There she was joined by other women, who taught her how to wrap her flow in a soft buckskin bundle lined with cattail down. Then she placed her sacred bundle outside in a plum tree, the symbol of fertility and hospitality. As she did so, she prayed silently to White Buffalo Woman, who brought the Bison Calf Peace Pipe to the Lakota Nation. When the girl returned to her family, they hosted a large public ceremony during which the myth of White Buffalo Woman was retold.[20]

Long ago White Buffalo Woman appeared to two young hunters as a beautiful woman. She was without clothing of any kind except for her long hair that fell over her body like a buffalo robe. One of these men thought of having sex with her, and since she could read his thoughts, she encouraged him.

As they embraced she surrounded herself with white smoke. When the smoke cleared, all that remained of him was his skeleton.

She told the second young man to return to camp and tell the elders that in a short time they would see four puffs of smoke directly under the sun at midday. When they saw this sign they should prepare a feast and she would arrive.

When she appeared, as promised, she presented the chief's family with a pipe, and taught them its ritual use. Then she instructed a shaman to place sweetgrass on the coals. It made a swirling cloud of smoke and as she entered it she rolled over four times. The first time, she became a black buffalo, the second time a brown buffalo, the third time a red one, and the fourth time she rolled over, she turned into a white female buffalo calf and galloped away across the hills.

In puberty rituals a Lakota girl assumed the mythical role of the great woman shaman, White Buffalo Woman. Thus she imparted to her people a mysterious or sacred power called *wakan*. For the remainder of her fertile years, for several days each month, she withdrew into the women's lodge, where she undertook visionary journeys together with the other women in the lodge.

When a young girl first began her feminine bleeding among the Ojibwe and their neighbors the Menominee, she spent several days fasting in a small lodge her mother built for her in the forest. During this time she was called *wemukowa*, "becoming a bear." Her slightest glance or touch could bring destruction to the berry crop (the favorite food of bears), paralysis to adults, and death to infants. And even without any prior training, she had the power to heal. As a local man explained:[21]

When I was young I had many warts on my hands. I was almost covered by them. An old woman of my tribe advised me to go to a girl who had built a bakan ishkodawe *[menstrual lodge] at some distance from town.*

She warned me to approach the lodge from the side very carefully. If I reached it safely I was to pass my hands in front while saying, "I have come to you to cure my hands."

I approached the lodge, passed my hands in, and repeated the words. The girl wet her fingers with her saliva and touched the warts on my hands. When she completed this, I retraced my steps to the village. And in just five days all of my warts had totally disappeared!

In the early years of the twentieth century, in British Columbia, the Haida urged an individual in severe pain to seek out a young woman who was undergoing her first menses and ask her to massage the soreness. If she was able to cure in this manner during her subsequent flows, she was formally trained and initiated as a shaman by an older woman.[22]

The idea that menstrual blood can heal is a widespread one. In Alaska, among the Koyukon, menstrual and birthing fluids are mixed with medicinal plants and used to concoct protective talismans for children. In Tibet the menstrual blood of young girls is offered to the goddess Tara and used as a potent medicine for the entire community. And on the Indonesian island of Java, the sarong a girl is wearing during her first menstruation is never washed or worn again but kept as a charm. Later, when one of her children falls ill, she treats the child by wrapping it inside the cloth. If the child recovers, the woman is recognized for her healing abilities and taught to be a shaman.[23]

According to a number of origin myths, a woman brought the cosmos into being by releasing sacred feminine blood. Such goddesses are typically associated with the color red, which symbolizes menstrual and birthing bloods, the source of their dangerous, mystical, and creative powers. At the Australian Aboriginal shrine of Ankota, the vulva of the earth, women worshipers visualize themselves standing on the edge of an underground pathway that gapes open before them like an enormous cavern. They see themselves as red like blood, like the heart of a flame.[24]

In Tibetan Buddhism the woman shaman known as Yeshey Tsogyel, or the Great Bliss Queen, is depicted as bright red. Her healing power is directly associated with her "mansion of flaming bliss," her vulva and womb. In south India the shamanic warrior goddess Bhagavati is also brilliant red; she is the epitome of feminine heat and sexual energy, and a red hibiscus flower is her symbol.[25]

The Barasana of the Amazon basin believe the first grandmother of us all, Romi Kumu or Woman Shaman, reaffirms her strength by painting her face red each month. But first she removes the old paint, taking off a thin layer of skin, which stands for her menstrual blood. Barasana shamans, like the Trio Indians of Suriname, are either postpubescent or premenopausal women, or else men who have undergone male puberty rituals of bloodletting from their penises. This blood is said to be the same as menstrual blood. In these and several other South American groups male shamans and menstruating women are considered equally powerful because of their great authority or their fertility.[26]

BLOOD AND SHAMANIC INITIATION

Wherever shamanism retained a distinctive feminine tradition, the trials and healing tied to puberty rituals often led to a young woman's initiation. Early in the twentieth century Lucy Thompson, a wealthy northern California woman of Yurok heritage, published a history of her people in which she explained that shamanism was passed only through the female bloodline. Young women with strong shamanic potential were selected as novices shortly after menarche and began training with their mothers and other female relatives. For two to ten years they visited sacred sites and canoed along the Klamath River to its mouth, where they fasted until they attained visions. A human or animal ghost placed a manifestation of subtle energy inside their bodies; it was visualized as a bloody, liver-colored mass called a "pain."[27]

Later, during her initiation ritual, a young woman went into the Klamath Mountains alone on ten consecutive days to bathe and seek a vision in a sacred pond. The first day she hiked up and bathed and meditated once. The second day she went twice and bathed and meditated twice, and so on until she completed the tenth and last day. Finally, she bathed at midnight, standing in the center of the pond, between the power of the water and the power of the full moon. She prayed aloud to Sky Woman, asking her for long life, strength, wealth, and a special gift or ability. Then she dived deep into the pond and brought up a shell as a token of her experience. When she returned she gave her talisman to her mentor and shared thoughts, feelings, sensations, images, and dreams from her ten-day quest.

In the late nineteenth century, Fanny Flounder, a famous Yurok basket weaver who wished to follow in the footsteps of her grandmother, mother, and sisters, undertook this form of shamanic initiation herself (figure 47). Years later, after she had become a successful healer, she told the story of her youthful shamanic quests to Robert Spott, a Yurok neighbor.[28]

For several summers I hiked to a peak overlooking the ocean near my home. There I danced for hours in the hopes of receiving a vision. One late summer afternoon, while dancing, I

47. *Fanny Flounder, a famous and wealthy Yurok shaman. The tattoos on her chin indicate that she had a puberty ritual when she came of age.*

became unconscious. While sleeping I dreamed I saw the sky rising and blood dripping off its edge, like icicles. I heard the drops go ts, ts as they struck the ocean.

Then I saw a woman in an old-time dress made of maple bark, with her hair tied up like a doctor. The woman reached up as the edge of the sky went higher and picked off one of the blood icicles, saying, "Here, take it," and put it into my mouth. It was icy cold. Then I knew nothing more.

When I came to I was in the breakers with several men holding onto me. They carried me back to the sweathouse to dance. But I could not. My feet turned under as if there were no bones in them. Then they took turns carrying me on their backs and dancing with me. . . .

Finally, after five days of dancing in the sweathouse, I was resting when I felt a craving for crabmeat. An old kinswoman [also a shaman] went along the beach until she found a

washed-up claw and brought it back and roasted it in the ashes.
But at the first bite I became nauseated.

The old woman said, "Let it come out," and held a basket
under my mouth. As soon as I saw the bloody vomit, I cried,
"Eya."

Fanny acquired five pairs of "pains" and became a powerful
herbalist and sucking doctor who could move objects by her
thoughts alone. This combination of shamanic powers made her
one of the wealthiest shamans in all of northern California at the
turn of the twentieth century.[29]

Other Yurok shamans similarly dreamed of receiving watery,
bloody shamanic powers from their ancestors and guardian spirits.
A woman by the name of Merip Okegei accepted raw venison from
the hands of an unknown ancestor and vomited up a salmon's liver.
Such images—blood-filled icicles, pieces of raw venison, bits of
bloody salmon liver, and amulets enveloped in dripping blood—
all symbolically link these women's shamanic powers to menstrual
fluids.

Tela Star Hawk Lake, a practicing northern California shaman,
notes that historically when a young woman reached puberty in
Hupa society, there was a celebration during which she lived in a
specially constructed "moon lodge" with a holy woman. This woman
sat with the girl, burning herbs and roots in a sacred fire. Then she
covered the girl's head with a deerskin to help her focus her thoughts.
While the young woman prayed for a vision, dancers outside the
lodge sang songs in her honor. After two or three days of seclusion
she emerged and ran to the river. There she asked the moon and her
spiritual helpers, the water beings, to give her protection, wealth,
strength, and long life. Upon returning to the lodge, she gazed into
an abalone shell filled with water. The shifting iridescent images revealed her new spiritual status as a shamanic healer.[30]

Due to various cultural pressures fewer Native American women in California now spend time in menstrual seclusion or undergo puberty rituals. As a result, only a handful of these women undertake shamanic training and initiation. In its place, however, they have created an intertribal monthly ritual known as the moon time ceremony. Women who participate abstain from work, sex, and eating meat. They rest; drink soups, herbal teas, and fruit juices; and sing and pray in the moonlight. In the morning they bathe in cold water to build strength. During this ceremony they meditate, tell stories, and share their life experiences with other women.[31]

Early in the twentieth century in Greenland the custom was to send potential female shamans off alone into the wilderness during their first menstruation. They were told to seek contact with the spirit world. When the shaman Teemiartissaq was approaching puberty, her shaman father suggested that she ought to follow his path. Later, early in the twentieth century, she described her years of training.[32]

My father told me: "Train for angakok*" [the shamanic profession to which he himself belonged]. So I went inland into the mountains. When I arrived I saw a beautiful butterfly, all covered with blood, sitting on the ground. It looked as though it was ready to be whistled to, so I did. It possessed me and I clothed myself in its appearance.*

Once again I whistled. This caused the butterfly to leave me, to fly away.

Suddenly I heard someone say, "Since she whistles and begins to dress as the butterfly, she must be training to become one who can descend into the sea. I wonder if she will visit the ocean deity when she has become a fully-trained shaman."

Then I saw the butterfly lick herself all over, stroking away the blood. At that point I recovered my consciousness.

The bloody butterfly emerging from the chrysalis symbolized her tender coming of age. Just as her blood burst forth from her genitals, her spirit broke free and metamorphosed into a butterfly, soaring skyward on her initial shamanic journey. This is the most beautiful image of the power of feminine blood magic as an ecstatic form of shamanic power that I have ever encountered.

The symbol transcends culture, as Judy Chicago has shown in her complex work *The Dinner Party*. In this creative blend of sculpture, needlework, ceramic tile, and painted china, she developed a symbolic history of the feminine. The sexual imagery intrinsic in the thirty-nine plates on Chicago's dinner table provoked an extraordinarily negative response on the part of male art critics when it was first exhibited in 1979. As one female reviewer noted, "Perhaps this overt symbolism hits too close to home in a society that continues to try to control women's bodies through an ongoing battle over reproductive rights." But for the artist, one of the most crucial elements of the work was the plate she called a "butterfly vagina."[33]

THIRTEEN

The Sacred, the Dangerous, and the Forbidden:

MENSTRUAL TABOOS AS FEMININE POWER

ALONG WITH THE power of feminine blood comes a complex and varying set of beliefs that have too often been misinterpreted. In many cultures ethnographers have recorded that menstruating women and feminine blood are considered "taboo"; they must be avoided so as not to contaminate men, their activities, or their possessions. But these researchers have failed to fully understand these prohibitions; they've certainly missed their positive values. Yes, menstruating women may be subject to restrictions, but they are also considered sacred and powerful.

During my shamanic apprenticeship in Guatemala I learned firsthand about menstrual taboos. Early in my training Don Andrés and Doña Talín asked me if I had been menstruating during any of my visits to the outdoor shrines. Luckily I had not. It turned out that a noninitiated menstruating woman must not approach the burning copal incense at these shrines because the odor of her blood would readily mix with the incense smoke and be carried to the homes of the ancestors. Such an offering is considered a powerful form of "feeding" the dead. This should be undertaken only by a woman who has been formally introduced to the ancestors and therefore can be trusted to continue to feed them for as long as she lives. If a woman were to begin such a lifetime obligation and fail in her training, then her menstrual blood would become a poison for the ancestors, who would be killed once and for all.

The word *taboo*—meaning "marked thoroughly" or "set apart and forbidden to profane use because of dangerous sacred powers"— came into English from the Polynesian islands of Tonga. There and elsewhere in the Pacific the concepts of the sacred, the dangerous, and the forbidden are all closely linked.

In the Marquesas the first menstruation of a woman chief called for elaborate taboos that celebrated her *mana,* or sacred power. These rituals were as important to the women's authority as the men's taboos about warfare were to a male chief. In Fiji a menstruating woman is referred to as *dra tabu,* meaning "sacred blood" or "forbidden blood." Her menstrual blood, too, is infused with *mana.*[1]

On the Great Plains of North America, during pre-reservation times, women left their men during their menstrual periods and set up special lodges where they sought contact with spiritual beings. The men, believing that menstrual blood could drive away game animals and affect the power of their guardian spirits, withdrew to their own lodges. However, neither women nor men viewed menstruation as shameful or unclean; rather, it was powerful, magical, and dangerous. A menstruating woman could be taboo, but she was not impure.[2]

COYOTE MISCHIEF

The creation stories of native North Americans reveal their cultural attitudes toward women and menstruation. Many of these myths feature a trickster hero known as Coyote. According to an early-twentieth-century narrative, Coyote created the first menses in order to punish a beautiful maiden's refusal of a sexual favor. We pick up the story—collected by anthropologist Alfred Kroeber from a Yurok woman shaman in California—when the girl rebuffs Old Man Coyote's outrageous sexual advances.[3]

She rejected him and Coyote became very angry and went to Pulekukwerek [the culture hero] and said, "I think [it would] be best if a woman has flowers. When she has flowers she will see blood."

The deity agreed with Coyote and cut his ankle. Then he spread his own blood on the girl's thigh.

"You got flowers now," Coyote said.

"No!" cried the girl.

"Yes, I see blood on your legs," insisted Coyote.

Then, as Coyote began outlining a set of taboos, Sky Woman spoke from the center of the heavens saying:

"We are around here in [the] sky, all we women, flowers. We are never afraid because we have medicine for it. Now look upriver. I always wash there myself. Now look at that lake in the middle of the sky, you can see how many trails come to that lake. Now look where I stand. You can see blood all around me because I'm that way now. I'm flowers. I will go out in the lake and wash, and then I will have good luck. Tell her I wash in the sky."

Despite Coyote's actions, Sky Woman taught the girl not to fear her bleeding but to think of it as beautiful flowers.

A woman from another California Indian culture recently told a slightly different menstrual origin story to the shaman Tela Star Hawk Lake.[4]

One day long ago Old Man Coyote was out hunting with his bow and arrow. He saw some beautiful young women gathering herbs by the side of a pond. "Maybe I will shoot at them to get them to run away," he said to himself.

You see he wanted to get them to run so that he could see how developed their buttocks and breasts were becoming.

So, he sang his love song and pretended that he was going to shoot them. He was enjoying himself so much. Then he suddenly fell down, and his arrow slipped, hitting one of them in the crotch. The young girl lay there bleeding and crying.

Older women came running and shouting at the top of their lungs. They chased Coyote away.

He became furious and said: "You can't talk to me in that way. I'll show you how much power I have. I am putting a curse on all young women. From this day forward whenever girls get to this age they will bleed, get scared, and become sick."

But the women elders had power and so they set about healing the girl. First they gathered willows from the creek and constructed a special lodge, similar to the men's sweat lodge. Then they went inside and sang, danced, and prayed over the girl, asking Grandmother Moon to heal her. They doctored her with herbs and flowers, and then taught her how to contemplate, meditate, and learn from her dreams.

So it was that medicine women changed menstruation from Coyote's Curse into a Medicine Woman's Blessing.

The analytical psychologist Carl Jung described Coyote as an asexual "collective shadow figure, an epitome of all the inferior traits of character in individuals."[5] His analysis downplays the gender of the ultramasculine Coyote, who is portrayed in these myths first as a culture hero who purposely originates menstruation and second as a fool who does so accidentally. In both cases women overcome him, turning his menstrual taboos into puberty rituals and his hunting curse into a menstrual blessing.

This difference between men's and women's attitudes toward menstruation is also emphasized in other Native American traditions. In Creek mythology, corn grew because the primordial mother scrubbed her legs once a month, causing her blood to flow as corn gruel. Ever since then masculine sun rays have struggled to emerge from this watery feminine menstrual abundance. Such a metaphor suggests that to encourage the growth of food, men should separate from women each month. Creek men disdain the odor of menstrual blood as "stink lying down" and say it indicates a dangerous or uncontrolled woman who can ruin both their hunting abilities and their health. Creek women, on the other hand, believe that menstrual flows give them power and therefore force a separation of the sexes. Historically women lived apart from men during menses, ate with separate dishes, and sat on different mats. Contemporary men and women sleep in different bedrooms, or in warm weather the men may stay outside in a brush arbor. If a family neglects to live by these rules, the men are said to be vulnerable to a number of illnesses, including diabetes, stroke, cancer, and rheumatism.[6]

Bleeding women are portrayed in many cultures as life-giving goddesses or polluting demons. Sometimes they're a bit of both. The negative view is most likely found where a hierarchical male priesthood closely controls religious ideology. The Hindu practice of tantra includes rituals that worship female menstrual flow; in mainstream Sanskritic Hinduism, however, these rituals are considered polluting. In Japanese Shinto—where the religious leaders are mostly female—menstruating women are said to embody the feminine divine. The clerical Buddhism practiced in Japan, China, Tibet, and India—where the priests are mostly male—declares menstruating women unclean.[7]

MENSTRUAL SHAME, FEAR, AND ENVY

Generations of social scientists have paid more attention to the words and actions of men than of women. As a result, the ethnographic record is overflowing with descriptions of men's fear, disgust, and anger at menstruating women. Women ethnographers may have had difficulty accepting these attitudes, but because they so often allow themselves to become "honorary males" in the societies they study, their points of view have become tainted.[8]

Ruth Landes, in her classic book *The Ojibwa Woman* (1938), let her disgust with menstruation affect what she was seeing. She described first menses among the Ojibwe as a time when a young woman is a menace to herself. She also claimed that a girl's vision quest is culturally unimportant. "While a boy's puberty vision quest is a hopeful striving for broader horizons, hers is a conscientious withdrawal of her malignant self."[9]

Another ethnographer, Ruth Underhill, admitted she had a problem understanding and accepting menstrual taboos. She asked a Tohono O'odham (Papago) woman who was undergoing her days of separation, "Do you mind being sent out of the house?" The woman laughed at her, saying, "Mind! Why, it's a holiday for us women. No work to do, no matter how the men may want it." Underhill continued to push the point, however: "You don't mind—er—people knowing?" The woman was truly amazed. "Why should we?" was her reply. "That is the time when we are powerful and the men are afraid. We like to see them slinking past with their backs turned."[10]

By simultaneously displaying her own embarrassment and the woman's clear answers to her foolish questions, Underhill furnishes an easily remembered teaching story about intercultural sensitivity. The unease that so many Western women feel about their menstrual cycles springs from a combination of masculine sentiments and religious sanctions.

In the Christian tradition the menstrual curse and the pain of childbirth are legacies of Eve's disobedience in the Garden of Eden. Her eating of the fruit of knowledge, offered by the serpent, brought these punishments to all mortal women. To this day feminine blood is considered impure in the Roman Catholic Church. One reason Church fathers give for refusing to allow the ordination of women as priests is that their uterine blood could pollute the holy altar.[11]

In the Jewish tradition, too, menstruation was the result of Eve's actions in the Garden of Eden. As a result, a menstruating woman, called *niddah* in Hebrew, must follow specific legal codes forbidding sexual relations. Each month she counts five days for menstruation, then adds seven days of purity, during which she must verify that no menstrual blood has flowed. At the end she immerses her body in the *mikvah*, or ritual bath. Talmudic law stipulates that while a woman is permitted to cohabit with her husband after bathing, on the eighth day, she is not permitted to take this bath during the Sabbath, even if it is her eighth day.[12]

In Western society women hide their menstrual bleeding in their language—through euphemisms—and in practice. Studies have shown that many young women conceal menarche from their mothers and share their experience with other young women only after several periods. The psychologist Melanie Klein suggested that girls do this because they unconsciously identify menstrual blood with urine and feces, and therefore with contamination.[13]

There has also been a societal reason for women to downplay their menstrual cycles: in the early days of the industrial revolution, men doubted that women in the workforce were actually able to carry out their tasks day in and day out. Social reformers hired researchers to prove that women could perform their work when they were menstruating as easily as when they were not. They concluded that women showed no inefficiency in motor skills or word associations during their periods. More recent scientific studies reveal something slightly different: evidently routine physical skills do decline somewhat, but creative thinking and problem solving actually improve just before and during menstruation.[14]

Psychoanalysts have contributed to widespread feelings of shame over menstruation. Sigmund Freud, who was generally dismissive of women, reduced all esoteric inclinations to an infantile longing for the "oceanic" feeling of the womb. Bruno Bettelheim, however, suggested that the hostility between men and women, which frequently results in disgust with menstruation, is closely linked to vagina or womb envy.[15]

The overall result has been that for far too long women in Western society have had to apologize for their feminine blood. It is time for women to embrace their difference; only then will men learn to respect the power of menstruation.

WOMEN'S MENSTRUAL PRIDE

The menstrual shame that seems such a part of Western society is a matter of culture at war with nature. From members of other traditions we hear again and again about the value of feminine bleeding and menstrual seclusion. Philip Deere, a Muskogee holy man from Oklahoma, expressed it this way: "Woman is the same as man—but at a certain age she changes into another stage of life. During this stage she naturally purifies herself each month. During their monthly time women separate themselves from men. Men must take a sweat bath once a month while women are naturally purifying themselves to keep their medicine effective."[16]

Similarly, Aymara women who live near Lake Titicaca, in Bolivia and Peru, believe menstruation cleanses and empowers them spiritually. Ethnographers have described these women, who travel all over the Andes to practice their shamanic healing skills, as more powerful than male healers. In the opinion of these women, the monthly flow of blood purifies and strengthens them, making them especially effective in curing reproductive problems such as sterility and infertility, as well as removing other misfortunes, including trouble with lovers.[17]

In societies where women are perceived as a threat to men, masculine menstruation rituals have developed, perhaps to partake of female power. Melanesian men, for example, fervently believe that any contact with feminine substances—especially menstrual blood—is dangerous. At the same time they envy women, who are freed of "contamination" through menstruation. To compensate, they invented bloodletting rituals that imitate women's monthly flow. Beginning in puberty and continuing throughout their lives, men induce bleeding from their noses or genitals.[18]

In Australia Aboriginal males were traditionally circumcised during puberty ceremonies in which adults of both sexes participate. At the beginning of the ritual the boys were smeared with menstrual blood, and a womb-shaped hole was prepared in the ground. One by one the boys were placed in the cavity and told that Karwadi, the "mother of all," would swallow and regurgitate them—that is, they would die and be reborn. All the while the sound of a bull-roarer (a flat board tied to a string swung rapidly in circles above the head) emulated Karwadi's voice.

Several years later these same boys underwent subincision, a painful operation that involves using a knife to split the ventral surface of the penis along most of its length; thus they gain symbolic vaginas. As the final step in their initiation they were swallowed and regurgitated by Julunggul, the rainbow snake. They crawled through the legs of their initiators and were reborn as androgynes from this collective male womb. From then on their penis wounds were broken open once a month with a thorn; the combined flow of blood and semen was released as the vital essence of life.

According to British ethnographer Ashley Montagu, subincision was considered valuable because it allowed men to menstruate so that they could get rid of the "bad blood" that resulted from sex and other dangerous activities. Women lost this bad blood naturally through menstruation, while men had to take action to obtain the same effect.[19]

During male puberty rites in Wogeo, New Guinea, the tongues of initiates were cut to rid them of their mothers' blood, which was passed along through nursing. This ritual bloodletting, or induced menstruation, was said to make young men's tongues supple and help them play the sacred flute. The ceremonies took place at the same time as the initial bleeding of pubescent girls. During the new moon, as the girls left the village for their menstrual seclusion, the boys reentered the settlement.[20]

To a person born and bred in a society that has exalted the achievements of men and deprecated the role of women, these emulations of feminine bleeding may seem bizarre or far-fetched. After all, women in Western society, who were supposedly fashioned from Adam's rib, strive to imitate men. In New Guinea culture, however, where men feared women's ability to bring forth life, it was they who tried to imitate the superior power.

COUVADE

Nothing epitomizes female reproductive life force more than childbirth itself, and in some places men vicariously share that power by practicing certain birth precautions called couvade. The tradition was first noticed among Basques, and the name comes from the French word *couver,* meaning "to hatch." After giving birth a woman went about her chores, while her husband lay in bed recovering.[21]

Couvade was illustrated in sixteenth-century Spanish colonial paintings. And according to Celtic tradition, whenever a fairy queen gave birth, her husband, too, lay in bed to share her pain. Some rural people of Celtic descent living in France, Germany, and the British Isles still maintain the custom. In Canada, where Celts intermarried with Native Americans, this tradition is honored in myth, ritual, and occasionally in practice. The Tupinamba of Brazil and the Quichua of Ecuador followed a similar custom: the husband of a woman who had just given birth wore his wife's clothes and reclined in his hammock, receiving congratulations from his kin. Meanwhile his wife was up cleaning, washing, and cooking.[22]

In medieval times, Europeans believed that physical pain and suffering could be shared by the exchange of clothing. A woman in labor wore one of her husband's garments; the man would put on one of her dresses and roll on the ground, moaning and groaning. In some communities in southern India men wear their wives' saris during childbirth to transfer the pain to themselves. These rituals have been interpreted in various ways—as a man's indirect experience of birth, as a form of emasculation and submission, or as a jealous reaction, since males cannot give birth.[23]

Husbands and wives together practice postpartum rituals in some indigenous societies. Among the Wayapí of South America today new parents take elaborate precautions concerning what they can eat and where they can go. Indigenous peoples in California had a similar set of parental restrictions called by ethnographers "the semi-couvade." Here the couple was considered physically as one; thus the man, instead of being injured by the woman's power, partook of it. He gave up male activities such as fishing and gambling, withdrew from other people, and guarded his own safety, just as his wife did. However, instead of resting during his couvade, he kept busy performing women's tasks, such as gathering firewood. He bathed every day and had a man attend to him, just as his wife had a midwife to take care of her. A man who deeply identified with his wife's experience might also develop symptoms of pregnancy, such as lethargy and nausea. Then he might take to his bed at the time of birth. When his wife cried out as she tried to push the baby into the world, he, too, would feel her labor pains.[24]

Sometimes couvade caused actual physical pain. In northern California, Native American men withdrew into a separate building when their wives had babies. They abstained from socializing, ate only acorn soup, and called upon the spirit world to help during childbirth. That way, as the woman suffered, her husband suffered as well. And as she bled, he cut himself with a white quartz flint to take on a portion of her discomfort.[25]

According to Huichol tradition, when a woman gives birth to her first child, her husband must squat in the rafters directly above her, with ropes attached to his testicles (figure 48). As the woman goes into labor, she tugs vigorously on the tethers and her husband shares in her painful, but ultimately joyous, experience of childbirth.

A similar ritual has been recorded in Estonia. There a husband

48. *Huichol yarn painting of the birthing ritual. This yarn painting by Guadalupe de la Cruz Ríos shows a woman giving birth. She is pulling on ropes tied to her husband's testicles so that he shares her pain.*

sits on a high platform with his testicles tied to a thread that runs to his wife's childbirth bed. Whenever the woman moans, her midwife pulls hard on the thread, evoking groans from the husband. The idea behind these rituals is to transfer some of the genital pain to the father so he can empathize with and encourage his wife.[26]

FEMININE SHAMANIC PATHS

Most students of shamanism have followed Mircea Eliade in focusing their attention on masculine shamanic paths—dismemberment, evisceration, and symbolic death leading to rebirth—as necessary to shamanic initiation. Women on feminine paths focus their attention around birth: they receive their shamanic calling during menarche or pregnancy and are symbolically born into the profession. In a number of traditions in Siberia, Southeast Asia, and China women shamans not only serve as midwives in their communities but during their séances tie long white ropes to ceiling beams in order to coax their spirit helpers down into their bodies before they begin shamanizing (see chapter fourteen).

Judeo-Christian belief has portrayed menstruation as a form of punishment or defilement rather than a time for spiritual awakening and natural cleansing. And anti-menstrual attitudes have distorted our understanding of the power of menstrual blood and the celebrations conducted by menstruating women. The withdrawal of women into special places during menses has been interpreted as a sign of female degradation instead of representing the positive aspects of seclusion. To truly comprehend the healing potential of women's blood, we need to pay closer attention to traditions in which women practice as shamans.

Women today, regardless of their ethnic and religious affiliations, might do well to develop moon time rituals celebrating the divine feminine. During this special period they might make pilgrimages to sacred locations to come into harmony with their natural biorhythms and menstrual flows. By freeing themselves from the damaging idea of menstruation as a "pollution" or "curse," and by realizing that moon time rituals can encourage intuitive and spiritual powers, they might also empower themselves in other aspects of their lives.

With the recent entry of women into leadership roles in the Reform and Conservative rabbinates, Jewish women now can join together in Rosh Hodesh groups to celebrate the new moon and to practice spiritual healing. Many of the women involved in this movement feel that these celebrations link the moon to their menstrual cycles.[27]

Women in the goddess spirituality movement gather their own menstrual blood and use it to feed houseplants, or drip it on paper as works of art that they exhibit publicly. These activities invert the understanding of menstruation as Eve's "curse." Instead of something embarrassing, ugly, and evil about women, menstrual blood becomes the material form of subtle energy—clean, beautiful, creative, and powerful—that it is.[28]

Perhaps the most basic lesson of all is that women can achieve mystic states of awareness—and serve as shamanic healers—by considering their bodies and bodily fluids as integral to their spirituality, not as obstacles to it. When feminine blood is felt as a materialization of vital energy, menstruation provides women a special pathway toward spiritual understanding and healing.

FOURTEEN

Calling Forth the Spirits:

BIRTH, RITUAL, AND
THE MIDWIFE'S ART

IF MENSTRUATION IS a powerful time for women, then pregnancy magnifies their shamanic abilities greatly. In many cases, not only are they connected to the creative force in their bodies, but they also may be more attuned to an alternative reality. Bayar Odun, the Mongolian shaman I introduced in chapter five, explained to me that being pregnant and having a baby were the most powerful ways for a woman to access the creative and transformative powers of the natural world. During each of her pregnancies she noticed that she was more easily connected to the spirit of her own dead mother, who had been a famous shaman. She also noted that her shamanizing was stronger or weaker depending on the nature of the child in her womb. Bayar knew, for example, that her second daughter, Baljir, had the shamanic gift because Bayar's own powers of clairvoyance and healing were greatly intensified during this pregnancy. This had not been the case during her first pregnancy, when she found herself weak and unable to shamanize with intensity. When her first daughter was born the child was pale and weak, and unfortunately lived only a few weeks.

Bayar suggested that since I had never become pregnant, serving as a midwife was one way I might tap into this most feminine of shamanic powers. As a result of our conversation, I began to pay closer attention to the overlap between midwives and shamans. In culture after culture I have found that—like my Ojibwe grandmother—women shamans are nearly always midwives. The act of helping souls to transform themselves in order to cross from the other world into this world turns out to be at the heart of feminine shamanic traditions worldwide. While the masculine traditions focus on a shaman's symbolically dying into shamanhood, the feminine traditions focus on the shaman's being born into it. For that reason pregnant women and new mothers all over the globe are often inspired to become prophets, diviners, healers, or shamans.

In northeastern Brazil a Quichua-speaking woman began receiving prophetic messages in 1963 from the baby in her womb. In a matter of weeks she became the center of a religious cult that soon supplanted the traditional all-male political leaders in her community. More than fifty retainers carried her in a sedan chair from village to village. Everywhere she stopped, worshipers kissed her abdomen, and after she gave birth, both she and her baby were declared to be great shamans.[1]

In the Siberian region of North Asia, women are commonly selected as shamans immediately after childbirth, an event that may be real or symbolic. In the mid-twentieth century a Nanai woman named Gara Geiker told how moments after her infant came into the world, she gave birth to something else. First she hid it; then, realizing it was the placenta, she threw it away. In subsequent dreams, though, she saw that she had foolishly gotten rid of a baby girl, a spirit daughter who promised to help her in her shamanic practice. Not long after, Gara dreamed that she gave birth again—this time from her mouth—to a child with a catfish tail. The fish-child promptly rowed away in a small boat. Later, when Gara began performing as a shaman, the fish-child became her helping spirit, who enabled her to spiritually travel along the Amur River.[2]

Sophia Anga, a seventh-generation shaman and healer from the neighboring Ul'ichi group, as a teenager often dreamed that she gave birth to tigers. When she was twenty, twin tigers took her to the lower world, where she saw seven burning mountains. The animals tried to keep her there, but her deceased grandmother, who had been a famous shaman, helped her to tame the creatures. Eventually the girl released the tigers from the underworld and they became her spirit helpers. Since then, when Sophia experiences her spiritual journeys, the flying tigers are her steeds.

Sophia's specialty is curing reproductive disorders. One of her patients, Chana, had had several miscarriages before she again became pregnant and decided to ask for help. She was giving birth when Sophia arrived. Discerning that the soul of the unborn child had been stolen, the healer blew the soul back through the woman's fontanel. "It was as if my skull opened up. I remember the feeling well; it was cold. Her breath was very cold. Such a feeling! I will never forget it," Chana said.[3]

Matryona Petrovna Kurbeltınova, an Evenki shaman, relied on symbols of childbirth for her séances. She began by putting on a special gown, apron, and fur shoes, then lashed a symbolic birthing rope—the cord women hang on to during labor—to the top horizontal pole of her tent. Singing softly, "Ko-ko-ko, tut-tut," she lured her spirit helpers, a cuckoo and a hoopoe, down into her body.[4]

Women shamans in Southeast Asia and China also use birthing ropes to assist in their soul travel. In Vietnam and northern Thailand long white cloths are attached to ceiling beams during both childbirth and shamanic séances. Pregnant women hold on to them as they deliver their babies, and women shamans do the same when they consult their ancestral spirits. Since babies are considered reincarnated ancestors, the birthing rope symbolism aptly fits both activities.[5]

The ancient profession of midwifery is still practiced so widely today that midwives deliver nearly 80 percent of the world's babies. Besides the nurturing and supportive role they take with pregnant women, midwives regularly administer treatments for sterility, give massages and sweat baths, and provide herbal remedies and advice on nutrition and childcare. They know how to concoct herbal aphrodisiacs and abortives, and how to treat female ailments and children's illnesses. (Among the ancient Aztecs, midwives even functioned as marriage brokers, and later baptized and named the children of the couple. They then officiated at puberty rituals, engagement ceremonies, and marriages of the children they helped bring into the world.)[6]

Most important, in many cultures midwives may enlist spiritual aid before, during, and after birth. Thus they are shamanic healers in their own right. They join fertility experts, herbalists, and bonesetters among the ranks of Mongol shamans; for the Manchu and other neighboring North Asian peoples, shamanic specialties include midwifery. This also holds true in Mesoamerica, where midwives, bonesetters, and snake- and spider-bite specialists all practice as healing shamans.[7]

Yet midwifery has rarely been acknowledged as a shaman's art. Instead midwives have been classed together with barber-surgeons and homeopaths as "empirical practitioners" or labeled as "traditional birth attendants," a lesser category of healer that is used for women outside the Western biomedical tradition. Why were such mistakes made and perpetuated? During the early years of ethnographic field research, men, who were usually denied access to pregnant women and the scene of childbirth, carried out most studies. Only as the number of women ethnographers increased has this record been corrected.[8]

The ethnographer Lois Paul, for example, discovered that among the Tzutujil Maya living on the shores of Lake Atitlán in Guatemala, midwives were shamans who became possessed by their guardian spirit, a patron deity, or the moon. The first sign that a woman might be destined for the midwife's shamanic path was a nighttime dream or daytime vision in which a powerful figure announced her calling. If she disregarded the first message, similar dreams would recur. During the day the woman might find an unusual rock, shell, marble, or fragment of an ancient figurine. These objects were said to speak for the spirits. If she took it home and placed it on her family altar, she received herbal cures and other remedies during her sleep. Eventually she might be taken away, during dreams or waking reveries, to a distant mountaintop or cave, for more training and eventual initiation as a shaman.[9]

SHAMANIC INITIATION INTO MIDWIFERY

In the Mexican state of Oaxaca, a young Cuicatec woman by the name of María Malinche gave the late ethnographer Eva Hunt a detailed narrative of her own shamanic initiation. Eva, who was a friend of mine, passed it to me shortly before her death. She told me that María's father was a well-known bonesetter, and that if María had been male, she might have inherited his practice. Instead, when she was eight, María was summoned by a female spirit. The girl's story opens as she moves away from her playmates and sits down alone under a giant oak tree.[10]

I went out late one afternoon to gather blackberries with some children. While the older children were picking berries, I got tired and sat in the shadow of a tree.

I was hungry, so I ate some of the berries I had collected in my basket. When I finished I found that I could not hear the older children anymore. I got scared and started calling to them, yelling loud.

A woman wearing a long white embroidered huipil *[traditional dress] appeared before me and asked, "Did you call me? You woke me up!"*

I knew this woman. She was a friend of my mother's who had recently died. Some people in the village had seen her late at night roaming around her old homestead.

The woman smiled and said to hold onto her dress. I did so and we flew away. It was like in a dream when one moment one is one place and the next moment somewhere else. All of a sudden we were at the doors of a cave. They were gigantic doors. She knocked and we entered, passing an old man standing there with a big orange-colored dog.

Inside there was an enormous city in a high long tunnel all lit with torches. On the right side were row upon row of two-floor houses, and on the left side was a row of women making tortillas to feed the people and the sick souls.

After entering we were received by Lord Lightning Thunderbolt. I was scared, actually terrified, but he was gentle and very kind to me. He told me that he had chosen me to become a healer. Then he asked me which ways I wanted to use in curing. I refused to answer him and asked to be sent back home. But he insisted that it was not my choice, for I had the ability and the power. Besides, I was ready to learn.

I refused. He insisted. I refused five times. And five times he insisted, until I gave in, and we walked together into the interior of the earth, into the cave city.

We moved along a line of sick people. In front of each one Lord Lightning Thunderbolt asked me to say what was wrong with the person. I gave my opinion and he gave me his, together with healing instructions. Sometimes he said to light candles or to take the pulse and say what I felt. Sometimes he said to massage the patient with wild tobacco.

Then he gave me some herbs and told me, "This is for making tea. This is for rubbing with. This is for fanning."

The first sick person I was to heal turned out to be a woman who had been in labor for a long time. She had eaten cold foods [avocados, lard, and other fats] and now she was dying. I saw her weakness, the sweat, and the swollen legs. Lord Lightning Thunderbolt told me to put my hands over her belly, softly. When I did so, immediately the child was born.

Then he said: "Never put your hands inside the woman. That is not the way. Just massage her outside and help her push. Tie *her with a shawl. Hold her. If you pray and give her your strength the baby will be born."*

He taught me the language of prayer, the sacred language of the caves. At every step he gave me things: herbs and stones for my collection, and instructions for the order of things in curing. After each cure I was paid in copper coins, one or two for each person. He told me to always charge for healing because if the patients did not pay, I would lose my power. But I was not to charge much. Then, after many cures, he said, "You are tired and weak."

I had not eaten or slept and my power was gone. But he told me that I was going to attend a banquet. There was a long table covered with a beautiful woven cloth. Everyone was there that I had cured. It was like when the town leaders are given their staffs of office. I was being given a job there. I was becoming a healer.

At the banquet they served turkey and tortillas, liquor, and wild-tobacco cigars. I ate, drank, and smoked a cigar. After awhile the woman who brought me to the cave reappeared. She told me it was time to go home.

I was given a cloth bundle. Inside was my curer's kit as well as some tortillas, turkey meat, and on top were the coins. I put the bundle, which was tied with a double knot, inside the berry basket that I was still carrying with me. The doors opened, and the woman and I left. Then I blacked out.

The next thing I remember is waking up under the tree. It was sunset. The place was quiet and getting dark. I was very afraid, for the other children were nowhere to be seen.

I stood up and saw that everything had truly happened. There in my basket was a bundle sitting on the blackberries. I opened it to see what was inside. The money was still there on top. The stones were there. The herbs were still there, but now they were dry. The most curious thing of all was what had happened to the turkey and the tortillas. Instead of tortillas, there was a pile of leaves. Instead of turkey, there were chunks of rotten wood, white and soft.

When María returned home that evening, her mother asked her where she had been. She described what had happened, and her mother became angry, accusing her of lying. But her father defended her. "That is the way one begins," he explained. "I know because I did it too. It was a friend of my father who took me there, because I am a male. She is too young and will have to wait. Later she can come with me when I do my curing and maybe she can help. You should respect her now because she is different from your other children." The girl became her father's helper, and on his death some years later she became a well-known shaman.

María's mythic journey is a classic example of shamanic soul flight. Lord Lightning Thunderbolt's detailed instructions about assisting at birth, together with her consecration as a shaman, clearly indicate that midwifery is a woman's shamanic specialty among the Cuicatec, as it is among the Tzutujil.

In recent years, as I have read primary sources and communicated with ethnographers worldwide, I have begun to find extensive archaeological and ethnographic evidence for midwifery as a branch of shamanism in other times and places.

JAGUARS

Ancient jade sculptures, terra-cotta figurines, and vase paintings that depict rulers, priests, and midwives with jaguar characteristics abound throughout the American tropics. Jaguars, like bears in temperate regions, are animals of great strength, majesty, and power. As the largest spotted cats in the world and the glory of the forest, they are key symbols of shamanic transformative power. The shaman shares so much with the jaguar that in many indigenous languages of the Americas they are called by the same name. In both Central and South American traditions the soul of a dead shaman takes the form of a jaguar that roams near the village.[11]

In hieroglyphic writing painted on Classic Mayan vases, a sign interpreted as *way,* meaning "jaguar lord" or "hidden lord," stands for a shaman's companion spirit. The glyph consists of an *ahau* facial sign with a mouth and two eyes, meaning "lord," half covered with the pelt of a jaguar (figure 49). This is just one case of a symbolic association between large predatory cats, warfare, and high social status that has a long history in Mesoamerica: images of humans with feline attributes have been found all the way from the Pre-Classic Olmec (1250–400 BCE) to the Post-Classic Aztec (1350–1521 CE).[12]

Archaeologists have excavated numerous clay figurines of Chak Chel, the Mayan goddess of childbirth and the midwife of creation as well as the deity of the waning moon, water, weaving, sexual relations, and healing. These figurines often have jaguar features. Many were found in women's graves on the island of Jaina, off the coast of Yucatán, a burial place heavily used during the Late Classic period (600–1000 CE). Some of the little statues show a woman giving birth or a midwife helping her.

One terra-cotta figurine, currently located in the Princeton University Art Museum, particularly caught my eye. It portrays the midwife who attended the original birth of humankind during the creation of the Fourth World (figure 50). She wears the snakeskin headdress of immortality and has a jaguar's ear. In her left hand she holds a warrior's rectangular shield and in her right hand a weaving

49. *Early Classic Mayan "jaguar lord" glyph consisting of a highly stylized face partly covered with a jaguar pelt. The use of the glyph indicates that a shaman's nagual, or "spirit double," is a jaguar.*

50. *Figurine of a mythic Mayan midwife.*

heddle. Thus she combines the creation of new life through her weaving with the warrior's skills needed to overcome the dangers of childbirth.[13]

And there is a Classic Mayan polychrome vessel from the sixth century whose pictures and text tell the mythological story of birth itself. One side of this rectangular vessel shows a young goddess wearing a long sarong, with a jaguar-skin design, tied around her chest below her breasts (figure 51). She holds a twisted birthing rope similar to those still used today.[14]

The goddess giving birth in the painting is firmly embraced around the waist from behind by a midwife who is identified by a badge of office tucked into her headdress: a spindle whorl with a dangling bit of cotton. Her right hand is changing into a jaguar paw, which indicates her shamanic powers and also suggests that she can shape-shift into this, the most powerful of animals. Standing before her, holding a bowl, is a second, older midwife with a large spotted jaguar ear, pendulous breasts, and a wrap-around skirt with a crossed-bone design.

This same elderly goddess is pictured and identified in the *Dresden*

51. *Mayan birth vase, side one. The midwife's badge of office, a spindle whorl, is visible just over the birthing goddess's left shoulder.*

Codex, an ancient hieroglyphic book, as Chak Chel. Here, in the vase painting, we recognize her by her wrinkled face and the spindle whorl stuck into her knotted serpent-skin headdress. (The serpent is a key birth symbol in this and many other cultures, thanks to its tendency to swallow its food whole—making it look as engorged as a pregnant woman—and to its ability to slither out of its skin.)

On the second side of the vase three mythic midwives perform similar birth rituals that Mayas carry out today (figure 52). Two of them hold vessels for bathing the newborn, while the third one reaches out for the baby. The figure emerging from the mouth of the bearded dragon at the upper left is both the *nagual,* or spiritual essence, of the newborn baby and Mam, a dwarf deity whose presence is conjured today during births.

By showing that before there were midwives among humans,

52. *Mayan birth vase, side two. Three midwives assisting during the birth of a deity. The standing midwife on the right wears jaguar-paw gloves and has a spotted jaguar symbol over her left eye.*

there were midwives among the gods—and emphasizing their jaguar-shaman attributes—midwifery is represented as shamanic at its very foundation.

The third scene on the birth vase (not shown here) is virtually a mirror image of the second one. The fourth and final side, however, is broken into two registers, just as hieroglyphic books often were (figure 53). In the upper portion a young woman leans across a vessel filled with flint knives. She faces an old man wearing a bound cloth headdress. In the lower scene three other naked old men with knotted headdresses sit around a pottery incense burner. These masculine figures, which have no shamanic characteristics, are directional aspects of a deity known as Pawahtun.

The censer, with its dozens of spikes, represents the trunk of a ceiba, which is the Mayan cosmic world tree. The censer would be

53. *Mayan birth vase, side four. A woman is consulting a male deity in the upper register. Three other male deities are gathered around an incense burner in the lower register.*

placed in the middle of the house to mark the navel of the earth, the place ultimately reached by the hanging umbilical rope on the first side of the vase. The bowl held by the Pawahtun figure on the right side may contain the placenta and birth blood. If so, he will sprinkle the blood on the fire and then bury the placenta under the hearth. Traditional Mayas today still bury the umbilicus of baby girls and the placenta of both girls and boys under the cooking hearth in their homes. They place the umbilicus of baby boys on a tree branch or bury it in their cornfields. Thus, though the four sides of the birth vase portray mythic events, they follow the same pattern as birth rituals currently observed by the Maya, whose midwives follow this shamanic calling.[15]

MIDWIFERY IN SOUTHEAST ASIA

The fact that midwives in Malaysia are shamans was recently discovered by accident by my friend and colleague Marina Roseman, who teaches at Queen's University in Belfast. She was conducting an interview with Uda Tengah, a Senoi Temiar midwife, when the woman began to tremble uncontrollably as her spirit familiars bubbled through her body. Marina instantly realized that the woman must also practice as a spirit medium or shaman as well as a midwife. This came as a complete surprise, since researchers previously had reported that only males became shamans in Malaysia. Men, they said, traveled great distances in order to trade, unlike women, and on those journeys they encountered the spirits. When Marina told Uda about this, the Malaysian woman smiled and gestured toward her machete. "Women travel long distances, too," she said. "We gather ceremonial flowers, medicinal herbs, far off in the forest, and meet spirit familiars."[16]

On the Indonesian island of Java, however, the connection had been made thirty years earlier, when the ethnographers Hildred and Clifford Geertz reported that midwives, mediums, diviners, masseurs, acupuncturists, herbalists, and wedding specialists all belonged in the single category called *dukun*, meaning "shaman" or "ceremonial specialist." They also noted that one person usually engaged in several of these specialties. Thus while a woman might initially act as a marriage broker, she later would assist the couple as a midwife.

As part of their work, these ethnographers followed the course of one woman's pregnancy. They were there when a midwife arrived at the home of the woman shortly after she discovered she was pregnant. The midwife massaged and bathed her, together with the father of the child, in a tub of fresh springwater sprinkled with multicolored flower petals. The Javanese say that gods and goddesses always bathe this way, and so the married couple was momentarily viewed as divine.

After the bath the midwife produced a string, and the woman tied it loosely about her waist. The man took a dagger that belonged

to his mother-in-law's ancestors, lifted it high above his head to
honor it, then lowered it and cut the string. All the while the midwife chanted:

> *My intention is to cut open a young unopened leaf.*
> *But I really am not cutting open a leaf*
> *I am cutting open the way for the baby to emerge.*
> *I limit you to nine months of meditation*
> *within your mother's womb.*
> *Come out easy. Go in easy.*

At this point the midwife dropped a weaving shuttle inside the
woman's sarong. The husband's mother caught it at the bottom and
carried it off as though it were a baby. Speaking to the cradled shuttle, she said, "Oh, my grandson," while the woman's mother said,
"Oh, my granddaughter."

The midwife then set before the husband two green coconuts
painted with images of the mythical Djanaka and Sumbadra, the
most beautiful couple who ever lived. Hidden inside the fruit were
male and female figures. She told him to slash the coconuts with a
knife. If both split, it would mean an easy birth. If only one split,
then the child would be the sex of the figure inside the whole one.
If neither split, the birth would be very difficult.

Several months later, when labor pains began, the midwife was
called back to the house. She rolled out a sleeping mat on the floor,
sat the mother on it, and began her prenatal massage. As the moment of birth neared, she rubbed turmeric *(Curcuma longa)*, an herb
known for its anti-inflammatory properties, onto the mother's
vagina.

After the baby was born and the placenta was delivered, the midwife cut the umbilical cord with a bamboo knife and rubbed
turmeric on it, too, then washed both baby and mother. She salted
the cord and afterbirth, wrapped them in white muslin, and placed
them in a jug, which she buried outside. To keep animals away, she
put a wicker fence around the spot, and to prevent evil spirits from

disturbing the jar, she lit a candle and told the family to keep it burning for forty-five days.

The Javanese believe the amniotic fluid that precedes the birth is an infant's spiritual older sibling, while the umbilical cord and placenta are its spiritual younger sibling. These two spirits protect the baby against illness and remain guardians for the rest of the child's life. The bamboo knife and the turmeric play similar roles. Thus, every individual begins life with four spirit guardians, who may appear in dreams or waking visions with advice or other information. When help is needed, the spirits may be summoned through mental concentration, fasting, and wakefulness.[17]

BIRTHING COSMOLOGY

As is obvious from the examples above, the symbolisms and rituals surrounding birth are rich and complex. Preserved in myths and incorporated into cosmologies, they constitute a feminine vision of the world that has been illustrated on drumheads, on clay vessels, in paper manuscripts, and particularly through the women's arts of spinning, knotting, weaving, and embroidery. In one worldview, for example, the arrival of new life—which calls upon the spirits of ancestors—links the realms of past, present, and future in a mysterious sacramental act. The midwives, as they bring forth these spirits, are shamans who access the other world. And just as the world may be defined by time, so the cosmos may be divided into three spatial realms: the upper sky world, the middle earth world, and the lower watery underworld. From this perspective, too, midwives help women bring forth a new being from the ancestors who live in the upper or lower realms.

Since hunting can be viewed as a shamanic practice that calls animal spirits from the land of the dead, midwives who call human spirits from the land of the dead are sometimes illustrated together with hunters on shamans' paraphernalia from North Asia and Scandinavia. For example, the classic Scandinavian cosmology of the upper, middle, and lower realms appears on a seventeenth-century Saami drumhead (figure 54). The upper realm is the home of the thunder god, who is represented as a double-sided triangle, together with the sun and moon, drawn as circles with rays, and a number of other deities. Linking the three realms along the entire right side of the drumhead, a reindeer draws a sledge filled with a shaman's drum, costume, and other regalia.

In the middle realm, a woman stands on the left and a man on the right. The man is a hunter. The woman is Madder Akka, the great-grandmother who is said to dwell under one's house floor. She is the head midwife at the delivery of a baby, the keeper of all human and animal souls, and the guardian of women during their menstrual periods and pregnancy.

On the lowest level of the drumhead we see Madder Akka's three daughters. The eldest, holding staves on the right, is Sar Akka, the Old Woman of Spinning. She lives under the hearth, and she assists in childbirth and the fawning of reindeer that remain central to

54. *A cosmological drawing on a Saami shaman's drumhead from the seventeenth century.*

Saami economy. Her job is to separate a child from its mother's uterus. The two figures to her left are her younger sisters, Urs Akka and Juks Akka, the Old Woman of the Door and the Old Woman of the Bow. They live near the entrance of a house and protect infants and fawns in their new home on earth.[18]

All across Eurasia, feminine deities—thought of as "mothers," "wives," or "sisters"—create and deliver human and animal young. In North Asia, among the reindeer-herding Selkup, the mother goddess has two daughters who carry out her functions. One creates the fetus; the other serves as the protector of the newborn. Labor and birth are considered forms of shamanizing, because during these times the ancestral and natural worlds penetrate the human domain.[19]

Throughout North Asia ancient cults still flourish that are devoted to female fertility spirits, the keepers of the souls of unborn children. These spirits are portrayed as birds sitting in the world tree, waiting to be reborn, and they have their own iconography and rituals as well as their own shamans. In the Amur basin, where most of the shamans are women, these cult leaders are identified by poles with painted birds set up in their house yards. Women embroider their wedding dresses with trees of life; on each limb lie birds' eggs containing the souls of fetuses. These lovely trees, together with other figures—fish, ducks, swans, loons, eagles, tigers, and bears— serve as amulets containing the power of helpful spirits and protect the wearer from evil ones.[20]

There are two other great metaphors for women's powers of birth and creation. Weavers and sky goddesses play unique roles for shamanic women, as we'll see in the next chapter.

FIFTEEN

Tied to the Fabric of the Sky:

WEAVERS AND CELESTIAL GODDESSES

FOR MILLENNIA, WOMEN the world over have sat together spinning, knotting, weaving, and sewing. These rhythmic acts of unraveling and tying together can be seen as expressions of unity and hope in the face of the reality of change, destruction, and death. Since almost every object connected to these activities is considered feminine in most cultures, weaving tools and sewing kits have become badges of female honor and signs of feminine authority.[1]

Women's rituals surrounding the weaving of cloth often evoke those performed during childbirth, and the feminine shamanic path addresses both activities, as it equates spinning, knotting, and weaving a textile with the development and birth of a fetus. It's important to realize that the very processes of spinning and weaving, like those of birth, call for the ability to access the spirit world for the power to create something new.

In many societies the spinning of thread out of an amorphous mass of fiber—and the tying, knotting, or weaving of this thread into a net bag or a piece of cloth—is linked symbolically to sexual intercourse and pregnancy. Centuries ago Aztec spinners in Mexico described their spindles as "dancing in a bowl" (figure 55), and an ancient riddle goes: "What is it that they make pregnant, that they make big with child in the dancing place?" The answer is "spindles." The dancing place is a "bowl" (vagina) in which the spindle (fetus) is placed. To this day in many Mesoamerican societies when a fetus's body is growing (is being spun or woven), a woman must not engage in spinning or weaving. This is because the crossing and intertwining of threads during weaving symbolizes sexual intercourse. Thus a textile is not merely woven but is "conceived" and eventually "born."[2]

Among the Warlpiri of Australia, women spin and knot thick cotton threads and weave them around sticks as fertility charms (figure 56). These amulets are called *makarra*, meaning "womb," "afterbirth," and "umbilicus." They are used during all-female ancestral ceremonies that celebrate birth and reincarnation. In Oceania, all things associated with weaving, pregnancy, and birth are infused

55. *A Pre-Columbian image of an Aztec woman hand-spinning cotton in a bowl placed on a woven mat.*

56. *Australian fertility amulet. This amulet is made and used during women's coming-of-age and ancestral ceremonies. The Huichol of Mexico make a similar fertility symbol known as a "god eye."*

with moral authority and sacred power, called *mana* in Polynesia. In New Zealand, the poles traditional Maori women use to support themselves during delivery are similar to those they use for weaving. And the sacred cloaks that women knot and weave are called *kahu*, meaning "placenta."[3]

In Mongolia the clients of Bayar Odun knot cloth strips and silk streamers to her costume. The streamers on her right side recognize her important service to clan members, those on her left side are for her immediate family, and the ones that hang down the center are for outsiders, neither clan members nor family. According to the Mongolian logic of symbols, if shamans travel to the world of the spirits, then the souls of their clients need to be tied to their gowns with knots so that they do not fall off during the long celestial journey.[4]

WEAVING IN MESOAMERICA

Weaving, which has long been a principal women's activity among the indigenous peoples of Mexico and Guatemala, was and still is a source of wealth and prestige. During pre-Columbian times textiles were collected as tribute and given as gifts to rulers. Cloth making brought great honor to the weavers, whose artistry provided the central metaphors for world creation and social order.[5]

Because the backstrap loom played such a large role in Meso-american myth and imagery, it helps to understand how a loom is constructed and used. A typical backstrap loom consists of a thick rope with a loop at one end, a strap that passes around the weaver's back, and a set of sticks that includes two end bars for stretching out the warp yarns. The rope hitches the upper end bar to a house post, rafter, or tree. The backstrap, usually woven from maguey fiber, is tied to the lower end bar and passes around the woman's back at hip level. The weaver regulates the tension of the warps by leaning backward to tighten it and then forward to loosen it enough to insert the weft threads.[6]

During the early days of my shamanic apprenticeship I was sent by my teachers to study in the Mayan town of Santa Catarina Ixtahuacán. María Tzep Catinac, a prominent woman shaman living there, told me that I should pay attention to backstrap weaving. "We not only weave our textiles but we also birth them. This is an important part of a woman shaman's education," she said. She showed me how she assembled the yarns and warped them, then began her textile at the bottom. After several inches she turned it upside down, explaining that she was placing the bottom of the weaving at the top in the same way she turned a baby around in the womb to ensure a head-first delivery (figure 57).

In a nearby Tzutujil Maya community I learned from the women that a group of thirteen goddesses created the framework of the world through weaving: "They wove their children, birds, jaguars, and snakes." And according to my hostess, the goddess of Lake

57. *A Mayan woman shaman from Santa Catarina Ixtahuacán in her court-yard weaving on her backstrap loom. Moments before this photograph was taken she flipped her loom around and began weaving again from the other end.*

Atitlán was the midwife who attended the birth of the three volcanoes that rose out of the water. She wove the fabric of the night sky and the mantle of the earth on her backstrap loom. Today, the forward-and-back motion of the weaver is thought of as a feminine movement similar to making love or having labor contractions. If the midwife notices that the baby is in a breech position, she may use a weaving batten or a loom bar to press on the woman's stomach above her womb to coax the fetus to realign itself head downward.[7]

How long has weaving been central to feminine shamanic practice in Mesoamerica? The discovery of the body of a woman shaman in a hilltop tomb in Monte Albán, Mexico, suggests it extends back at least to the Classic period of Mixtec culture (between 100 and

58. *Ivory weaving batten found in tomb seven at Monte Albán, Oaxaca, Mexico. This tomb, which contained the body of a woman shaman, was built during the Classic period. It was later opened and more offerings were added during the Post-Classic.*

700 CE). Laid out near the shaman's remains were a large number of jaguar and eagle bones exquisitely shaped into miniature weaving tools: picks, awls, and battens (figure 58). The battens were carved with illustrations of creation myths, calendar signs, divination, marriages, conquests, and royal descent.[8]

A number of the battens show an important goddess—known as both Lady Nine Reed and Lady Ten Reed—who is recognizable in several painted Mixtec codices or books. In the center of the first batten is a newborn baby lying on a raised bench with its long umbilicus arched over its body (figure 59, left). On the right end of the batten the goddess-midwife wears characteristically feminine clothing: a triangular blouse over an elaborately woven skirt (figure 59, right). She is flying toward the left with a pair of serpents twisted into her long hair. In her nose she wears a butterfly ornament. (Butterflies, like snakes, are considered symbols of new life because living souls burst forth from old skins or cocoons.) The woman holds

59. *Details of the previous weaving batten showing Lady Ten Reed. She is holding a rattle in her left, or feminine, hand and her warrior's shield in her right, or masculine, hand as she flies toward the infant resting on the altar.*

her shamanic rattle in her left, or feminine, hand. In her right, or masculine, hand she grasps a warrior's shield with her calendar day name, in this case Ten Reed, attached to it as though it were a bundle of arrows. The day number is indicated by ten dots, three above her shield and seven beginning at the left and descending below her shield.[9]

This goddess is portrayed as a warrior with a protective shield because birth is considered a dangerous battle for both mother and child. That she is flying toward the baby at the center of the batten indicates her shamanic abilities and her role as a midwife.[10]

On another batten found in the tomb (figure 60), the top figure is the same goddess, this time called Lady Nine Reed. She is depicted as the patron deity of the mythic tree said to stand in Apoala,

60. *The Mixtec emergence myth carved on an ivory weaving batten found in tomb seven at Monte Albán. Lady Nine Reed, the creator deity, stands at the top of the image, holding her weaving batten above her head as her staff of office. She used this instrument to cut open the diamond-shaped hole in the tree trunk below, from which gods and nobles were born.*

Oaxaca. (From this tree both the deities and humankind were originally born.) Again, she wears a triangular blouse, and she is standing on her birth date, which is represented by nine dots. In her right hand she holds a weaving batten in a menacing gesture. Directly below her is a small naked figure emerging from a tree, which is swollen as if pregnant. At the center of the swelling a diamond-shaped outline surrounds a jagged hole, or vagina. According to Mixtec mythology, Lady Nine Reed is the creator deity who cut open this tree, from which gods and noble men and women emerged.

These ancient images all mesh with the continuing Mixtec belief that certain places—caves, rivers, trees—engender children whose souls are conceived and carried in the womb of their "real" mother, the earth. Later each is transferred to a human woman in the symbolic form of a butterfly. She nurtures this living being until it transforms itself into a human baby that she births.

Another Mixtec codex depicts twin creator goddesses holding a spiderweb between them, with a captured butterfly soul in its center. The goddesses are closely associated with the earth, represented here by a spotted skull (figure 61), and they themselves are the implied spiders, responsible for forming and placing living souls into human bodies.[11]

6I. *Mixtec creator goddesses as illustrated in the* Codex Fejérváry Mayer. *The spiderweb contains a captured butterfly hanging above a skull.*

STORIES OF SPIDER WOMAN

To the north, at Acoma pueblo in New Mexico, the first two human beings were said to have been female. They lived in the dark underworld, where Grandmother Spider taught them their language as she nursed them. Then she gave each of them a basket filled with seeds and small images of the plants and animals they were to bring out into the world. Trees sprouted from the seeds that the sisters planted. They grew very slowly in the darkness until they punched a hole through the surface of the earth, permitting rays of sunlight to enter the dark world below. But the hole was too small for the women to get out, so they created Badger Old Woman, the first midwife. She used her claws to make an opening large enough for the twins to climb through. When they emerged, Grandmother Spider taught them the prayers and songs with which to create all living beings. A mist impregnated one of the sisters, who in turn gave birth to twin sons. The other sister adopted one of the boys, and he grew up to become her husband. Some years after that, they gave birth to all of the Pueblo people.[12]

The neighboring Diné have a different story about Spider Woman. She taught human women to weave on a loom that Spider Man taught them how to make. The crossbeams were constructed of sky and earth cords, the warp sticks of sun rays, and the heddles of rock crystal and sheet lightning. The batten was a sun halo, and the comb was made of white shell. There were four spindles. One was made of zigzag lightning with a whorl of coal. Another was formed of flash lightning with a whorl of turquoise. A third was of sheet lightning with a whorl of abalone. And a stream of rain formed the fourth, with its whorl of white shell.[13]

When the loom was finished, Spider Man said to the first woman weaver: "Now you know all that I have named for you. It is yours to work with and to use following your own wishes. But from now on, when a baby girl is born to your tribe, you shall go and find a spider web, which is woven at the mouth of some hole; you must take it and rub it on the baby's hands and arms. Thus, when she grows up she will weave, and her fingers and arms will not tire from the weaving."[14] And to this day, that ritual is performed for baby girls soon after their birth.

SKY GODDESSES

Not all the deities who nurture and protect women are associated with the earth. Although sky gods have often been described as uniquely masculine, in fact there are a number of important exceptions. In ancient Egypt the feminine sky deity, Nut, and her brother Geb, the earth deity, were created together, locked in a deep sexual embrace. Shu, the goddess of air, separated them, and so gave the universe its proper form. Nut is most often depicted as a giant celestial woman who overarches the entire earth, with the moon, stars, and constellations passing through her body.[15]

The constellation known as the Pleiades was envisioned in ancient China as a set of feminine deities known as the Seven Celestial Midwives. They evolved out of an even earlier Manchu tradition in which the sky deities were Three Heavenly Midwives or the Three Celestial Maidens. Their three pairs of eyes looked in all directions, enabling them to see and know everything happening on earth, so that they could act as holy warriors and keep the peace. In 1993 the Chinese archaeologist Fu Yuguang discovered a two-hundred-year-old wooden icon that depicts these three sky goddesses. It had been carefully preserved in Jilin province and was still being worshiped by a clan of midwives in Huichun.[16]

An early North Asian myth, "The War in Heaven," records the existence of sky goddesses called Abuka Hehe. (*Abuka* means "sky," and *hehe* means "woman's genitals.") And all across the region, from the Altai in the west to the lower Amur in the east, a celestial warrior deity by the name of Ome Niang-Niang, or the womb goddess in the sky, reigns supreme. A painting displayed on a Mongol shaman's altar (figure 62) shows the womb goddess standing

62. *Painting on paper of the Mongolian womb goddess, known as Ome Niang-Niang. A lotus flower is on a low table in front of her, and she is surrounded by her daughters, the Pleiades.*

behind a low table covered with an open lotus blossom, surrounded by the Pleiades, her seven celestial children.[17]

Among the Daur Mongols female shamans, called *otoshi*, worship the womb goddess, as well as other sky deities concerned with fertility, childbirth, growth, and childhood diseases. One of these is an old woman with snow-white hair who lives in a nine-story house in the midst of nine white tents. In her courtyard are gold and silver pine trees; two phoenixes guard the gate. Outside the door nine mineral hot springs bubble out egg-filled water. The goddess takes the eggs and raises them in her courtyard. When the babies mature, she spanks them and sends them down to be born in the human world below.[18]

Studies of shamanism that focus on the sky have ignored the existence of such celestial goddesses and the practices associated with them. Mircea Eliade, in discussing the shamanic symbolism of ascent to the sky, asserted that "the supreme gods of archaic peoples are called 'He on High,' 'He of the Sky,' or simply 'Sky.' "[19] The truth is that North Asian celestial cults focused on bringing babies into the world and nurturing them. The fact that the celestial goddesses were oriented around fertility was abhorrent to Buddhist missionaries, who set out in the twelfth century to destroy the feminine cults. Their efforts at suppression were only partly successful, although the celestial goddesses were expunged from many written historical records.[20]

Similar celestial fertility cults are found in other Asian countries. Korean women shamans today lure Samshin Halmoni, the Great Birth Grandmother, into a gourd dipper filled with grain (representing the Big Dipper constellation). Then they give the dipper to a young woman who wants to become pregnant. The woman holds it in her hands until it begins to shake, indicating the Birth Grandmother's presence. After the ritual she hides the dipper in the room where she sleeps with her husband. During the final stages of her pregnancy she makes a special offering of seaweed soup and cooked rice to this deity. Later she will hire a woman shaman to conduct an exorcism to drive off family ghosts that might harm her baby.[21]

In Southeast Asia pregnant women are assisted not only by human midwives but also by sky goddesses. A young Malaysian woman named Noh told my colleague Carol Laderman, from the City University of New York, that the Bidandari, or Seven Celestial Midwives, attended her own birth. Her mother, who had been in labor for seven days, was all alone, since her husband was at work and the midwife had given up waiting and went home. Finally, seven beautiful smiling ladies descended from the sky. They eased her pain, delivered her baby, and washed her and her infant. When they finished they ascended back to the heavens. The neighbors heard the baby crying and came over to find the mother clean and comfortable, and the infant washed and swaddled. Her auspicious birth left Noh with the ability to see spirits. And it encouraged her father-in-law, an important shaman, to offer to train and initiate her as a shaman. Fearing that a shaman's long hours would conflict with family demands, Noh declined to be trained, a decision she later regretted.[22]

Among the Huichol, in Mexico, a celestial goddess provides aid in pregnancy and childbirth. My colleague Stacey Schaefer of California State University at Chico learned that if a Huichol woman was having difficulty becoming pregnant, she and her husband might consult a midwife. The woman would instruct the couple to go to a sacred spring and collect water, candles, votive gourds, and prayer arrows left by previous visitors. In the words of one midwife's daughter, "We have to sing and look for the place where the Goddess Nivetuka exists; she is called the Goddess of Children. She is in the sky. The *mara'akame* [shaman] has to sing to ask for the *kupuri* [soul] of the child. When it appears the *mara'akame* has to gather it in a gourd bowl."[23] The woman is cured when she dreams the cause of her infertility.

Once a Huichol midwife is certain the woman is pregnant, she instructs her not to weave on her backstrap loom, so as not to strain her lower back and cause a miscarriage or premature birth. Her weaving might also induce the umbilical cord to wrap around the baby's neck and strangle the child. Shamans who specialize in fertility are said to be able to change the sex of a baby early in the pregnancy through rituals. Over five days the midwife, with the aid of holy water and pieces of cotton placed in a votive gourd, communicates with the sky goddess Nivetuka. As she prays, the midwife traces the desired shape of the baby's genitalia on the mother's abdomen and sprays it with cool water drawn from a sacred well.

How powerful—and beautiful—are these metaphors of weaving

creators and nurturing sky goddesses. Their meanings and connections to the feminine shamanic path grow naturally out of the physical elements—blood, menstruation, pregnancy, and birth—that make up the woman's cycle. And they counterbalance and complete the masculine shamanic path already mentioned in chapter thirteen—and which, as we will see in chapter seventeen, is rooted in death and rebirth.

SIXTEEN

Lightning in the Shadows:

A MIDNIGHT HEALING SÉANCE

LATE IN MY apprenticeship in highland Guatemala I learned about a shamanic séance that would be taking place in a small rural community one hour's drive from Momostenango. It was to be conducted by a woman who had been initiated into one of the most powerful Mayan traditions, the *ajnawal mesa,* meaning "the spiritual essence of the healing table-altar." And although I knew that Don Andrés and Doña Talín deeply distrusted this form of shamanic practice—they thought it might involve witchcraft—I nevertheless decided to attend Doña Josefina's ceremony.

So one chilly evening Dennis and I joined a small group of spirit seekers in an ancient adobe house next to a cemetery at the foot of a volcano. Its single room had a ten-foot ceiling with rounded rafters and tiny mica windows. Along the eastern wall under a mass of dusty crepe-paper streamers stood a rickety table covered with a long tapestry. In the center was a cement cross embedded with green and blue stones. Stacked around the cross and in each corner of the table were strangely shaped quartz crystals, fulgurites, potsherds, and black obsidian blades.

On the left, or feminine, side of the table was a wood and glass box containing a carving of Santa Ana, the patron deity of midwives. On top of the box were a large multifaceted crystal and an embroidered bag. Vases of white calla lilies and tiger-striped daylilies, together with rusted tin cans planted with bright red geraniums, surrounded the statue.

On the earthen floor under the table, peeking out from between cut pine boughs, were fierce-looking snake-headed stones glistening with fresh offerings of liquor. *This must be Doña Josefina's healing altar,* I thought. But before I could study it more carefully people began to arrive and mill around the room. When a copper bell chimed we quickly took our places on an adobe bench plastered to the western wall.

We sat silently, huddled together as the atmosphere grew clammy. The odor of mildew mixed with pine pitch and coffee grounds kept me wakeful and wary. At the stroke of midnight a chorus of three women sitting in a shadowy corner of the room began chanting monotonously in an eerie minor key. Although I knew how to speak this Mayan language by now, I could not understand the words they were singing. Maybe they weren't words at all but simply syllables of sound floating without meaning in the cold night air.

As the flames flickered out in the three-stone cooking hearth in the center of the room, leaving behind a mass of murmuring coals, I started feeling panicky. It was so quiet in this darkened house. The only sounds were the uncanny chanting and the crackling of electricity in my long auburn hair.

After what seemed like half an hour of waiting in the blackened room for something, anything, to happen, I smelled burning incense and heard rain splattering on the roof in huge drops. As I looked up toward the noise I saw a translucent blue ball of light slide across a ceiling beam, then come crashing down into the smoldering hearth. An acrid odor, something like the smell of ozone or burning hair, filled the room.

My breath caught in my throat. Had it not been so clearly inappropriate and disrespectful, I might have run out of the house right then.

The pulsating ball rose about three feet off the ground and began circling the fire, moving rapidly in a counterclockwise direction. I remained seated, closed my eyes, and held my breath. After a moment or two I opened my eyes and saw that the strange ball of light—no bigger than my open palm—was still whirling around, periodically illuminating the altar. Perhaps it was one of those ghostly lights my grandmother called "Indian lights" or "will-o'-the-wisps." She had told me that ancestral souls returning to earth sometimes travel inside these mysterious illuminations.

I was still holding my breath when the light suddenly disappeared. Momentarily relieved, I inhaled deeply. But then I heard what sounded like sobbing, followed by the rattling of a long metal chain scraping across the dirt floor.

An intense electric jolt pushed me backward on the adobe bench, and the middle of my torso began tingling. I felt as though a strong electrical force field had entered my stomach through the abdominal wall. The strange but not altogether unpleasant sensation eventually resolved into the wavelike tremors of a low-intensity earthquake with rolling thunder that spread throughout my body. More odd sounds came from the roof; this time I heard the flapping of wings. Was it a dove, an owl, or perhaps an eagle? I looked around at the group. Everyone, even Dennis, looked calm and focused inward.

Then, just as fear began to wash over me again, a deep, masculine voice in the purple-black gloom said, "Good evening, my children. What favors do you wish to be granted?"

I was taken aback and wondered who could be speaking. Despite my ongoing apprenticeship with Don Andrés and Doña Talín I couldn't believe a spirit was actually speaking to us, or rather speaking through Doña Josefina to us. Since I had been taught long ago to place the spiritual world in the realm of the imagination I became edgy and suspicious. Was she tricking us and just imitating a spirit voice? At that point I still subscribed to the idea that spiritual beliefs and other religious superstitions were in opposition to logical thought and rational science.

The shaman must have sensed my skepticism, but instead of

challenging me, she merely ignored me as she began her round of questions. Starting on my left, she addressed every person in a deep voice: "Do you know me?"

"Yes," each replied, and then asked for help of some kind, either with practical issues such as children, money, or health or with spiritual matters such as intuition or creativity. Doña Josefina then asked each of us for a gift in the form of tallow candles and incense. These would be used as offerings to the Holy World—the mountains, valleys, trees, volcanoes, lakes, springs, and caves.

To an anxious young woman sitting next to me she said in a booming voice, "Yes, my daughter, I am the *iyom* [midwife] who will help you give birth to many children. With herbs, incense, and wax candles I will arrange all this for you with Santa Ana. Remember my words, my child, for I speak as the holy mountains and plains, and the weasel is my helper in birthing."

A young boy about ten, whom I could barely see in the dim light, asked in a halting mixture of K'iche' Maya and Spanish for guidance in his future life path. The shaman addressed him in a softer, more feminine-sounding voice. "While you may travel many leagues in this life, my dear, it seems you will never become rich," she said. "But you will be respected for your family, for your home, and for your business. Ten bundles of incense, ten wax and ten tallow candles, and five bottles of *kuxa* [the local bootleg alcohol] will be needed to arrange all this for you, my son."

The teenage girl next to him had recently lost her brother. To her the shaman offered the solace of a final conversation. "My sister," she began in the high-pitched voice of an adolescent boy, "I have not abandoned you. Do not cry, for I am the little bird that sits singing on your weaving loom. Feed me flower nectar and petals, candles and incense, sugar and the sap of pine boughs." Overcome with grief and joy, the girl began sobbing softly.

The shaman turned next to an elderly man. "You wish news of your wife?" she asked gently in yet another voice, one that sounded like that of a middle-aged woman. "She is among the thousands of tiny stars swirling around the three hearthstones in the sky."

That must be the triangle of stars that encloses the smoky nebula in the constellation of Orion, I thought.

"Soon she will be reborn as a new baby girl in your family. This requires twenty-five tallow candles, one pound of brown sugar, two bottles of *kuxa,* and twenty bundles of incense."

When the shaman finished answering all the questions, a second ball of blue light began circling the hearth. This time I thought it might be a lightning ball. Although some meteorologists might dismiss ball lightning as an optical illusion, others believe that it is formed from a small mass of highly charged gas produced by the electric discharge of a lightning flash. Or perhaps I was seeing what geologists call an "earth light." Such strange beams occur naturally on mountain peaks or near fault lines during earth tremors. Guatemala was certainly earthquake country.

My reverie was interrupted when Josefina began speaking in a high-pitched, unintelligible babble. Slowly her voice resolved into that of a man speaking Spanish with a heavy English accent. "My daughter is here in this room somewhere," the voice intoned. "But she does not speak."

I felt a cold chill run up, then down, my backbone. The voice sounded like that of my own dead father. I sat there completely still, unable to move or speak.

A moment or two passed. The room was utterly silent except for the hissing blue light and spitting orange coals. Although I could not reply, I nevertheless hoped the voice might say more. When it did not, I realized, with a sense of deep regret and terrible loss, that I had missed an opportunity to reach through the veil of sorrow that separated me from my deceased parent. I had thrown away my chance for a last goodbye.

The iron chain rattled once again across the floor, and in the shadows I could see someone walk over to throw a fresh log on the fire. Then the figure began lighting, one by one, the kerosene lanterns that encircled the room.

In the brightening light I saw that the person was young—about twenty-five, I guessed, with a firm jaw and straight black hair that fell a couple of inches past her shoulders. There was something masculine about her, and she was dressed in a farmer's white poplin shirt, loose-fitting white pants tied at the waist with a wide woven red and black sash, and black men's shoes with cut-out toes. So this was our mystery shaman. She was hardly the image of the stereotype. Was I disappointed or relieved?

Before I could answer that question, the ball of light suddenly whirled toward her, quickly expanding and engulfing her in orange flames. As it entered her body, I heard a muffled sound, something like a distant thunderclap. Then all was silent, and Doña Josefina stood there as if nothing had happened.

We were all still sitting in stunned silence as she walked over to the front door and slowly lifted the heavy iron bar that held it closed. The sky was the same black crystal I'd seen when we arrived, but now the stars were a little higher. If a thunderstorm had produced the lightning balls, there was no sign of it now.

I shivered and wrapped my sweater tighter around me, in part because of the sudden chill and in part because I felt that I had intruded into something important, even sacred. I didn't fully understand the significance of this shaman's performance, with her luminescent lightning balls and many disembodied voices, nor did I care to understand—at least not yet. I was confused and more than a little frightened. My father's voice had been so real that I was certain he had spoken.

Impatient to distance myself from this bizarre event, I wanted to get home as quickly as possible to write up an accurate scientific account of the séance. But as I motioned to Dennis and stood to leave I realized that the women in the chorus had just finished making offerings to Santa Ana and the altar stones and were now removing tamales from a large willow basket.

They were dressed in traditional multicolored embroidered blouses and wrap-around skirts and were placing these bite-size tamales on a sizzling circular *comal,* a clay griddle balanced on three hearthstones that formed a triangle around the fire. Nestled in the coals was a glazed ceramic bowl of red chili sauce and a pitcher filled with *atole,* or corn gruel.

It would have been ill-mannered to forgo the communal feast. So I sat next to the open fire, eating the spicy food and watery gruel, and I slowly began to feel ashamed of myself. I had questions, of course, about my future, and I also had dead relatives of my own. But after years of science courses, I wasn't sure if I believed in spirits or prophecy anymore or not. And even if I did believe, I certainly wouldn't speak with my own ancestors in front of a group of total strangers.

In the weeks that followed I spent a great deal of time trying to understand this shamanic performance with its strange altar, eerie lights, and spectral voices. I came to understand more about the way Mayan shamans monitor their bodily energy. In fact, shamans use the same word for the electrical energy that surges through their bodies and the streaks of pink, purple, green, and red sheet lightning that flicker along the horizon and are reflected in the sacred lakes.

Depending on where and when it moves, the electricity within a shaman's blood, flesh, and muscles—sudden twanging, twitching, and burning sensations—calls attention to matters that have been overlooked. Similarly, sheet lightning flashing over the sacred lakes highlights occurrences in the outer world: pink flickering over Lemoa, the eastern lake, indicates sunrise, meaning new business and other opportunities; white lightning over Najachel (or Atitlán), the southern lake, stands for happenings in the watery underworld through which humans emerged, and brings blessings in the form of babies and curses in the form of illnesses; green lightning over Pasokob', the western lake, indicates rain and thus crop fertility; purple lightning over Pachi'ul, the northern lake, means that the rain will stop and that it is time to harvest, both literally and metaphorically.

Over time I came to understand that Doña Josefina was so advanced in her shamanic practice that she not only knew this cosmology and felt the lightning within her body but was able to manifest it externally for the benefit of her clients. The illusion of a translucent blue ball of light circling the fire was a segment of cosmological energy that she had somehow gotten firmly under her control.

But the lightning was just one aspect of her performance. The masculine clothing she wore, her many male and female voices, her forceful predictions—all of these were clues to the importance of gender shifting in shamanism and the transcendent roles of the woman warrior and prophet, which are the subjects of the chapters that follow.

PART FOUR

The Power of Gender and Shamanic Revitalization

SEVENTEEN

Uniting Separate Realms:

GENDER SHIFTING IN SHAMANISM

AS DENNIS AND I worked with Don Andrés and Doña Talín, we were taught to perceive our personalities, and indeed our very own bodies, as "co-gendered"—that is, the left side of each one of us is female, while the right side is male. We were also encouraged to behave in both feminine and masculine ways and, from time to time, to take on the social role of the opposite sex. Dennis was urged to spend time with the women learning how to make tortillas, and he was sent down to the river to pound our laundry on the rocks— much to the amusement of the village children. I, on the other hand, was expected to take masculine risks, such as walking along slippery stones above a waterfall and driving our jeep into Mexico without proper car papers or personal identification.

This part of our shamanic training was difficult for us, since, like most people, we had learned about gender very young. Gender is one of the most fundamental psychological expressions of social identity, and in contemporary North America it's primarily deter-mined by physical genital characteristics. Whenever a hermaphro-ditic or intersexed baby is born in a hospital, physicians almost always perform surgery to correct the child's sexual ambiguity. Thus, many people equate sex with gender, and gender identity is simply assumed to be "natural."

Societies that exist outside of, or on the edges of, monotheistic religious and biomedical systems hold quite different views. The quintessential Western insignias of sex—dress, voice, authoritativeness—have little meaning in other times or other cultures where sexual and gender identities are impermanent and alternating. And gender rather than sexuality is the primary element that makes up shamanic personhood. Shamans embody and perform the tasks of multiple social and spiritual genders, regardless of their anatomical sex and sexual practices.[1]

In a number of traditions, the ideal gender may be embodied in an androgynous deity, in a creator with a shifting gender, or even in a co-gendered culture hero. According to Aztec cosmology, for example, the paramount deity is Ometeotl, the self-generating god-goddess of duality. In this deity masculine and feminine principles are joined together, and he-she provides the model for the unity of complementary aspects that has been central to Aztec shamanism for centuries.[2]

In ancient Aztec society a child did not become fully feminine or fully masculine until early puberty, when its heterosexual reproductive role emerged. Thus the sixteenth-century *Florentine Codex* depicts an Aztec midwife baptizing and instructing a newborn about both genders. By following her footsteps around the central mat in a counterclockwise direction, we see that she first shows the baby the feminine tools, then circles around to the masculine warrior's shield and arrows and the male tools of the feather worker, sculptor, and goldsmith (figure 63). She must point out both sets of instruments to the baby, since it is born ambiguously and is said to change sex from day to day, even from hour to hour. In this way the midwife teaches the baby the potential of shamanic shape-shifting between genders.[3]

In addition to shape-shifting, shamans travel between realms that are otherwise separate—sky and earth, as well as the female and the

63. *Aztec midwife baptizing an infant. The footprints around the baptismal water basin, sitting on fresh rushes, show the counterclockwise path she walks during the ritual. She stops first at the bottom to show the infant the female occupational tools: a broom, spindle with cotton fiber, and a workbasket. Then she walks to the top to show the infant the warrior's shield and arrows and the male occupational tools including a chisel and paintbrush.*

male—in order to improve disturbed conditions. These apparent opposites define one another through interaction rather than by separation. Shamans in many traditions believe that human beings are a combination of masculine and feminine aspects, with a female soul and a male soul, as well as membership in a mother's clan and a father's clan. The most powerful shamans, of either sex, work with both masculine and feminine forms of energy. So while women shamans are usually nurturing, they can also be brave and powerful—when they help with a difficult birth, for instance, or take on the warrior's role in healing.

In general, each one of us, in our lifetime, takes on many social identities, which are constantly being created, erased, and re-created. Separating gender from sexual characteristics and associating it with occupations and social roles creates the possibility of having more than two genders. As a result, in a number of societies there are four genders: woman, man, woman-man, and man-woman.

Some researchers have suggested that a shaman is neither masculine nor feminine but rather a mediator between the sexes, a third gender that is either woman-man or man-woman. While this idea is intriguing, at least at first, it's far too static a description for what is, in fact, an extremely changeable situation. It is not membership within any one of these gender categories per se that is directly linked to shamanic practice but rather the transformation of gender or the frequent gender switching, bending, blending, or reversing that is important and that enables shamans to manipulate potent cosmic powers during rituals, as Doña Josefina did during her midnight séance.[4]

The theme of gender reversal frequently occurs in mythology and rituals, but its significance varies greatly and affects beliefs about shamans, animal spirits, and the manipulation of their energies. Some shamanic rituals enforce the differences between genders, others encourage ambiguity, and still others imply that a shaman is actually transformed, either partly or completely. The widespread practice of shamanic transvestitism offers some clues to these beliefs. While shamans may dress as the opposite gender, they nearly always also display their own gender either symbolically (a woman may wear a tiny earring) or else by their behavior (she may speak in a high-pitched, feminine voice while dressed as a man).[5]

In Siberia during the eighteenth and nineteenth centuries, shamans wore cloaks patterned after women's clothing during their séances. On Alaska's Kodiak Island, Konyag boys who were destined to become shamans received female names and were dressed and raised as girls. And some male Chukchi shamans in northeastern Siberia identified with their female spirits so strongly that they always dressed as women, did women's work, and used a special language spoken only by women. Others combined men's garments with women's dress and acted out a feminine role only during their shamanic performance.[6]

In an extreme instance of a male shaman's identifying with women, an Inuit shaman by the name of Asatchq performed a birth ritual before a large audience in Alaska during the early years of the twentieth century. While someone drummed he rubbed his belly until it swelled. Removing his pants, he knelt in the traditional childbirth position and with much effort pulled a bloody rag doll from between his legs. This birthing ritual not only displayed his gender-shifting abilities but also encouraged the audience to be more flexible in its attitudes toward sexual identity. In Siberia, Sakhá shamans of both sexes were said to be able to give birth, at least to animal spirits. Beginning at puberty a shaman's training entailed birthing a raven or loon, which instantly flew away. In the second year the shaman brought forth a pike, which swam away. And in the third and final year of training, a truly great shaman gave birth to a bear or a wolf.[7]

It's crucial to realize that shamanism acknowledges the importance of both masculine and feminine energies and traditions. Birth and death are the key metaphors and actions. In many societies shamans are said to "be born to" or to "die into" the profession, and in their subsequent practices they often assist at actual births and deaths.

A number of investigators of shamanism, including the Colombian anthropologist Gerardo Reichel-Dolmatoff, followed Mircea Eliade in claiming that the only path to "rebirth" as a shaman was a single enormous ejaculation, followed by a symbolic death, dismemberment, and skeletalization—the masculine tradition. This path may begin with a heroic journey through mountains, rivers, and valleys and end with a sexual climax. It can also take the form of a mythic voyage into the cosmic uterus, or even into the very body of a female client, as Claude Lévi-Strauss described for the Kuna of Panama. Healing within this tradition is said to focus on the symbolism of the movement of massive external energy fields, such as those released during thunderstorms. The psychedelic shamanic path taken by males among the Mazatec, as described in chapter eleven, typifies this masculine tradition. Meteorological forces are contacted and channeled through the mind and psyche of the shaman and then into the body of the patient, symbolically killing the patient as a way of healing her.[8]

In the parallel feminine path, which has been ignored until now by most researchers, the focus is on the capacity for multiple sexual orgasms, trembling, the ability to create new life, and the bliss of nurturing an infant. The emphasis on birth, rather than rebirth, provides a powerful metaphor that carries over to other rituals. Thus, when Huichol families undertake a pilgrimage to gather peyote, for example, each person confesses his or her wrongdoings and ties a knot in a long cord. Just as a midwife ties off the umbilical cord of a newborn, so first-time pilgrims have the knot tied for them by the shaman who guides the pilgrims. As my friend and mentor the anthropologist Peter Furst pointed out, "The shaman in a very real sense acts as a midwife for this passage into the Otherworld."[9]

Feminine shamanic training begins within the body and centers on mindfulness toward dreams and the movements of internal thoughts, fluids, and vital energies. Novices are encouraged to produce mental images of sexuality, and through these daydreams they learn potent healing techniques. By entering a trance and through dream rituals, they can contact and embody a spirit. Shifting their attention to hands and breath, they experience a connection with the earth's electrical fields and an erotic merging with other humans, animals, plants, and elemental life forces. The souls of shamans traveling along this feminine path eventually leave their bodies and "fly" by means of their imaginations to upper or lower cosmological worlds. When these shamans are engaged in healing, they may see into the minds, hearts, souls, and bodies of their clients.

Nursing mothers sometimes enter into a similar deeply peaceful state of consciousness, during which their ideas and impulses float past without impact, leading to a feeling of transcendental bliss. Vicki Noble, an ethnographer of the Huichol, described her blissful feelings as she rocked and nursed her newborn son. She was shocked to later learn that several Huichol men had given this most feminine form of shamanic ecstasy a derogatory name: "milk mind."[10]

As shamanism flows from the masculine to the feminine and back, it sets up a kind of dialogue between men and women. Thus, among the Kulina of western Brazil, it is not necessary to become a shaman in order to be an adult man, but only shamans—in their practice as masters of game animals as well as village protectors and leaders—achieve the full potential of maleness. Similarly, among the Yurok of northern California, it is not necessary to become a shaman in order to be an adult woman, yet only shamans in their practice as midwives, doctors, and village protectors achieve the full potential of femaleness.[11]

In southern Chile nearly all the Mapuche shamans are female, and in fact the anatomical sex of these women is important to their practice. According to my colleague Mariella Bacigalupo at the State University of New York at Buffalo, Mapuche midwives and mothers are "givers of life" who obtain powers from the moon in order to bring fertility to land, animals, and people. Unlike most local women, though, these shamans also head their households; their families perform domestic chores for them and arrange their lives around the ritual duties of the shamans, who travel as they please, without asking permission of their men. During healing they use both feminine and masculine symbols and actions. The female symbols nurture, heal the body, and integrate the self. Male symbols exorcise, defeat, and kill the "other." Mapuche shamans dramatically weave together these seemingly incompatible themes and in so doing embody multiple genders as they cure.[12]

Julia, an East African healer who was in her mid-forties in 1979, also nicely illustrates the co-gendered shamanic path. As reported by the ethnographer Martha Binford, Julia began her healing séances by tying back her long black hair with a beaded string. Then she hung a tiny ivory trumpet and a long medicine pouch around her neck. These power objects dangled over her bare breasts as she began drumming. Pausing briefly, she put on her ancestral Zulu warrior costume: a gazelle-skin helmet with ostrich-feather brush, a fly whisk, a small cowhide shield, and a sharp knife. She drummed, sang, and danced more and more wildly, slipping into a trance as the ancestral deities possessed her body. One moment she talked of love, family, and health in a lilting voice, only to be interrupted by an impatient, angry voice growling out death threats. These feminine and masculine energies alternated, mixed, and mingled, bubbled, pulsed, and boiled through her body. Julia was famous all over Mozambique for her powerful dancing and her successful shamanic healing.[13]

Watching shamans such as Julia, one can come to see that during these rituals femininity and masculinity are not opposite ends of a single sexual spectrum with women on one side, men on the other, and shamans in between. Shamans are taught not to negate or destroy either their masculine or their feminine side. Instead, by shifting genders and embodying characteristics of each gender, they manipulate the male-female polarity itself. Shamans are able to hold incompatible things together, because each of the apparent opposites is necessary and in some sense "true."

EIGHTEEN

Brave Acts and Visions:

WOMEN WARRIORS AND PROPHETS

DURING THE CIVIL WAR in Guatemala, in the early 1980s, the military intimidated Mayan religious and secular leaders. Doña Josefina, like many other shamans, was fearless in the face of this danger and continued to hold her healing midnight séances in open defiance of the curfews the military government imposed. When I returned to Guatemala in 1988 I learned that she, like many other brave shamans, had been killed by the military for daring to continue her shamanic activities.

Years earlier and half a world away, Siberian shamans also faced intimidation by military state power, sometimes winning and sometimes losing. One story still told in Siberia illustrates how an extraordinary woman named Alykhardaakh combined her feminine cunning with a masculine fearlessness to overcome the violent Soviet persecution of shamanism that was rampant in the late 1920s. Pressured to confess that she was a charlatan, Alykhardaakh challenged the men who ran the local village soviet. She invited them to her home and sat them down on long benches. Then she stood next to her roaring fire and began singing, dancing, and drumming to summon her spirit helpers.

First she called forth water, and the men's ankles were covered with the liquid. Next, she called forth a pike and caught it with her bare hands. Finally, she told the men to remove their pants and grab hold of their male organs. Then she snapped her fingers, and as they came out of their trance, she pointed out what they were doing: sitting there in front of a woman with their pants off and penises erect. Deeply embarrassed, they begged forgiveness for doubting her power and vowed never again to disturb her.[1]

Alykhardaakh had shown that she could force the men to enter an altered state of consciousness that she created and controlled. She also demonstrated that even though these men had embraced Communism, they were still vulnerable to a shaman's powers. The spiritual fish that she caught with her bare hands was made manifest in the naked penises they held in their hands. This brave woman shaman was one of only a few who during the dark years of Communism were spared public denunciation, confiscation of property, and deportation to a gulag.

WARRIORS OF CHILDBIRTH

Women have learned bravery in the face of childbirth. After all, bringing a child into the world is a painful and dangerous activity, one that many women dread and others openly fear. In Western societies women may opt out of part of the experience by choosing drugs. By contrast, women in many indigenous cultures expect to face the pain of labor and delivery with valor.[2]

In South Africa a fifteen-year-old San girl explained to my friend the ethnographer Marjorie Shostak her understanding of childbirth. Though she had not yet begun to menstruate, she was already mentally preparing herself for the rigors of the birth experience. "People tell me that I am female and that I will marry and give birth to a child one day," she said. "They also say that giving birth is like something that kills. Those who fear die and are buried. Those who don't fear, live."[3]

In this girl's society the ideal birth is unassisted, at least after a woman has had her first child. The San believe so strongly in the need to face childbirth bravely that women who behave in a cowardly manner are openly ridiculed. "A woman who isn't afraid sits quietly; she doesn't walk around or even brush the flies off her face," the girl explained. "If she does, others will say that she is afraid and will laugh at her. Her husband will yell at her, too; he will search for a wife who isn't afraid, and their marriage will die."[4]

Those who give birth "properly"—alone and without aid—are models for the younger women. In reality, of course, most women welcome assistance, at least in delivering the afterbirth, cutting the umbilical cord, and wiping the baby clean.

Among the Aztecs the metaphor of giving birth as a form of symbolic combat extends back to ancient times. A pregnant woman facing childbirth was described as a warrior going to fight. The *Florentine Codex,* an illustrated manuscript of the sixteenth century, describes how a young woman was prepared for her first "battle." Her pregnancy was announced before a large gathering. It was a joyful occasion because the woman had in her womb "a precious stone, a quetzal feather" that promised to continue the family line. Yet the event was also solemn, because birth is mysterious and fraught with danger.

During the seventh or eighth month of pregnancy, the families met to feast and discuss the hiring of a midwife, "an artist, a craftswoman" who received her powers from the female deity of the *temazcalli,* or bathhouse. During times of birth the bathhouse was called *xochicalli,* or "house of flowers."

When the young woman's contractions began, the midwife gave her a toy shield and weapons—including weaving battens—and encouraged her by uttering war cries.

When the woman feels pain, when she is soon to give birth, the midwife promptly gives her a vapor bath. Then she has her drink a potion of an herb called cihuapahtli [Montanoa tomentosa] *which is an impellent, an expellant. If the woman's labor is causing her great suffering, she has her drink a potion of about two small pieces of an opossum's tail and she expels it completely, with this she gives birth easily.*

Both the herb and opossum tail have been found to be excellent oxytocics, inducing contractions of the smooth uterine muscles and hastening parturition.[5]

When the woman waged her battle successfully and gave birth, her fame was attached to motherhood and her prize was the baby. If there were problems, however, the midwife prayed aloud and held the woman up, shook her, and used her feet to pummel her back.

My daughter, the battle is yours.
What are we to do for you? Here are your mothers.
Yours alone is the task.
Take up the buckler, daughter, my little one.
You are a woman warrior, be like one!
This means put forth all your strength.
Emulate the woman warrior, the valiant woman.

If, after an entire day and night, the woman did not give birth, the midwife rearranged the baby in the womb and placed the woman in the sweat bath. If the woman died, the midwife blessed her and gave her the name Mocihuatquetzque, meaning "woman warrior." Hers was considered a noble death, and she, like the valiant eagle and jaguar warriors who died in battle, went to live forever in the House of the Sun.[6]

AMAZONS IN LEGEND AND IN FACT

The most famous stories of females in battle go back to the Greek historian Herodotus, who reported in 450 BCE that he had heard tales of women warriors skilled both in hand-to-hand combat and with weapons. They rode the steppes of southern Russia, he said, and he gave them the name *Amazons,* meaning "those who are not breast-fed"—not, as popular culture has it, "those without one breast." For many years Herodotus's report was considered merely a fanciful tale that had been used to rationalize the patriarchal Greek society. According to their ideal, men fought battles in faraway lands while women stayed home alone rearing children. The Amazons, a "nomadic matriarchal culture," reversed those gender roles, and they became a powerful mythic archetype as the antithesis of Greek women.[7]

In the early 1980s, however, archaeologists excavating Iron Age burial mounds that dated from 800 to 250 BCE in central Europe and the southern Ukraine noticed that there were many female graves that contained swords, spears, daggers, arrowheads, and armor. To their surprise, it appeared that Herodotus might have been correct after all and that there actually were Amazons in this part of the world.[8]

During the past several years a Russian-American archaeological team headed by Jeannine Davis-Kimball of Berkeley, California, has excavated more than fifty such burial mounds outside the town of Pokrovka, a river port near the Russian border with Kazakhstan. She has found that each burial originally contained a single grave, of either a woman or a man. The individual was placed in a pit four to six feet deep in the center of the mound with offerings that included bronze-pointed arrows in quivers, bronze mirrors and jewelry, stone altars, pottery, pieces of colored stone, and horse trappings. A side of mutton lay either at the head or at the feet, ready to provide food during the long journey to the land of the dead.[9]

Davis-Kimball has also noted that the women were buried with more artifacts, and a wider variety of them, than the men. There were three different classes of female burials. The first contained spindle whorls, fragments of broken mirrors, and stone or glass beads. The second group had many of these objects, as well as stone altars, bone spoons, and seashells. These women might have been priestesses or shamans who presided over the spiritual and cultic affairs of a family. The grave goods of the third group included some of the above items but also had iron swords or daggers, bronze arrowheads, and whetstones to sharpen weapons. These were the graves of the women warriors, concluded Davis-Kimball.[10]

Researchers now believe that Bronze Age women in Central Asia controlled much of the society's wealth, performed rituals for their families or clan, rode horseback, and hunted antelope and other small game. In times of crisis they took to their saddles carrying spears, bows, and arrows. They were ready and willing to defend their animals, pastures, and clans.

Warrior queens, who both ruled and waged war, are known to have lived in Persia, China, Ireland, Egypt, and Africa. However, most of them fought alongside men. Roman soldiers confronted Celtic tribes in which females and males stood shoulder to shoulder. And the nomadic tribes of Eurasia—Huns, Mongols, Tatars, Uzbeks, Tajiks, and Scythians—all had women warriors among their horsemen. In China, the swordplay of a woman known as Madame Kung Sun was immortalized by a Tang dynasty poet.[11]

> *Her swinging sword flashes like the nine falling suns*
> *Shot by Yi the legendary bowman.*
> *She moves with the force of a team of dragons*
> *Driven by the gods through the sky.*
> *Her strokes and attacks are like those of terrible thunder.*
> *And when she stops*
> *All is still water reflecting clear moonlight.*

Centuries later, in the West African kingdom of Dahomey, an elite company of women served as the king's personal bodyguards, diviners, healers, and oracles. Richard Burton, in his account of his

1863 mission to the area, devoted an entire chapter to these Amazon troops of King Gelele. He estimated there were about twenty-five hundred of them, and noted, "Their masculine physique enabled them to compete with men in enduring toil, hardship and privations."[12] Later, during the Franco-Dahomean War of 1892, they fought valiantly with knives, muskets, and blunderbusses. And even though the kingdom was defeated by France during this war, the Amazon tradition of martial readiness continues today in the women's sword dance performed in the region.[13]

The Igbo women's war of 1929 in Nigeria illustrates once again how shamanic activities may be closely connected to war. According to one of the few surviving written reports of the uprising, multitudes of women protested the colonial resident's imposition of taxes; more than ten thousand were shot down with machine guns in a single incident. They were wearing sacred palm fronds, which signal danger because of powerful spiritual engagement. Thus these women were acting not only as warriors but also as shamans. The Europeans misunderstood their actions as profane acts of resistance, however, entirely missing the fact that the women were holy warriors battling not only economic and political oppression but also the colonial assault on Igbo spirituality and cosmology.[14]

WOMEN WARRIORS IN NORTH AMERICA

Native North America, from the Great Plains to Alaska, has also produced many famous women warriors. The most prestigious of them possessed supernatural powers that helped ensure their success. The Kiowa, Cheyenne, and Nootka had all-female warrior societies that lasted for many generations. And among the Cherokee, women warriors were so respected that during the nineteenth century special offices—with the titles Beloved Woman, Pretty Woman, and War Woman—were created to honor them. These women attended tribal councils, offered advice on military matters, led religious celebrations, and healed the sick. The most famous Cheyenne woman warrior, Yellow Haired Woman, is remembered today for leading a battle against Shoshoni horsemen. Mounted on her favorite stallion, she fought for hours, and for her bravery she was initiated into a secret shamanistic society composed solely of women warriors. Because the meetings were closed to the public, little is known about them today.[15]

During the early nineteenth century, a Gros Ventre girl who had been captured by the Crow was raised as a warrior by her adoptive father. From the age of ten, she carried a gun and hunted deer and bighorn with the men. When her father was killed in battle, she assumed charge of his family lodge and performed the duties of both mother and father for her orphaned siblings. In time she joined in raids on the Blackfeet, and her daring feats elevated her to the third-ranking position in the band. Eventually she married four women who cooked, tanned hides, and looked after her large family. After numerous vision quests and initiation as a shaman, the tribal elders raised her to the most prominent rank ever achieved by a woman: from that day on she was called Woman Chief.[16]

Some years later Pretty Shield, a famous Crow shaman, described another powerful woman shaman and warrior, named Strikes-Two. She rode out bravely against Lakota tribesmen who attacked her village.[17]

I saw Strikes-Two, a woman sixty years old, riding around camp on a gray horse. She carried only her root-digger, and she was singing her medicine song as though Lakota bullets and arrows were not flying around her.

Then I heard her say, "Now all of you sing: 'They are whipped. They are running away.' Keep singing these words until I come back."

When the men, and even the women, began to sing as Strikes-Two told them, she rode straight out at the Lakota waving her root-digger, and singing that song. I saw her, I heard her, and my heart swelled, because she was a woman.

The Lakota, afraid of her medicine, turned and ran away. The fight was won, and by a woman.

Sitting-in-the-Water Grizzly Bear was a famous woman warrior among the Kutenai of Washington state. As a "two-spirit" person—a Native American term for a lesbian or transgendered person—she married a white man, but soon ran away and returned home to her own people. There she put on men's clothing and weapons, assumed a masculine name, took a woman as her wife, and became a famous shaman and warrior. In 1837, while she was mediating peace between the Flatheads and her people, Blackfeet warriors attacked her. She was shot several times, then stabbed, but due to her remarkable shamanic healing abilities her wounds kept closing up by themselves. Only after a portion of her heart was cut out did she finally die.[18]

A number of Apache women shamans were highly respected both for their spiritual powers and for their leadership in raiding and warring expeditions. Two of them, Dahteste and Lozen, were friends and lovers who worked together during the 1880s as messengers and warriors with Geronimo's band. Dahteste was married at that time to a Chiricahua Apache warrior, but after Geronimo's band surrendered to American troops, her husband abandoned her. Later she married an Apache scout and raised her children on the Mescalero Reservation in New Mexico.

While Dahteste was bisexual, her friend Lozen, or Little Sister, was a two-spirit person. At puberty she had visited shamans and gone on a vision quest into the mountains. On the fourth night she was awarded with the knowledge of how to deliver babies and heal wounds, as well as the clairvoyant ability to locate the enemy: she would stand with her face toward the sky and her arms outstretched and begin to sing, and as she slowly moved in a circle, her palms turned purple and started to tingle, indicating where the enemy hid.

Lozen's brother Victorio, the famous Warm Springs chief, described her as his own right hand: "Strong as a man, braver than most, and cunning in strategy. Lozen is a shield to her people and I depend upon her as I do Nana [his brother]. She is skillful in dressing wounds; when I got a bullet through my shoulder she burned the thorns from a leaf of *nopal* [cactus], split it and bound the fleshy side to the wound. The next day I rode."[19]

In what is now Montana, the Blackfeet followed a great woman warrior by the name of Brown Weasel. She, like Dahteste and Lozen, possessed spiritual power that greatly enhanced her value as a warrior. When she was a child, her father gave her a bow and arrows and took her hunting. Later she joined him in a war party, and when her father had his horse shot out from under him, she braved enemy fire and rode back to save him. That was her first act of valor. After her first expedition Brown Weasel sought a vision and was rewarded with a guardian spirit and increased powers. She joined the Braves Society of Young Warriors, was allowed to speak at the Medicine Lodge ceremony, and after many successful exploits earned the war title Running Eagle.[20]

The Nez Perce had their own woman warrior: during Chief Joseph's last battle in 1877, when the tribesmen were almost out of bullets, an eighteen-year-old girl named Ah-tims told the men that she had a mighty guardian spirit and offered to run into enemy territory in order to bring back new cartridges. Yellow Wolf, a relative of hers, later recounted the event. [21]

Ah-tims had a strong Power: a Power to protect her in dangerous undertakings. She told the people of her Power, and said: "I will bring the cartridges!" The distance was about four hundred steps.

She ran, but not swiftly. Shots came about her, but she was not hit. Gathering up the cartridges, she ran for the rifle pit. Bullets struck about her, throwing up snow and dirt. She reached the rifle pit in safety. Her Power had protected her.

Bullet holes were in her clothing, in her red shawl. But she had no wounds. The warriors now had ammunition for their rifles. They were no longer useless. Everybody recognized Ah-tims as a brave woman and respected her.

WOMEN PROPHETS

At times the valorous deeds of women warriors extended beyond shamanic acts. These women took on the roles of visionaries and prophets and led their people in broad spiritual movements. In the Great Lakes region during the late nineteenth century, as growing numbers of European settlers pushed indigenous peoples off their land, a Dakota woman warrior by the name of Wananikwe, who had recently come to live among the Ojibwe, began having powerful shamanic experiences: she saw herself as a member of a band that was massacred by Custer's army at Little Big Horn in May 1876. She escaped by jumping into a stream at the approach of the soldiers and spent four days beneath the waters. There she beheld two deities, one good and the other evil. After choosing the good one she received a large drum and other ritual paraphernalia. She then learned an entire repertoire of songs and dances, which she performed for her followers. Her shamanist religion, which became known as the Dream Dance and the Drum Religion, condemned alcoholism and promised a rejuvenation of the indigenous world. She prophesied a time in the not-too-distant future when an immense drum would sound in the heavens; all whites and Catholic Indians would be paralyzed, and Indian traditionalists would take possession of the land.[22]

In Africa at about the same time—a troubled era of intertribal and colonial wars there as well—a number of women warriors in the Upper Nile Valley were suddenly able to divine the future and lead their people. Nyacan Ruea, a young Nuer woman, had an ecstatic experience in which she was seized by a divinity and then ran, shouting, from her parents' home. She was transformed from a shy young woman into a fearless spiritual warrior who led many successful raids on the Dinka, her people's traditional enemies. Over the years she performed dozens of shamanic ceremonies in which she "tied up," or hypnotized, her foes. As she taught this ability to other young women and created a shamanist warrior cult, her reputation grew until she became widely known as Mandong, or Grandmother.[23]

In the mountains of eastern Peru during the mid-twentieth century, a powerful Shipibo woman shaman by the name of Wasdëmëa (or Vasámea) began to publicly predict that white people would soon be swept away. What was the reason? They did not know how to cook properly, she said. They were using a red flame, instead of the blue one that symbolized the dawn of a "new age," which was totally different from the world the whites had created. As part of her prophecy she also pioneered an innovative asymmetrical curvilinear pottery design known as the *vero-yushin-quene*, or eye spirit design (figure 64), characterized by bold symmetrical lines filled in with delicate nonsymmetrical brushwork around a central cross. When the millennium she prophesied did not materialize, Wasdëmëa's movement faded, but her dynamic painting style remained; today it is very popular and is often painted on women's skirts.[24]

While Wasdëmëa and many other women warrior prophets preached ethnic and racial separation as the only way to avoid an apocalypse, a few other women began to advocate racial reconciliation and blending. In the years between 1831 and 1835, when the Australian government removed the last Tasmanian natives to an island in Bass Strait, one of their woman shamans prophesied, "We will die on that island. But sometime in the future we will

64. *Pottery design created by the woman shaman and prophet Wasdëmëa during the early 1950s. It consists of sets of interlocking curved lines arranged around a cross. The pattern is known as the "eye spirit design," named for the spirit that leaves a person upon death through the pupil of the eye.*

pop up again as white people." Echoing the sentiment behind her words, tribal elders in 1976 proclaimed that all Australians with any Aboriginal blood should consider themselves Aboriginal people. They believed that as Aboriginal blood became increasingly diluted in the ocean of white blood, its spiritual essence would increase in potency and cause the ancient consciousness of their race to reemerge in time to save the world from utter disaster.[25]

In Japan in the late nineteenth century a woman prophet named Nao Deguchi founded an all-embracing shamanist religion called Oomoto. Her first *kamigakari,* or creative trance, occurred without warning in 1892; she was fifty-five years old when a spirit possessed her. Both frightened and enlightened by this experience, she rushed home, stormed into her house, and loudly ordered her daughters to go pray at a local shrine. When they returned, they found her by the well in the backyard, dousing herself with buckets of cold water. For fifteen days she did this, all the while speaking in a deeply resonant masculine voice. She told her daughters that a living being had entered her body and lodged itself in her lower abdomen. Feeling heavier and stronger than she had in years, she stood erect with her chest thrust forward. The tension in her body made her tremble, and when she sat down on the floor, her feet vibrated, producing a thumping sound. On New Year's Day in 1893 the woman's trembling ceased, and though previously illiterate, she could now take dictation from the spirit of the Holy World, which issued this prophecy:[26]

The Great World shall burst into full bloom as plum blossoms, simultaneously. The World has hitherto been that of beasts, the stronger preying upon the weaker—it is satanic. You are so cheated by evil as to be quite unconscious of the truth. A dark age!

If things are left as they go now, order shall never prevail. Through the manifestation of Divine Power, the earth shall be reconstructed and transformed into an entirely New World. After going through cleansing, the world shall be changed into the Kingdom of Heaven, where peace will reign through all ages to come.

Since its founding the religion has been handed down through the female line and is now headed by its fifth woman spiritual leader, a direct descendant of Nao Deguchi. Practitioners of Oomoto maintain shrines and administrative facilities in the cities of Ayabe and Kameoka. They emphasize traditional Japanese arts—the tea ceremony, calligraphy, ceramics, and Noh drama—

and pursue peace through active participation in worldwide movements.[27]

Recently women's prophecies have taken on a new ecumenism with feminist overtones. Brooke Medicine Eagle, an intertribal healer who trained with a Cheyenne woman shaman, insists that a return to women's traditions is necessary for balance, growth, and healing. Rose Auger, a Woodland Cree prophet, agrees. At a 1995 international meeting of elders she demonstrated the power of feminine spirituality. During the council one of her spider guardians, who always accompanies her to listen and help, hopped onto the lap of a young holy man, who began to tremble. As he reached out to swat the spider—an unthinkably brutal act—an elder sitting next to him gently picked the creature up and handed it back to Rose. She smiled and prophesied that during the final days of the earth's forthcoming purification, Spider will return to correct what has gone wrong with the younger generation.

As we come to understand that shamanism worldwide is based on the emotional power of the entire cycle of birth, life, and death we cannot help recognizing that women warriors and prophets, like midwives and healers, are following important shamanic pathways. In these transcendent roles, powerful women are able to draw on both the feminine and masculine dimensions of shamanism in their minds and flesh, truly exemplifying the woman in the shaman's body.

NINETEEN

Rekindling the Flame:

SHAMANIC REVITALIZATION
AND RECONSTRUCTION

DURING THE TIME that I have been researching and writing this book, I have found myself invited to speak at many national and international gatherings. The interest in and reaction to what I was saying has been positive, and although I initially thought this was the result of my building an audience for my work, I now realize that we are in the midst of a major shamanic healing and religious movement. My colleague Mihály Hoppál, the director of the Institute for European Folklore in Budapest, recently observed that even after years of oppression from Islam, Christianity, Buddhism, and Communism, shamanism is very much alive and will go on living. Many shamanic practices have not only survived but are being re-created today as increasing numbers of people abandon atheism and established religions, seeking instead individual or small-group spiritual practice.

In the Siberian and Central Asian heartland, shamanic traditions are currently undergoing revitalization. In Europe and North America members of postindustrial societies—the very civilizations that persecuted tribal shamans in the past—are supporting research about shamanism, embracing indigenous shamans, and reconstructing shamanic traditions for themselves. The Foundation for Shamanic Studies, a nonprofit organization created in the 1980s by the anthropologist Michael Harner, is dedicated to the study, preservation, and transmission of shamanic knowledge. The foundation sponsors basic research and assists indigenous people in their attempts to recover lost shamanic traditions. It also carries out an experiential training program in which it teaches members of Western societies shamanic techniques.[1]

A supportive but nonparticipatory orientation toward shamanism is adhered to by Cultural Survival, a nonprofit organization founded in the 1980s by the anthropologist David Maybury-Lewis. Rather than encouraging Western experimentation with shamanic traditions, it supports the cultural privacy and exclusive rights of indigenous people to practice their own form of shamanic spirituality. In the fall of 2003 they published a special issue of their journal, *Cultural Survival Quarterly,* focusing on the topic "Shamanisms and Survival." In this gathering of essays various types of shamanic practice are described as powerful tools currently used by indigenous political leaders. Examples include Native Americans in northern British Columbia who use their shamans' deep hereditary knowledge to regain their lost territories and the San peoples of South Africa who use their weekly shamanic trance dances to enhance their ethnic pride and self-determination.

SHAMANIC REVITALIZATION

In the Siberian and Central Asian heartland the revitalization of local forms of shamanism began in the mid-1980s as *perestroika* took hold in the Soviet Union. During more than seven decades of repression, shamans who dared to drum or prophesy in public were rounded up, their drums were destroyed, and their tongues were cut out; then they were sent off to gulags or killed. These brutal acts nearly destroyed the hereditary transmission of shamanism.

However, an alternative inspirational shamanic path, practiced for generations by Turkic and Khakass peoples, enabled shamanism to survive. Shamans traveling this path received healing knowledge directly from the spirits of earth, water, and sky.[2]

Turkic peoples living in the Republic of Tuva continued throughout the Communist era to privately worship the White and Black Skies, located behind the Blue Sky that we see with our eyes. This reverence for the sky is beautifully inscribed in the prayer of a woman shaman by the name of Targyn-Kara.[3]

> *I am Targyn-Kara*
> *A worshipper of the Sky*
> *I am burning my pine incense for you.*
> *I am offering my milk to you.*
> *I am sanctifying my White Sky.*
> *Make my people happy and rich.*
> *I am sanctifying my Black Sky.*
> *Make my people safe and proud.*

As soon as Soviet repression was lifted dozens of shamans suddenly emerged into public life as fully initiated healers and ceremonial leaders. In 1987 Nadia Stepanova became the first Buryat shaman to publicly confess her years of covert practice of shamanism. Joining together with other shamans, she performed mass public healings and blessings in state-run theaters. By 1992 she had gathered together a large number of practicing shamans and became the founding president of the Khese Khengereg Association of Shamans.[4]

After the fall of the Soviet Union in 1992 many other shamans in Siberia and Central Asia went public about their healing activities. My colleague Marjorie Balzer of Georgetown University was conducting anthropological research in the Sakhá Republic at that time and observed shamanism exuberantly burst forth as a backlash against seven decades of stultifying Soviet rule. At a conference entitled "Shamanism as Religion: Genesis, Reconstruction, and Tradition," held at the Academy of Sciences in Yakutsk, she observed that the star was a Soviet-trained woman surgeon, Aleksandra Chirkova, whose father had been a famous shaman.[5]

When Aleksandra was a child she and her eight siblings were labeled "children of a shaman-charlatan." Because of this her father urged her, as his only child with curing potential, to be trained in modern medicine so as to avoid accusations of illegitimacy. In so doing, he hoped, she would be able to merge the best of Sakhá traditional shamanic medicine with European techniques. She was a dutiful daughter and attended medical school, where she joined the Communist Party. However, upon her father's death, when she inherited his shamanic drum and costume, she suddenly experienced a profound understanding of her spiritual healing abilities. As a result of this epiphany, she founded a center of folk medicine in the city of Yakutsk. At her clinic she and the other doctors and nurses she hired began healing people using shamanic techniques. From the moment they opened their offices they had a large number of clients since 80 percent of all Sakhá people, both urban and rural, still believed that some aspects of shamanic practice were effective medicine.[6]

Similar centers of folk medicine were also set up and licensed by local ministries of public health in many other post-Soviet communities. In Almaty, the capital of the Central Asian republic of Kazakhstan, a clinic was opened in 1992. By 2002, there were thirty Kazakh shamans who practiced spiritual and hands-on healing working in the center; twenty of them were women. A folk medicine center was also founded during 1992 in the Russian Republic by the Düngür Federation, or Society of Tuva Shamans. The ethnographer Kenin-Lopsan Mongush Borahovich, who was the grandson of a famous woman shaman, became its founding president. Initially he registered nearly forty shamans, twenty-eight of whom were women. He tested all new shamans and gave them certificates in folding red leatherette cases like the ones that had once held Communist Party membership cards. When the numbers of certified shamanic healers had grown to nearly one hundred, the Center for Non-Traditional

Medicine was formed and opened its doors directly opposite the municipal hospital at 41 Lenin Street. The head of the center was Ala Sergeevna Chunan, a Soviet-trained gynecologist and alternative healer. In her clinic each treatment room had a sign above the door giving the name of the healer followed by the number of generations in the shaman's direct lineage. To this day the majority of clinicians who practice there are women.[7]

In the central Russian republic of Khakassia there is today a small group of educated shamans who heal clients. Tatiana Kobezhikova is such a shaman. She has postgraduate training in archaeology and engages in shamanic soul retrieval. This practice involves finding lost parts of personalities, which she blows back and massages into the bodies of her clients. Even as a teenager, she saw auras around people and could predict what was about to happen. Her parents tried to dissuade her from developing her prophetic talents, but Tatiana persisted. After the fall of the Soviet Union, she traveled first to Tuva and then to Mongolia to study shamanism. In Mongolia a group of hereditary shamans trained and consecrated her as a shaman. Today she spends her time guiding visitors around Khakassian archaeological sites. When her clients begin to feel the sacred energy of the earth, she encourages them to develop rituals that combine ecological awareness with personal growth.[8]

Although the Chinese form of Communism, known as Maoism, also worked hard to exterminate shamans and their ceremonies, in some regions of this vast land traditional hereditary shamanism survived with minimal disturbance. This occurred because shamans filled official niches as folk healers within the country's "barefoot doctor" medical system. While these individuals never made their real ritual identities public, they nonetheless continued to heal in a shamanic way, and their clients believed in their powers. More recently in Manchuria and Xingjiang, hereditary priest-shamans came forth to orchestrate large communal gatherings and small family healing ceremonies, as their ancestors had for thousands of years.[9]

Not only has shamanism survived as a healing modality in post-Communist societies, but it is also undergoing a renaissance as a cultural and religious phenomenon. This is due to the work of artists and intellectuals who have created cultural revival movements in Russia and Mongolia. In the Sakhá Republic an organization known as Kut-Sür (the name means "consciousness-soul," "heart-mind," or "intuition") was formed by a group of writers, film directors, historians, anthropologists, biologists, and physicians. They immediately began to explore shamanism as the ancient wisdom of their people and felt that it might help them to understand and rebuild their ethnic identities in a postcolonial world. A similar cultural movement, known as Negdsen Hudelguun, or United Movement, was also created at about the same time (1995–1996) by intellectuals in Mongolia. The leader, Gongorjav Boshigt, suggested that instead of following the philosophy and economics of the colonizing powers (Russia and China) that had imposed their views on the region, his people should reach deep into their own historical traditions for models for their future. The main work of the United Movement has been to advocate the application of shamanic principles and practices to the ongoing social, political, and religious reform of Mongolian society.[10]

When I talked with the Buryat shaman Nadia Stepanova in Ulaanbaatar, during the Fifth Conference of the International Society for Shamanistic Research, she told me that while the Soviet campaign against shamanism had never been very effective in silencing all of the healing shamans, it had, however, seriously disrupted traditional clan rituals. As a result, it was now the duty of all consecrated shamans to compare their memories of prayers, songs, and rituals so that they could restore as many of the pre-Soviet shamanic ceremonies as possible. During the conference she actively encouraged the Buryat and Mongolian shamans in attendance to share their memories of the rituals for the Thirteen Northern Deities, spirits of the mountains, cliffs, rivers, woods, lakes, and islands. She also told me that she hoped one day to find a way to have shamanism officially recognized as a religion.

All over Siberia shamans worship trees that symbolize the center of the world where heaven and earth touch. Some trees—especially large and strangely shaped ones, or trees growing in unusual places—are honored by tying ribbons or pieces of cloth containing tobacco or other offerings to their branches to recognize the spirits residing in the tree. On a steep cliff above the Tapsy River in Tuva, shamans today venerate a majestic, three-hundred-year-old pine tree. Remains of offerings—bits of food, pieces of cloth, horsehair, beads, and empty bottles of milk and brandy—intertwine with its roots. Not long ago, when a young girl became ill, a woman shaman named Dygdaa laid the child out at the foot of this sacred tree. In so doing she reconnected the girl to her lost spirit guide and dedicated her future life to the service of her ancestors, who had worshiped there for centuries.[11]

In northern Mongolia, many shamans are still selected today in the traditional fashion, by their clan leaders. In Ulaanbaatar when I interviewed Byambadorj Dondog he explained to me that his shamanic line extends back to the twelfth-century shamans of Chinggis Khan's mother's Olkhon clan. When he was presented to the leaders of his clan the chief of the water spirits appeared in the form of a long yellow snake. This was a clear omen that he was to become a great shaman or *zaarin*. In 1996 he and a few colleagues, including Bayar Odun, founded an organization called the Center Golomi of Mongolian Shamanism to promote the training and healing practices of shamans. The Mongolian word *golomi* refers to the fire at the center of the tent, and the organization is dedicated to the view that shamanism is the spiritual fire at the center of the Mongolian nation. Like the feminine spirit of fire at the center of the home that warms, feeds, and sustains the family, the spirit of shamanism, too, must be kept burning.

SHAMANIC RECONSTRUCTION

In Western Europe, Australia, and North America shamanism is actively being reconstituted from archaeological, anthropological, and historical records. This interest in reconstructing lost shamanic traditions is connected with the insight that the Western world-view has become overly material in religion, medicine, and psychotherapy and needs to be either abandoned altogether or else expanded in a more spiritual direction.

In North America there is a growing number of people of Celtic heritage who are leaving their various denominational churches and returning to pre-Christian shamanic traditions. To reconnect with their suppressed spirituality they visit Ireland and join shamanic congregations dedicated to worshiping the earth, trees, and animals. By fasting, dancing, and praying in groves of trees and at rock shrines, they hope to reclaim at least some of their shamanic knowledge so that they can heal themselves and others. A few also make pilgrimages to Scotland and Wales, where they undergo dream incubation rituals in the shaft tombs of their ancestors.[12]

For these people of Celtic descent reconstruction is a difficult process because shamanism was nearly destroyed there by Christian missionaries a very long time ago. Although various local forms of shamanism were violently repressed during the early Middle Ages, in the United Kingdom today the spirit world, the Otherworld of the Celts, includes the ancient World of Faerie, where one can meet talking foxes and other spirit guides. Individuals who are open to such encounters and who long to reconnect to their pre-Christian religious identities have begun to study the remains of Bronze Age shamanism together with shamanic traditions mentioned in folklore and history. The contemporary nature-based shamanic religious and healing traditions that have emerged include Wicca, Goddess Spirituality, Druidry, and Heathenry.

Wicca, or modern witchcraft, is a reconstruction of the form of European shamanism that was practiced from the Paleolithic to the Middle Ages. It is today an initiatory religion in which practitioners revere divinity as manifest in the polarity of a goddess and a god. Wiccans refer to their religion as "Shamanic Wicca," "Shamanic Craft," or "Wiccan-shamanism." In New Zealand during the 1980s feminists of Celtic heritage adopted the label "witch" rather than "Wiccan" as a defiant symbolic gesture. For these women the word *witch* is synonymous with "wise woman," and for them becoming a witch is an affirmation of a focused, woman-centered spirituality in which material reality is perceived as swirls of energy. They further believe that when their own energy is concentrated and channeled it can influence the energy in the world surrounding them. Their rituals celebrate an annual round of seasonal festivals and rites of passage in women's lives: menarche and menopause, birthdays and the birth of children, retirement, and death.[13]

Goddess Spirituality is closely related to this strongly feminist branch of Wicca. As a social movement of more than a million members, it is devoted to the reemerging spirituality of Mother Earth and women's closeness to her and to the planet. In its formative stages the movement was influenced by the work of Marija Gimbutas and her goddess-oriented interpretations of the famous archaeological site of Çatalhüyük in Turkey. Starhawk and others in this movement have engaged with the critiques of Gimbutas's research and explained how they perceive the link between pre-patriarchal matrifocal societies and contemporary feminist agendas. They point to the strange notion that nature and human bodies need to be dominated as an unfortunate legacy of Judeo-Christian ideology and claim that goddess worship is the oldest religion of all, dating back to the Paleolithic and closely associated with shamanism and other primal religions. Carol Christ, a leader in the goddess movement, has argued that religious symbol systems, such as those of Christianity, that focus almost exclusively around male images of divinity create the impression that female spirituality can never be fully legitimate.[14]

Druidry centers on nature-oriented forms of shamanic spirituality that are bound to local (originally Celtic) landscapes. The rituals and beliefs are based on artifacts from the Celtic Iron Age and literature from the medieval period in England, Wales, Scotland, and Ireland. The major groups in English druidism grew out of the Ancient Druid Order (ADO), a fraternal organization founded in 1717. It focused on charity work and reviving disappearing lore and music. The Order of Bards Ovates and Druids (OBOD) split off from ADO, developing druidism into a philosophy and becoming the largest druidic organization in the world with over seven thousand members. American druidism took a different route; the Reformed Druids of North America (RDNA) started at Carlton College as a rebellious way to fulfill the school's religion requirement. The Henge of Keltria and A Druid Fellowship follow in this tradition, focusing on the individual's relationships with the land, deities, spirits, and ancestors. In both of these organizations women have leadership roles.[15]

Heathenry (the name means "people of the heath") is also called "Ásatrú" (allegiance to the gods) and "Nordic shamanism." This is a set of shamanic traditions that originated with the Germanic, Scandinavian, Anglo-Saxon, and Icelandic settlers of northwest Europe. It includes such shamanic practices as mediumship, weather-working, and shape-shifting as well as runic and oracular divination. Heathenry is actively being reconstructed today from information found in Norse and Icelandic mythology, Viking and Anglo-Saxon migration histories, and archaeological sources. In Scandinavia groups of shamanic practitioners undertake vision quests in which they journey to healing springs during the full moon or at midsummer and spend an entire night "sitting out." As part of their shamanic rituals, they search for a plant helper and practice soul retrieval and divination with stones or long wooden sticks. They access the alternative world through breathing exercises and meditation techniques, spiritually connecting with the moon and with the *vølve* or "wise women."[16]

Some of the shamans in this tradition have merged the cosmology of Wyrd (Old English for "fate" or "destiny"), the worship of Odin and Freyja as shamanic deities, and the divinatory use of runes (from Old English *rün*, meaning "mystery" or "hidden knowledge"). In Norse myths Odin rides his eight-legged horse, who serves as his spirit helper, to the shamanic otherworlds comprising the Yggdrassill tree. There he hangs in the tree and after nine nights receives the wisdom of the runes.[17]

Others have taken up the practice known as Seidr (Seiðr), which consists of remnants of several shamanic traditions practiced among ancient Scandinavian peoples. These traditions, which are based primarily on information in the Icelandic sagas, are currently being reconstituted in both North America and Europe. My anthropologist colleague Jenny Blain, of Sheffield Hallam University in the United Kingdom, describes Seidr traditions, of which she is a practitioner, as involving a change of consciousness: light trance for audience members and deep trance for "seidworkers." The tradition she follows is what has come to be known as "high seat" or "oracular" Seidr. It exists not only in the United Kingdom, where she lives, but also in Berkeley, California, where an organization known as Hrafnar, meaning "the ravens," was founded in 1988 by the medieval scholar and novelist Diana Paxson.[18]

In this reconstructed form of Norse shamanism a group of practitioners undertakes shamanic séances together during which the woman seer and her followers drum and sing themselves through a tunnel of trees until they arrive at the great tree Yggdrassill. They pause to honor the tree, then go below one of its roots, through several earthen chambers, across an echoing bridge, and arrive at the gates of the Land of the Dead (Helheim). Here the seer leaves the others behind and travels alone, assisted only by her spirit allies or "power animals," and attempts to make contact with the shamanic deities to help her clients and to establish healing relationships for them. Today, as in the Nordic saga traditions of more than one thousand years ago, most seidworkers are female.[19]

During the same years that these neopagan traditions were being reconstructed, a number of spiritual and hands-on healers in the United Kingdom organized themselves as charities, with Web sites, newsletters, and meetings. The president of one of these organizations, the National Federation of Spiritual Healers (NFSH), explained: "I feel it is important to remember that as an organization we are a charity. This means that, while healing under the NFSH banner in public, we are offering healing as a service. Members voluntarily and willingly devote time and effort to this important work." The organization formed the International Healer Support Group on the Internet, through which conferences are announced and issues of ethics in healing are discussed.[20]

In the United States, a similar organization, the Society for Shamanic Practitioners, was founded in 2004 by Bonnie Horrigan, author and editorial director of the international medical journal *Explore: The Journal of Science and Healing;* Alan Davis, MD, PhD, a physician specializing in physical rehabilitation; and Sandra Ingerman, MA, author and shamanic teacher. The society consists of individuals who use various shamanic skills in healing illness. Ed Tick, a member of the board of directors, said that "the purpose of the Society is to gather people working in various shamanic and spiritual practices to do serious clinical work, scientific analysis, networking, exploring, and developing shamanic practice in responsible ways." Like the National Federation of Spiritual Healers, the Society for Shamanic Practitioners has conferences and a Web site where issues of ethics in healing and ecological approaches to health are discussed.[21]

FEMININE AND MASCULINE SHAMANIC TRADITIONS

We are at the beginning of a worldwide spiritual movement—one in which women and men trained in various shamanic traditions insist on their right to openly practice ancient religious rituals as well as complementary and alternative medicine to restore themselves to a healthy balance with the world around them. To do so, they have instituted shamanist organizations that will enable them to survive in male-oriented educational, medical, and religious environments. The appeal to women who follow this path is apparent: they are not submerged or dominated, and thus they do not have to struggle with men for spiritual or healing equality. Equality does not mean sameness, however, since as we have seen in previous chapters, there are important differences between feminine and masculine shamanic traditions.

As a general rule, women shamans, and men trained within a feminine tradition, have an interpersonal orientation; they coax their clients to become active participants in their own healing. Male shamans, and women trained in a masculine tradition, take on a heroic role; they encourage their clients to take the role of passive spectators at their dramatic performances. It is vital that we understand both paths, crucial that we focus on the entire life-death-rebirth continuum.

Because women who attempt to join the ministry or to practice as midwives and physicians are still struggling for legitimacy, it is important for them to know the history of how and why women were excluded from these areas of knowledge. For too long, evaluations of women's religious beliefs and healing practices were based on opinions refracted through the eyes of men and explained by concepts taken from male-oriented religious and academic traditions. It is time to reclaim the areas of wisdom that were, until the spread of patriarchal world religions and the establishment of Western biomedicine, strongly feminine.[22]

This is an exciting time for those of us who study, work with, and practice as shamans. We can look with new insight at the archaeological and historical record, at groundbreaking physiological and psychological research, and at the practices of living shamans. Various shamanisms—including transcendent roles for women—have miraculously survived for millennia in revitalized and reconstructed forms. With the hearts and minds of the twenty-first century, we can now watch them take their rightful place as major religious healing systems in our time.

Notes

Chapter One
OLD WISDOM

1   For reports on this archaeological find see Bohuslav Klíma, "The first ground-plan of an Upper Paleolithic loess settlement in middle Europe and its meaning," in *Courses Toward Urban Life,* eds. Robert J. Braidwood and Gordon R. Willey (Chicago: Aldine, 1962) and "A triple burial from the Upper Paleolithic of Dolní Věstonice, Czechoslovakia," *Journal of Human Evolution* 16 (1988): 831–835. A discussion of these artifacts as well as a review of the archaeological dogma that fired clay was only invented during the Neolithic appears in Paul Bahn and Jean Vertut, *Journey Through the Ice Age* (Berkeley: University of California Press, 1997), 98–99.

Chapter Two
HEALING AND THE SEEKERS OF KNOWLEDGE:
WHAT SHAMANS DO

1   In "holistic medicine" there is a definition of health as a positive state, not merely as the absence of disease. There is also an emphasis on self-help and self-healing; a relationship between the health care providers that is relatively open, equal, and reciprocal; a concern with how the individual's health reflects the familial, social, and cultural environment; an openness toward using natural techniques wherever possible; an emphasis on physical and emotional contact between practitioner and client; and acceptance of the notion that successful healing transforms the practitioner as

well as the patient. See Michael Goldstein et al., "Holistic physicians and the recruitment of shamen [sic]," in *Yearbook of Cross-Cultural Medicine and Psychotherapy*, ed. Walter Andritzky (Düsseldorf: Verlag für Wissenschaft und Bildung, 1992), 119. The concept of "integrative medicine" that reconnects modern medicine with nature was developed by Andrew Weil and is currently being taught in the Program in Integrative Medicine at the College of Medicine, University of Arizona in Tucson, Arizona. See his books *Health and Healing* (New York: Fawcett, 1993); *Natural Health, Natural Medicine* (Boston: Houghton Mifflin, 1995); and *Spontaneous Healing: Eight Weeks to Optimum Health* (New York: Fawcett, 1997). He also publishes a monthly newsletter, *Dr. Andrew Weil's Self Healing*, and maintains a Web site at www.drweil.com. For excellent introductions to integrative medicine and holistic nursing as well as complementary and alternative therapies see Merrijoy Kelner et al., *Complementary and Alternative Medicine: Challenge and Change* (London: Routledge, 2000) and Bonnie Horrigan, *Voices of Integrative Medicine: Conversations and Encounters* (Churchill: Livingstone, 2003).

2   Discussions of the nature and origins of shamans and shamanism include Raymond Firth, "Shaman," in *Dictionary of the Social Sciences*, eds. J. Gould and F. W. Kolb (New York: Free Press, 1964); Åke Hultkrantz, "Ecological and phenomenological aspects of shamanism," in *Shamanism in Siberia*, eds. Vilmos Diószegi and Mihály Hoppál (Budapest: Akadémiai Kiadó, 1978), 27–58; John Grim, *The Shaman: Patterns of Religious Healing Among the Ojibway Indians* (Norman: University of Oklahoma Press, 1983), 11–14; Jane Atkinson, "Shamanisms today," *Annual Review of Anthropology* 21 (1992): 307–330; Marjorie Balzer, "Shamanism," in *Encyclopaedia of Cultural Anthropology*, eds. David Levinson and Melvin Ember (New York: Henry Holt, 1996), 1182–1186; Joan Townsend, "Shamanism," in *Anthropology of Religion: A Handbook*, ed. Stephen Glazier (Westport, CT: Greenwood Press, 1997), 429–469; Laurel Kendall, "Shamans," in *Encyclopedia of Women and World Religion*, ed. Serinity Young (New York: Macmillan, 1999), 892–895.

3   For a particularly nasty dispute about the presence or absence of shamanism in Africa see Cyril Hromnik, "A testament to the shamanistic hallucinatory trance theory of the Southern African Rock Art," *Rock Art Research* 8 (1991): 99–108. Some educated Africans trained in the ancient arts of divination and spiritual healing embrace the concept of shamanism, and also the term *shaman* to refer to their traditions. See Malidoma Patrice Somé, *Of Water and the Spirit: Ritual, Magic, and Initiation in the Life of an African Shaman* (New York: Jeremy Tarcher, 1994) and Susan Schuster Campbell, *Called to Heal: African Shamanic Healers* (Twin Lakes, WI: Lotus Press, 1998). Others have described similar healing traditions but have avoided using the term *shaman* to describe healers. See Yaya Diallo and Mitchell Hall, *The Healing Drum: African Wisdom Teachings* (Rochester, VT: Destiny Books, 1989). Even though a number of researchers have asserted that shamanism exists only in nomadic hunter-gatherer societies I have uncovered shamanism in all forms of ancient and modern human society. For discussions of the universal aspects and psycho-physiological dynamics of shamanistic healing see James Dow, "Universal aspects of symbolic healing: A theoretical synthesis," *American Anthropologist* 88 (1986): 56–69 and Michael Winkelman, *Shamanism: The Neural Ecology of Consciousness and Healing* (Westport, CT: Bergin and Garvey, 2000).

4   Daniel Moerman, "Physiology and symbols: The anthropological implications of the placebo effect," in *The Anthropology of Medicine*, eds. Lola Romanucci-Ross, Daniel E. Moerman, and Laurence R. Tancredi (New York: Praeger, 1983); Stanley

Krippner and Peter Welch, *Spiritual Dimensions of Healing: From Native Shamanism to Contemporary Health Care* (New York: Irvington Press, 1992); Margot Lyon, "Psychoneuroimmunology: The problem of the situatedness of illness and the conceptualization of healing," *Culture, Medicine and Psychiatry* 17 (1993): 77–97; Michael Winkelman, "Physiological and therapeutic aspects of shamanistic healing," *Subtle Energies* 1 (1991): 1–18.

5   See James Dow, "Universal aspects of symbolic healing," and Maria Dobkin de Rios, "A modern-day shamanistic healer in the Peruvian Amazon: Pharmacopoeia and Trance," in *Jahrbuch für Transkulturelle Medizin und Psychotherapie,* ed. Walter Andritzky (Düsseldorf: Verlag für Wissenschaft und Bildung, 1991), 41–54.

6   The efficacy of shamanic healing, as in other forms of complementary and alternative medicine (CAM), cannot be readily evaluated using randomized clinical trials since most CAM practitioners see the placebo effect as positive rather than taking the biomedical view that the placebo should be eliminated so as to ensure scientific rigor. See P. Pietroni, *The Greening of Medicine* (London: Victor Gollancz, 1991). The literature on the effectiveness of shamanic healing is vast. See Wolfgang Jilek, "From crazy witch doctor to auxiliary psychotherapist—the changing image of the medicine man," *Psychiatria Clinica* 4 (1971): 200–220, and *Indian Healing: Shamanic Ceremonialism in the Pacific Northwest Today* (Surrey, BC, Canada: Hancock House, 1982); Horacio Fabrega and Daniel Silver, *Illness and Shamanistic Curing in Zinacantan: An Ethnomedical Analysis* (Stanford, CA: Stanford University Press, 1973); Adell Johannes, "Many medicines in one: Curing in the eastern highlands of Papua New Guinea," *Culture, Medicine, and Psychiatry* 4 (1980); Jeanne Achterberg, *Imagery in Healing: Shamanism and Modern Medicine* (Boston: Shambhala, 1985) and "The shaman: Master healer in the imaginary realm," in *Shamanism,* ed. Shirley Nicholson (Boston: Sigo Press, 1987); Donald Joralemon, "The performing patient in ritual healing," *Social Science and Medicine* 23 (1986): 841–845; Carol Laderman, "The ambiguity of symbols in the structure of healing," *Social Science and Medicine* 24 (1987): 293–301; David Young, Grant Ingram, and Linda Swartz, "A Cree healer attempts to improve the competitive position of native medicine," *Arctic Medical Research* 41 (1988): 313–316; Walter Andritzky, *Schamanismus und rituelles Heilen im Alten Peru* (Berlin: Verlag Clemens Zerlig, 1989); Bernard Ortiz de Montellano, *Aztec Medicine, Health, and Nutrition* (New Brunswick: Rutgers, 1990); Anatoly Alekseev, "Techniques among Evén shamans for healing humans and animals," *Shaman* 2 (1994): 156–165, and "Healing techniques among Evén shamans," in *Shamanic Worlds, ed.* Marjorie Mandelstam Balzer (Armonk, NY: North Castle Books, 1997); Margaret Laurel Allen and Meredith Sabini, "Renewal of the world tree: Direct experience of the sacred as a fundamental source of healing in shamanism, psychology, and religion," in *The Sacred Heritage: The Influence of Shamanism on Analytical Psychology,* eds. Donald F. Sandner and Steven H. Wong (New York: Routledge, 1997); Romio Shrestha and Ian Baker, *The Tibetan Art of Healing* (San Francisco: Chronicle Books, 1997); Ana Mariella Bacigalupo, "The exorcising sounds of warfare: Shamanic healing and the struggle to remain Mapuche," *Anthropology of Consciousness* 9 (1998): 1–16; Michael Winkelman, *Shamanism: The Neural Ecology of Consciousness and Healing* (Westport, CT: Bergin and Garvey, 2000).

7   The literature on shamans and endorphins is large. For an intelligent and accessible introduction see Raymond Prince, "The endorphins: A review of psychological anthropologists," *Ethos* 10 (1982): 303–316, and "Shamans and endorphins: Hypothesis for a synthesis," *Ethos* 10 (1982): 409–423.

8   My discussion of these Siberian shamanic traditions draws on the excellent publications of Roberte Hamayon including *La chasse à l'âme: Esquisse d'une théorie du chamanisme sibérien* (Nanterre: Société d'ethnologie, 1990) and "Shamanism in Siberia: From partnership in supernature to counter-power in society," in *Shamanism, History, and the State,* eds. Nicholas Thomas and Caroline Humphrey (Ann Arbor: University of Michigan Press, 1994).

9   Uno Holmberg, *Finno-Ugric and Siberian Mythology* (New York: Cooper Square, 1964).

10 Ana Mariella Bacigalupo, "Mapuche shamanic bodies and the Chilean state: Polemic gendered representations and indigenous responses," in *Violence and the Body: Race, Gender and the State,* ed. Arturo Aldama (Bloomington: Indiana University Press, 2003), 322; Michel Perrin, "The *urukáme,* a crystallization of the soul," in *People of the Peyote,* eds. Stacey Schaefer and Peter Furst (Albuquerque: University of New Mexico Press, 1996), 407.

11 In some cultures, such as among the Mongols, goats, sheep, horses, camels, and yaks are inherited in the male line, or patrilineage, while shamanism is inherited in the female line, or matrilineage. In other cultures, such as among the K'iche' Maya, fields, orchards, houses, and shamanism are all inherited in the male line. In the north Asian nation of Nepal hereditary shamanism is combined with inspirational shamanism among the Sherpa, Tamang, Gurung, and Kirati. In these ethnic groups shamans are called to their practice by a summons from the primordial forest shaman, by illness, by visionary dreams, and by family tradition. See Larry Peters, *Ecstasy and Healing in Nepal: An Ethnopsychiatric Study of Tamang Shamanism* (Malibu, CA: Undena Publications, 1981); San Royal Mumford, *Himalayan Dialogue: Tibetan Lamas and Gurung Shamans in Nepal* (Madison: University of Wisconsin Press, 1989), 168–169; Claudia Müller-Ebeling, Christian Rätsch, and Surendra Bahadur Shahi, *Shamanism and Tantra in the Himalayas* (Rochester, VT: Inner Traditions, 2002), 25–28, 105–106.

12 Sendenzhavyn Dulam, *Darhad bog un ulamjilal* (Tradition of Darkhat shamans) (Ulaanbaatar: MUIS-iin Khevlel, 1992); and O. Purev, *Mongol boogiin shashin* (Mongolian shamanism) (Ulaanbaatar: Mongol Ulsyn Shinzhekh Ukhaany Akademiin Tuukhiin Khureelen, 1999).

13 Nicholas Humphrey, *The Inner Eye* (London: Faber and Faber, 1986), 130.

14 Juha Pentikäinen, "The revival of shamanism in the contemporary north," in *Shamanism in Performing Arts,* eds. Tae-gon Kim and Mihály Hoppál (Budapest: Akadémiai Kiadó, 1995), 271; Manabu Waida, "The land of the dead in Japanese shamanism," in *Shamans and Cultures,* eds. Mihály Hoppál and Keith Howard (Budapest: Akadémiai Kiadó, 1993), 85; Dorothy Kennedy and Randall Bouchard, "Bella Coola," in *Handbook of North American Indians,* vol. 7: *Northwest Coast,* ed. Wayne Suttles (Washington, DC: Smithsonian Institution, 1990); Alan Sandstrom, "Mesoamerican healers and medical anthropology," in *Mesoamerican Healers,* eds. Brad Huber and Alan Sandstrom (Austin: University of Texas Press, 2001), 319; Dorothea S. Whitten and Norman E. Whitten, *From Myth to Creation: Art from Amazonia Ecuador* (Urbana: University of Illinois Press, 1988), 24.

15 A. L. Kroeber, "The Yurok religion," in *Handbook of the Indians of California* (Washington, DC: Government Printing Office, 1925), 53–75; Marjorie Balzer, "Changing images of the shaman: Folklore and politics in the Sakha Republic (Yakutia)," *Shaman* 4 (1996): 5–16; Roberte Hamayon, "Buriat religion," in *The Encyclopedia of Religion,* ed. Mircea Eliade (New York: Macmillan, 1987); Peter Furst, "To find

our life: Peyote among the Huichol Indians of Mexico," in *Flesh of the Gods,* ed. Peter Furst (New York: Praeger, 1972).

16 Innuaimun and Inuit words for shaman, underscoring their ability to "see" or be clairvoyant, can be found in Knud Rasmussen, *The Intellectual Culture of Iglulik Eskimos* (Copenhagen: Gyldendalske Boghandel, Nordisk Forlag, 1929), 7:134, and Daniel Merkur, *Becoming Half Hidden: Shamanism and Initiation Among the Inuit* (Stockholm: Almquist and Wiskell, 1985), 41, 267.

Chapter Three
HANDPRINTS ON A CAVE WALL:
WOMEN SHAMANS IN PREHISTORY

1 J. T. Ozols, "Zür Altersfrage des Schamanismus," in *Sehnsucht nach dem Ursprung,* ed. Hans Peter Duerr (Frankfurt am Main: Syndikat, 1983); Mihály Hoppál, "Studies on Eurasian shamanism," in *Shamans and Cultures,* eds. Mihály Hoppál and Keith Howard (Budapest: Akadémiai Kiadó, 1993), 269; Ulla Johansen, "Further thoughts on the history of shamanism," *Shaman* 7 (1999): 46.

2 William Fitzhugh, "The tomb of a shaman," Arctic Studies Center, National Museum of Natural History, 2002, available at www.mnh.si.edu/arctic/features/croads/ekven1.html; Sergei Arutiunov and William Fitzhugh, "Contents of the burial," Arctic Studies Center, National Museum of National History, 2002, available at www.mnh.si.edu/arctic/features/croads/ekvens3.html; Sergei Arutiunov and William Fitzhugh, "Contents of the burial," Arctic Studies Center, National Museum of Natural History, 2002, available at www.mnh.si.edu/arctic/features/croads/ekven3.html.

3 Elizabeth Rega, "Age, gender and biological reality in the early Bronze Age cemetery at Mokrin," in *Invisible People and Processes: Writing Gender and Childhood into European Archaeology,* eds. Jenny Moore and Eleanor Scott (New York: Leicester University Press, 1997).

4 Some of the new technologies for sexing bones include macroscopic, microscopic, and chemical assessment of human skeletal remains. Misia Landau in her book *Narratives of Human Evolution* (New Haven, CT: Yale University Press, 1991) beautifully laid out the masculinist mythic structure of the story of human evolution. For work in the emerging area of gender studies in archaeology and paleoanthropology see M. P. Bumsted et al., "Recognizing women in the archaeological record," in *Powers of Observation: Alternative Views in Archaeology,* eds. Sarah M. Nelson and Alice B. Kehoe (Arlington, VA: American Anthropological Association, 1990); Dale Walde and Noreen Willows, *The Archaeology of Gender* (Calgary: Archaeological Association of the University of Calgary, 1991); Joan Gero and Margaret Conkey, *Engendering Archaeology: Women and Prehistory* (Oxford: Blackwell, 1991); Rita Wright, *Gender and Archaeology* (Philadelphia: University of Pennsylvania Press, 1996); Sarah Nelson, *Gender in Archaeology: Analyzing Power and Prestige* (Walnut Creek, CA: Alta Mira Press, 1997); Lori Hager, *Women in Human Evolution* (London: Routledge, 1997); Susan Kent, *Gender in African Prehistory* (Walnut Creek, CA: Alta Mira Press, 1998).

5 For the "pornographic" theory of Venus figurines see C. Chard, *Man in Prehistory* (New York: McGraw-Hill, 1975), 182; Desmond Collins and John Onians, "The origins of art," *Art History* 1 (1978): 12–13. It is instructive to note that nakedness

has different connotations when figurines are male rather than female. Thus, a Paleolithic naked male torso is described in a book under the heading "Figures of Authority." In the text we learn that "although male figures rarely appear among sculptures dug up, the few that do all seem to represent men of importance. There is a common theme, however varied the pieces themselves may be: regality or godliness." D. Hamblin, *The First Cities* (New York: Time-Life Books, 1973), 133.

6 Margaret Conkey, "Contexts of action, contexts for power: Material culture and gender in Magdalenian," in *Engendering Archaeology: Women and Prehistory*, eds. Joan M. Gero and Margaret W. Conkey (Oxford: Blackwell, 1991) and "Mobilizing ideologies: Paleolithic 'art,' gender trouble, and thinking about alternatives," in *Women in Human Evolution*, ed. Lori D. Hager (New York: Routledge, 1997).

7 It has been pointed out by the historian Ronald Hutton that Gimbutas was by no means the first person to suggest Great Goddess interpretations for European archaeological materials. He argued that the archaeological team of Jacquetta and Christopher Hawkes had by the mid-1940s portrayed Neolithic European communities as worshiping a Great Mother Goddess who personified nature. See Ronald Hutton, *Triumph of the Moon: A History of Modern Pagan Witchcraft* (Oxford: Oxford University Press, 1999), 278–279.

8 Marija Gimbutas's theories, research methods, and findings are summarized in three of her books: *The Goddesses and Gods of Old Europe* (Berkeley: University of California Press, 1974), *The Language of the Goddess* (San Francisco: HarperSanFrancisco, 1989), and *Civilization of the Goddess* (San Francisco: HarperSanFrancisco, 1991).

9 For critiques of Gimbutas's work by feminist archaeologists see Ruth Tringham's review of *Civilization of the Goddess* in *Archaeology* 95 (1993): 196–197; Lynn Meskell, "Goddesses, Gimbutas and 'new age' archaeology," *Antiquity* 69 (1995): 74–86; Margaret Conkey and Ruth Tringham, "Archaeology and the Goddess: Exploring the contours of feminist archaeology," in *Feminisms in the Academy*, eds. Donna Stanton and Abigail Stewart (Ann Arbor, MI: University of Michigan Press, 1995); Pamela Russell, "The Paleolithic mother-goddess: Fact or fiction?" in *Reader in Gender Archaeology*, eds. Kelley Hays-Gilpin and David S. Whitley (New York: Routledge, 1998). It ought to be remembered, however, that Gimbutas's work provided at least a partial corrective to the rampant androcentrism in the discipline and, perhaps more important, that it served as a stimulus to engender archaeology.

10 Alexander Marshack, *The Roots of Civilization* (New York: McGraw-Hill, 1972), 283; Patricia Rice, "Prehistoric Venuses: Symbols of motherhood or womanhood?" *Journal of Anthropological Research* 37 (1981): 402–414; Sarah Nelson, "Diversity of the Upper Paleolithic 'Venus' figurines and archaeological mythology," in *Powers of Observation*, eds. Sarah Nelson and Alice Kehoe (Washington, DC: American Anthropological Association, 1990); Costanza Di Capua, "Valdivia figurines and puberty rituals: An hypothesis," *Andean Past* 4 (1994): 229–279.

11 The recent recovery of a number of figurines found in graves was reported by Lauren Talalay, "Body imagery of the ancient Aegean," *Archaeology* 44 (1991): 46–49. For various new hypotheses about the possible functions of figurines see Talalay, "Rethinking the function of clay figurine legs from Neolithic Greece: An argument by analogy," *American Journal of Archaeology* 91 (1987): 161–169, and *Dolls, Deities and Devices: Neolithic Figurines from Franthci Cave, Greece* (Bloomington, IN: Indiana University Press, 1993). See also Tracey Cullen, "Social implications of ceramic style in the Neolithic Peloponnese," *Ancient Technology to Modern Science* (Columbus, OH: The American Ceramic Society, 1985); Alfred Kidder, "Preclassic pottery

figurines of the Guatemalan highlands," in *Archaeology of Southern Mesoamerica* (1965). Recent excavations at the Neolithic site of Kissonerga in Cyprus also suggests a religious use of figurines during birthing rituals. See Edgar Peltenburg and Elizabeth Coring, "Terracotta figurines and ritual at Kissonerga-Mosphilia," in *Cypriote Terracottas,* eds. F. Vandenabeela and R. Laffineur (Brussels: A. G. Leventis Foundation, 1991).

12   Catherine McCoid and LeRoy McDermott, "Toward decolonizing gender: Female vision in the Upper Paleolithic," *American Anthropologist* 98 (1996): 299–324; LeRoy McDermott, "Self-representation in Upper Paleolithic female figurines," *Current Anthropology* 37 (1996): 227–275.

13   The serrations found on this and two other figurines were first discussed as ropes and animal tails on a shaman's costume by Franz Hanchar, "Probleme und Ergebnisse der neuen russischen Urgeschichtsforschung," in *Bericht der Römisch-Germanischen Kommission,* 33 (1951): 25–60. The interpretation that at least some of the Venus figurines might therefore be representations of women shamans was suggested by Ivar Lissner, *Man, God and Magic* (New York: G.P. Putnam's Sons, 1961), 210. These serrations may also represent the type of skimpy string skirt preserved on the body of a young woman found at Egtved, Denmark, dating from the Bronze Age. Elizabeth Wayland Barber argues in *Women's Work: The First 20,000 Years* (New York: W. W. Norton, 1995), 54–59, that since a skirt made of loose strings cannot have been very warm and it certainly does not answer to our notions of modesty, it may have served to attract the eye precisely to the specifically female sexual areas by framing them and in this way, perhaps, indicate the childbearing ability of the wearer. However, discarded aprons found in Prehistoric Southwestern dry caves bear bloodstains and sometimes even the tiny bones of miscarried fetuses. See Kelley Hays-Gilpin, "Gender ideology and ritual activities," in *Women and Men in the Prehispanic Southwest,* ed. Patricia Crown (Santa Fe, NM: School of American Research Press, 2000), 120.

14   For an illustration of this famous masculine figure see Andreas Lommel, *The World of the Early Hunters* (Chatham, Kent: Evelyn, Adams and Mackay, 1967), 129. Lotte Motz, in the concluding arguments of *The Faces of the Goddess* (New York: Oxford University Press, 1995) 185–186, makes a doubly erroneous statement that "the hunt is a specifically male pursuit, and thus no female imagery, pointing to a feminine sacrality is to be seen in the Paleolithic caves." The fact that women worldwide have long been involved in "the hunt" is documented in chapter five, and that there is female imagery pointing to a feminine sacrality is clearly shown in the engravings at Pech-Merle.

15   André Leroi-Gourhan, *Préhistoire de l'art occidental* (Paris: Mazenod, 1965), 100. Andrée Rosenfeld, in "Profile figures: Schematization of the human figure in the Magdalenian culture of Europe," in *Form in Indigenous Art: Schematisation in the Art of Aboriginal Australia and Prehistoric Europe,* eds. Peter Ucko and Andrée Rosenfeld (Canberra: Australian Institute of Aboriginal Studies, 1977), rejected the bison connection altogether and mentioned the striking visual parallel with the engravings in Nubia. For more information on these African engravings see Peter Smith, "A preliminary report on the recent prehistoric investigation near Kom Ombo, Upper Egypt," in *Fouilles en Nubie 1961–1963* (Cairo: Antiquities Department of Egypt, 1967).

16   Paul Bahn and Jean Vertut, *Journey Through the Ice Age* (Berkeley: University of California Press, 1997), 16. However, it must be remembered that the interpretation of rock art is highly fluid and historically contingent.

17   The fact that Kalahari San draw and paint on rocks and trees was reported by Lorna
     Marshall, *The !Kung Bushmen of the Kalahari Desert* (New York: Holt Rinehart and
     Winston, 1965). Because there are currently no hunting and gathering peoples left
     in East Africa most rock art scholars today use the San from South Africa for ethno-
     graphic analogy in interpreting ancient African art. See A. Thackeray, "Dating the
     rock art of southern Africa," *South African Archaeological Society Goodwin Series* 4
     (1983): 21–26; Paul Bahn, "Pleistocene images outside Europe," *Proceedings of the
     Prehistoric Society* 57 (1991): 97–102. The most accessible book on Australian rock
     art is Josephine Flood, *Rock Art of the Dreamtime* (Sydney: Angus and Robertson,
     1997).

18   Wilhelm Bleek, "Remarks on Orpen's 'Mythology of the Maluti Bushmen,' " *Cape
     Monthly* (1874): 12; J. David Lewis-Williams, "Ethnography and iconography: As-
     pects of southern San thought and art," *Man* 15 (1980): 469; Thomas Dowson,
     Rock Engravings for Southern Africa (Johannesburg: Witwatersrand University Press,
     1992), 471.

19   J. David Lewis-Williams reports that "the two men are preceded by two Bushwomen,
     of whom one wears a cap on her head" ("Ethnography and iconography," *Man* 15
     [1980]: 469). But then he ignores the gender issue. Later, in his book *The Rock Art
     of Southern Africa* (Cambridge: Cambridge University Press, 1983), he says, "If about
     half the southern Bushmen were medicine men, as is the case among the modern
     Kalahari, it is very probable that at least some of them would also have been painters"
     (24). Since, as he and others have reported elsewhere, one-third of the indigenous
     women of the Kalahari are medicine women, why couldn't the painter have been a
     woman? This Western bias against women artists appears to be at least as strong as
     the bias against women shamans. In a critique of Lewis-Williams's interpretation one
     scholar illustrates this figure but then fails to reinterpret it. See Pieter Jolly "Symbi-
     otic interaction between black farmers and south-eastern San," *Current Anthropology*
     37 (1996): 277–305.

20   Richard Katz, *Boiling Energy: Community Healing Among the Kalahari Kung* (Cam-
     bridge, MA: Harvard University Press, 1982), 227; Richard Katz, Megan Biesele,
     and Verna St. Denis, *Healing Makes Our Hearts Happy* (Rochester, VT: Inner Tradi-
     tions, 1997), 114–119.

21   Wilhelm Bleek, "Remarks on J.M. Orpen's 'Mythology of the Maluti Bushmen,' "
     Cape Monthly Magazine 9 (1874): 15.

22   During a three-month expedition to the Kondoa district of central Tanzania Mary
     Leakey, her husband, and an Italian assistant recorded the rock art at 168 sites. In
     43 of these sites they traced over 1,600 figures. These three forms, painted in dark
     purple-red, were from the site of Kea Mtea, where some of the finest paintings and
     most interesting scenes were found. See Mary Leakey, *Africa's Vanishing Art: The
     Rock Paintings of Tanzania* (Garden City, NY: Doubleday, 1983), 99.

23   Richard Katz and Megan Biesele, "!Kung healing: The symbolism of sex roles and
     culture change," in *The Past and Future of !Kung Ethnography: Critical Reflections and
     symbolic perspectives,* ed. Megan Biesele (Hamburg: Helmut Buske Verlag, 1987). See
     Thomas Dowson, who describes the visual and somatic hallucinations the San ex-
     perience during trance, *Rock Engravings from Southern Africa* (Johannesburg: Wit-
     watersrand University Press, 1992), 67–75.

24   There is evidence of women as mural painters in a number of societies, among them
     the Vedda of Sri Lanka and some Australian Aboriginal groups. Ancient evidence is
     given by women's grave goods in the Neolithic city of Çatal Hüyük in Anatolia

(Turkey), which include shell painters' palettes, still filled with colored earth and vegetable oil binder, that are buried with females. H. R. Hays, *The Dangerous Sex: The Myth of Feminine Evil* (New York: Pocket Books, 1972).

Chapter Four
SUMMONING WHALES, SERPENTS, AND BEARS:
WOMEN SHAMANS IN HISTORY

1   Edith Turner, *The Hands Feel It: Healing and Spirit Presence among a Northern Alaskan People* (De Kalb: Northern Illinois University Press, 1996), 160. See also Tom Lowenstein, *Ancient Land: Sacred Whale* (London: Harvill Press, 1994), 44–46, 182–183.
2   Edith Turner, "Behind Inupiaq reincarnation: Cosmological cycling," in *Amerindian Rebirth,* eds. Antonia Mills and Richard Slobodin (Toronto: University of Toronto Press, 1994), 73.
3   Gilbert Herdt, *Sambia: Ritual and Gender in New Guinea* (New York: Holt, Rinehart and Winston, 1987) and "Spirit familiars in the religious imagination of Sambia shamans," in *The Religious Imagination in New Guinea,* eds. Gilbert Herdt and Michele Stephens (New Brunswick: Rutgers University Press, 1989).
4   Eleanor Leacock, *Myths of Male Dominance* (New York: Monthly Review Press, 1981), 277.
5   Lauri Honko, "Role-taking of the shaman," *Temenos* 4 (1969); 27.
6   This striped sash is also worn by an important male figure, Bird Jaguar IV, whose bloodletting is commemorated on Lintel 17 at Yaxchilán. See Carolyn Tate, *Yaxchilan: The Design of a Maya Ceremonial City* (Austin: University of Texas Press, 1992), 88.
7   Victoria Schlesinger, *Animals and Plants of the Ancient Maya* (Austin: University of Texas Press, 2001), 268–272. Davíd Carrasco, *Religions of Mesoamerica* (New York: Harper and Row, 1990), 112–113, noted that female blood, shed in a sacrificial manner from the tongue opens the passageway between heaven and earth. He also mentioned that Maya kings pierced their genitals and collected the blood "imitating the capacity of women to menstruate and to give birth." Maya kings are referred to as "Mother of the Gods," who give birth or bring the gods into being on earth through bloodletting. In this way the king becomes both a male ruler and a female nurturer of the gods. These dual-gendered rulers are common in Mesoamerica. See Rosemary Joyce, *Gender and Power in Prehispanic Mesoamerica* (Austin: University of Texas Press, 2000), 169–170, 191–192.
8   See Tate, *Yaxchilan,* 119–121, 203–208; Linda Schele, *Hidden Faces of the Maya* (New York: Alti, 1997), 19–22. Tatiana Proskouriakoff suggested that the scene represented a bloodletting ritual by the woman who had invoked an ancestor while holding a bowl of sacrificial objects. She also implied that the serpent was a personification of the sky where this ancestor lived. See Proskouriakoff, "Hand grasping fish and associated glyphs on Classic Maya monuments," in *Mesoamerican Writing Systems,* ed. Elizabeth Benson (Washington, DC: Dumbarton Oaks, 1973), and *Maya History* (Austin: University of Texas Press, 1993), 89–90. For a detailed discussion of this lintel see also Simon Martin and Nikolai Grube, *Chronicle of the Maya Kings and Queens* (London: Thames and Hudson, 2000), 122–137. A different scenario in which Lady K'ab'al Xook is the eldest wife of the king, Shield Jaguar II, and bitter rival of his co-wife, Lady Eveningstar, is found in David Freidel and Linda Schele,

"Maya royal women: A lesson in Precolumbian history," in *Gender in Cross-Cultural Perspective,* eds. Caroline Brettell and Carolyn Sargent (Upper Saddle River, NJ: Prentice Hall, 1997), 76–78. Rosemary Joyce suggested that she might have been a dual-gendered being, or a male ruler dressed in a combination of masculine and feminine clothing. See her book: *Gender and Power in Prehispanic Mesoamerica* (Austin: University of Texas Press, 2000), 86, 192.

9 Arthur Waley, *The Nine Songs: A Study of Shamanism in Ancient China* (London: George Allen and Unwin, 1955), 12. The sexual character of these songs was obscured by a number of commentators, who treated them as allegorical appeals by a presumably male author to his ruler. See Gary Seaman, "The dark emperor: Central Asian origins in Chinese shamanism," in *Shamanism in Central Asia and the Americas,* eds. Gary Seaman and Jane Day (Niwot: University Press of Colorado, 1994), 231.

10 Sarah Nelson, "Gender hierarchy and the queens of Silla," in *Sex and Gender Hierarchies,* ed. B. D. Miller (Cambridge: Cambridge University Press, 1993).

11 Won-Yong Kim and Richard Pearson, "Three royal tombs: New discoveries in Korean archaeology," *Archaeology* 30 (1977): 302–313; Won-Yong Kim, *Recent Archaeological Discoveries in the Republic of Korea* (Tokyo: UNESCO, 1981).

12 For more about mirrors in shamanism, including photo documentation, see Mihály Hoppál, *Das Buch der Schamen: Europa und Asien* (Luzern, Switzerland: Motovun Books, 2002), 94–105.

13 Virlana Tkacz et al., *Shanar: Dedication Ritual of a Buryat Shaman in Siberia as Conducted by Bayir Rinshinov* (New York: Parabola Press, 2002), 40.

14 See Caroline Humphrey, "Shamanic practices and the state in northern Asia: Views from the center and periphery," in *Shamanism, History, and the State,* eds. Nicholas Thomas and Caroline Humphrey (Ann Arbor: University of Michigan Press, 1994), 193–195; Manabu Waida, "Conceptions of state and kingship in early Japan," *Zeitschrift für Religions und Geistesgeschichte* 28 (1976): 97–112; "Notes on the sacred kingship in central Asia," *Numen* 23 (1976): 179–190.

15 Margaret Nowak and Stephen Durrant, *The Tale of the Nishan Shamaness: A Manchu Folk Epic* (Seattle: University of Washington Press, 1977); Stephen Durrant, "The Nishan shaman caught in cultural contradiction," *Signs* 5 (1979): 338–347. See also Fu Yuguang, "The transmission and value of the Manchu shamanic epic Wubuxiben Mama," in *Shamanism in Performing Arts,* eds. Tae-gon Kim and Mihály Hoppál (Budapest: Akadémiai Kiadó, 1995); Edward Schafer, *The Divine Woman: Dragon Ladies and Rain Maidens in T'ang Literature* (Berkeley: University of California Press, 1973). For more details about the history and cosmology of Manchu shamanism see Wu Bing-an, "Shamans in Manchuria," in *Shamanism Past and Present,* eds. Mihály Hoppál and Ogto von Sadovszky (Budapest: Ethnographic Institute, 1989); Guo Shuyun, "Social functions of the Manchu shaman," in *Shamans and Cultures,* eds. M. Hoppál and K. D. Howard (Budapest: Akadémiai Kiadó, 1993) and Daniel Kister, "Present-day shamanism in northern China and the Amur region," *Shaman* 7 (1999): 77–95.

16 Barbara Ehrenreich and Deirdre English, *Witches, Midwives, and Nurses: A History of Women Healers* (New York: The Feminist Press at The City University of New York, 1973); Carlo Ginzburg, *The Night Battles: Witchcraft and Agrarian Cults in the Sixteenth and Seventeenth Centuries* (Baltimore: Johns Hopkins University Press, 1983); B. P. Levack, *The Witch Hunt in Early Modern Europe* (London: Longman, 1987); Ruth Behar, "Sexual witchcraft, colonialism and women's powers: Views from the

Mexican inquisition," in *Sexuality and Marriage in Latin America*, ed. Asunción Lavrin (Lincoln: University of Nebraska Press, 1989); James Brain, "An anthropological perspective on the witchcraze," in *The Politics of Gender in Early Modern Europe*, eds. J. R. Brink, A. P. Coudert, and M. C. Horowitz (Kirksville: Sixteenth Century Journal Publishers, 1989); David Harley, "Historians as demonologists: The myth of the midwife witch," *Journal of the Society for the Social History of Medicine* 3 (1990): 1–26.

17   Joseph Deguignes, *Histoire générale des Huns, des Turcs, des Mogols, et des autres Tartares occidentaux*, 5 vols. (Paris, 1756–1758); John Bell, *Travels from St. Petersburg in Russia, to Diverse Parts of Asia* (London, 1763); Jean Chappe d'Auteroche, *A Journey into Siberia, made by order of the King of France* (London, 1770). Johann Gottlieb Georgi, *Beschreibung aller Nationen des Russischen Reichs, ihrer Lebensart, Religion, Gebräuche, Wohnungen, Kleidungen und übrigen Merkwürdigkeitrn* 4 parts (St. Petersburg, 1776–1780); William Coxe, *Account of the Russian Discoveries between Asia and America, To which are added, The Conquest of Siberia, and the History of the Transactions and Commerce between Russia and China* (London, 1780); Johann Anton, *Güldenstädt, Reisen durch Russland und im Caucasischen Gebürge* (St. Petersburg, 1781); Giuseppe Acerbi, *Travels through Sweden, Finland, and Lapland, to the North Cape in the Years 1798 and 1799* (London, 1802). For an overview of some of this material see Gloria Flaherty, *Shamanism and the Eighteenth Century* (Princeton, NJ: Princeton University Press, 1992).

18   S. Ia. Serov, "Guardians and spirit-masters of Siberia," in *Crossroads of Continents: Cultures of Siberia and Alaska*, eds. William W. Fitzhugh and Aron Crowell (Washington, DC: Smithsonian Institution Press, 1988), 347, Maria Antoinette Czaplicka, *Aboriginal Siberia: A Study in Social Anthropology* (Oxford: Clarendon Press, 1914), 199; Esther Jacobson, *The Deer Goddess of Ancient Siberia: A Study in the Ecology of Belief* (Leiden: E.J. Brill, 1993), 174–175. In Central Asia, Uzbek shamans, both male and female, wear a woman's dress. See V. N. Basilov, "Vestiges of transvestism in Central-Asian shamanism," in *Shamanism in Siberia*, eds. Vilmos Diószegi and Mihály Hoppál (Budapest: Akadémiai Kiadó, 1978), 283, figures 1 and 2.

19   Earl of Southesk, *Saskatchewan and the Rocky Mountains: A Diary and Narrative of Travel, Sport, and Adventure during a Journey through the Hudson's Bay Company's Territories in 1859–1960* (Toronto: James Campbell and Son, 1875), 329.

20   Matilda Coxe Stevenson, *The Zuñi Indians: Their Mythology, Esoteric Fraternities, and Ceremonies* (Washington, DC: Bureau of American Ethnology, 1904), 490–501.

21   Knud Rasmussen, *Intellectual Culture of the Iglulik Eskimos* (Copenhagen: Gyldendalske Boghandel, Nordisk Forlag, 1929), 38–39.

22   The Caucasian narrative abbreviated here is from Andrejs Johansons, "The shamaness of the Abkhazians," *History of Religions* 11 (1972): 251–252.

23   For a description of the goddess Grandmother Growth see Robert Zingg, *The Huichols: Primitive Artists* (New York: G. E. Stechert, 1938), 320–326. Discussions of these and other Huichol myths are found in Robert Zingg, *Huichol Mythology* (unpublished manuscript located at the School of American Research, Santa Fe, NM); Marina Anguiano Fernández, "Müüqui Cuevixa: 'Time to Bid the Dead Farewell,' " in *People of the Peyote*, eds. Stacey Schaefer and Peter Furst (Albuquerque: University of New Mexico Press, 1996), 380–384; Stacey Schaefer and Peter Furst, "Introduction," in *People of the Peyote*, 13–14.

24   All of Arrow Man's drawings, together with typed Spanish transcriptions of his oral narratives, are filed at the Huichol Center for Cultural Survival and Traditional Arts,

created by anthropologist Susan Valdez and her Huichol artist husband, Mariano Valdez. For a discussion of Arrow Man's shamanic drawing illustrated here see Susan Valdez, "Problem solving in a threatened culture: The practice of humanthropology among the Huichol," in *Mirrors of the Gods*, ed. S. Bernstein (San Diego: San Diego Museum of Man, 1989).

25 Barbara Myerhoff, *Peyote Hunt* (Ithaca: Cornell University Press, 1974), 279, and Stacey Schaefer, "The crossing of the souls: Peyote, perception, and meaning among the Huichol Indians," in *People of the Peyote*, 142–147, describe the practices of women shamans. For more about the gendered division of shamanic labor elsewhere in Mesoamerica see Barbara Tedlock, *Time and the Highland Maya* (Albuquerque: University of New Mexico Press, 1982), 47–85, and Brad Huber, "The recruitment of Nahua curers: Role conflict and gender," *Ethnology* 29 (1990): 170.

26 Yih Yuan Li, "Shamanism in Taiwan: An anthropological inquiry," in *Culture-Bound Syndromes, Ethnopsychiatry, and Alternative Therapies*, ed. W. P. Lebra (Honolulu: The University Press of Hawaii, 1972); Shirley Lin, *The Role of Shamanism in the Health Care System of Urban Taiwan*. MA Thesis, SUNY Buffalo (1985); Josiane Cauquelin, "The impact of Japanese colonialism on Puyuma (Taiwan) shamanism," in *Shamans and Cultures*, eds. M. Hoppál and K. Howard (Budapest: Akadémiai Kiadó, 1993).

27 However, when these languages are translated into another language, such as German, that requires gendered pronouns there is no excuse not to make a clear distinction between men and women shamans. This is indeed what the great modern student of shamanism, Mihály Hoppál, did in his wonderful illustrated book on shamanism, *Das Buch der Schamanen*. Here for the first time ever we see many (more than forty) photographs of women shamans in Europe and Asia.

Chapter Five
THE DISAPPERING ACT:
HOW FEMALE SHAMANISM WAS ECLIPSED

1 For a discussion of this whip or "hand icon [or idol]," see Ágnes Birtalan, "The *gariin ongon* 'hand-idol' of the Mongolian shaman," in *Shamanism and Performing Arts*, eds. Tae-gon Kim and Mihály Hoppál (Budapest: Akadémiai Kiadó, 1995), 135–136. Among Buryat Mongols the "whip" of five-colored silk cloths is known as the *tasiyur*. See Krystyna Chabros, *Beckoning Fortune: A Study of the Mongol Dalalya Ritual* (Wiesbaden: Otto Harrassowicz, 1992), 187.

2 Altayans are one of the three groups of nationalities in Siberia. They include the Mongols, Tungus (Evenki), and various Turkic peoples such as the Tuvans, Tatars, Khakass, Yakut, and Altai. They originated in the region between the Altai Mountains in the west and Lake Baikal in the northeast and share related languages. They have a mixed pastoral and hunting lifestyle and common shamanic traditions. For more about the history of women shamans among Altayan peoples see Vera P. Diakonova, "Shamans in traditional Tuvinian society," in *Ancient Traditions: Shamanism in Central Asia and the Americas*, eds. Gary Seaman and Jane S. Day (Niwot: University Press of Colorado, 1994), 245–248.

3 Klaus Hesse, "On the history of Mongolian shamanism in anthropological perspective," *Anthropos* 82 (1987): 403–413; Ulla Johansen, "Zur Geschichte des Schamanismus," in *Synkretismus in den Religionen Zentralasiens*, eds. Walther Heissig and

H. J. Klimkeit (Wiesbaden: Otto Harrassowicz, 1987) and "Further thoughts on the history of shamanism," *Shaman* 7 (1999): 40–58; John Lee Maddox, *The Medicine Man: A Sociological Study of the Character and Evolution of Shamanism* (New York: Macmillan, 1923), 88; M. Vasilevich, "Early concepts about the universe among the Evenks (materials)," in *Studies in Siberian Shamanism,* ed. Henry N. Michael (Toronto: University of Toronto Press, 1963), 75; and A. F. Anisimov, "Cosmological concepts of the peoples of the north," in *Studies in Siberian Shamanism,* ed. Henry N. Michael (Toronto: University of Toronto Press, 1963), 167–168.

4　Sergei Shirokogoroff, *Psychomental Complex of the Tungus* (London: Kegan Paul, 1935), 269, 422.

5　Joseph Campbell, *The Masks of God* (Harmondsworth: Penguin, 1959), 372; Waldemar Jochelson, *The Koryak* (New York: G. E. Stechert, 1908) and *The Yukaghir and the Yukaghirized Tungus* (New York: G. E. Stechert, 1926).

6　Mircea Eliade, *Shamanism: Archaic Technique of Ecstasy* (New York: Bolingen Foundation, 1964), 4, 124, 301, 363, 453, 455, 465. A Korean scholar has noted that Eliade's mistaken impression of Korean shamanism was partly due to his reliance on a single work by C. Hentze. See Hungyoun Cho, "An archetypal myth and its reality in Korean shamanism," in *Re-Discovery of Shamanic Heritage,* eds. Mihály Hoppál and Gábor Kósa (Budapest: Akadémiai Kiadó, 2002), 255–263. Early sources on Chinese shamanism include Jan Jacob Marie de Groot, *The Religious System of China* (Leiden, 1939), 6:1203; Han-yi Feng and John Schryock, "The black magic in China known as *ku,*" *Journal of the American Oriental Society* 5 (1935): 1–30; Eduard Erkes, "Der Schamanistische Ursprung des Chinesischen Ahnenkultis," *Sinologica* 2 (1950): 258–262. An early Chinese book, *Yijing,* links the word for shaman, *wu,* with a feminine trigram meaning "*dui,* the fertile marsh, the youngest daughter, the shamaness." From this and other sources it is clear that beginning as early as 1500 BCE, the shamans, called *wu* regardless of sex, were mostly women.

7　Eliade, "Recent works on shamanism: A review article," *History of Religions* 1 (1961): 180; Matthias Eder, "Schamanismus in Japan," *Paideuma* 6 (1958): 367–380; Carmen Blacker, *The Catalpa Bow: A Study of Shamanistic Practices in Japan* (London: George Allen and Unwin, 1975).

8　Carol Christ, "Mircea Eliade and the feminist paradigm shift," *Journal of Feminist Studies in Religion* 7 (1991): 75–94; Rosalind Shaw, "Feminist anthropology and the gendering of religious studies," in *Religion and Gender,* ed. Ursula King (Oxford: Blackwell, 1995).

9　Piers Vitebsky, *The Shaman: Voyages of the Soul, Trance, Ecstasy, and Healing from Siberia to the Amazon* (Boston: Little, Brown and Company, 1995), 32. See also Andreas Lommel, *The World of the Early Hunters* (Chatham, Kent: Evelyn, Adams and Mackay, 1967), 7.

10　Michael Ripinsky-Naxon, *The Nature of Shamanism: Substance and Function of a Religious Metaphor* (Albany: State University of New York Press, 1993), 127. See also Robin Fox, *Kinship and Marriage* (London: Pelican Books, 1967); Sherwood Washburn and Chet Lancaster, "The evolution of hunting," in *Man the Hunter,* eds. Richard B. Lee and Irven DeVore (Chicago: Aldine, 1968), 293–303.

11　George Murdock placed the sexual division of labor at the beginning of humanness in hunting-gathering societies and asserted that it was biologically determined. See George Murdock, *Social Structure* (New York: Macmillan, 1949), 7. Paleoanthropologists, however, have recognized the importance of narrative in their discipline, and a number of articles and books on the subject of bias in the study of fossil humans have appeared. See N. Eldredge and I. Tattersall, *Myths of Human Evolution* (New York: Columbia University Press, 1982) and Misia Landau, "Human evolution as narrative," *American Scientist* 72 (1984), 262–267.

12 Richard Lee, "What hunters do for a living, or, how to make out on scarce resources," *Man the Hunter*, eds. Richard B. Lee and Irven DeVore (Chicago: Aldine, 1968), 30–48. For more information on the specifics of hunting and gathering among the Bushman see Richard Lee, *The !Kung San: Men, Women, and Work in a Foraging Society* (New York: Cambridge University Press, 1979). See also Wayne Suttles, "Coping with abundance: Subsistence on the Northwest Coast," in *Man the Hunter*, eds. Richard B. Lee and Irven DeVore (Chicago: Aldine, 1968), 56–68. Marshall Sahlins in his book *Stone Age Economics* (Chicago: Aldine Publishing, 1972) examined statistics he abstracted from primary research reports on traditional hunting-gathering societies and published this information together with his interpretation of an incredibly short workweek for gatherer-hunters.

13 On the Labrador Peninsula a northeastern Algonkian-speaking hunting and gathering group, known as the Innu (Montagnais-Naskapi), lived matrilocally. See Eleanor Leacock, "Matrilocality in a simple hunting economy," *Southwestern Journal of Anthropology* 11 (1955). Until the late-1960s the patriarchal model was actively propagated by Julian Steward, "The economic and social basis of primitive bands," in *Essays in Anthropology presented to A. L. Kroeber in Celebration of His Sixtieth Birthday*, ed. Robert H. Lowie (Berkeley: University of California Press, 1936) and Elman Service, *Primitive Social Organization* (New York: Random House, 1962). They depicted hunter-gatherer social organization as patrilocal, exogamous, and territorial and related this to a scarcity of resources. This model was later rejected in favor of one that depicted fluid, constantly changing groupings in a world of affluence where gathering outranked hunting in its contribution to subsistence. See David Riches, *Northern Nomadic Hunter-Gatherers* (London: Academic Press, 1982), 56–106, and Nurit Bird-David, "Hunter-gatherers and other people: A re-examination," in *Hunter and Gatherers*, eds. Tim Ingold, David Riches, and James Woodburn (New York: Berg, 1988). The cross-cultural variation in hunter-gatherer residence patterns reveals that less than two-thirds of hunting societies are patrilocal and that it is even less frequent among non-equestrian, non-fishing-dependent hunters. See Kathleen Gough, "The origin of the family," in *Toward an Anthropology of Women*, ed. Rayna R. Reiter (New York: Monthly Review Press, 1975). The tendency toward matrilocality increases with women's relative contribution to subsistence and with increased dependence on gathering.

14 The gathering basket and the baby sling, as the first humanizing tools, were suggested by Sally Linton, "Woman the gatherer: Male bias in anthropology," in *Women in Cross-Cultural Perspective*, ed. Sue Ellen Jacobs (Champaign, IL: University of Illinois Press, 1971). See Frances Dahlberg's edited volume entitled *Woman the Gatherer* (New Haven: Yale University Press, 1981) for more information on the lives of female foragers.

15 Joan Gero, "Genderlithics: Women's roles in stone tool production," in *Engendering Archaeology: Women and Prehistory*, eds. J. M. Gero and M. W. Conkey (Oxford: Blackwell, 1991); Alice Kehoe, "Points and lines," in *Powers of Observation: Alternative Views in Archeology*, eds. Sarah Nelson and Alice Kehoe (Washington, DC: Archaeological Papers of the American Anthropological Association, 1990); Simon James, "Drawing inferences: Visual reconstructions in theory and practice," in *The Cultural Life of Images: Visual Representation in Archaeology*, ed. Brian Leigh

Molyneaux (London: Routledge, 1997). Patricia O'Brien, "Evidence for the antiquity of gender roles in the Central Plains tradition," in *The Archaeology of Gender,* eds. Dale Walde and Noreen D. Willows (Calgary: Archaeological Association, University of Calgary, 1990) argues that women in the thirteenth century produced some of the stone tools at the Holidome site near Manhattan, Kansas.

16   For more information about the lives of these new women hunters see Christine Thomas, "They became outdoors women," *Deer and Deer Hunting,* June 1992, 49–54; Kathy Etling, "Women afield," *American Hunter,* January 1992, 30–33, 66–67; Mary Zeiss Stange, "Women afield: The invisible hunters," *Sports Afield,* January 1994, 98–99; Michelle Leigh Smith, "Club of legal huntresses kills to network," *The National Law Journal,* April 25, 1994, A10; Sharon Begley, "Let's talk turkey," *Newsweek,* October 30, 1995, 71–72; and Mary Zeiss Stange, *Woman the Hunter* (Boston: Beacon Press, 1997).

17   A rendition of this drawing, found in a rock shelter near Oenpelli, Northern Territory, Australia, together with mention of women in other hunting scenes, can be found in Josephine Flood's *Rock Art of the Dreamtime* (Sydney: Angus and Robertson, 1997), 274–278.

18   Lyn Wadley, "The invisible meat providers: Women in the Stone Age of South Africa," in *Gender in African Archaeology,* ed. Susan Kent (Walnut Creek, CA: Alta Mira Press, 1997); Colin Turnbull, *Wayward Servants: The Two Worlds of the African Pygmies* (Garden City, NY: American Museum of Natural History, 1965); M. Ichikawa, "An examination of the hunting-dependent life of the Mbuti Pygmies, eastern Zaire," *African Studies Monographs* 4 (1983): 69; T. Hart and J. Hart, "The ecological basis of hunter-gatherer subsistence in African rain forests: The Mbuti of Zaire," *Human Ecology* 14 (1986): 29–55.

19   Agnes Estioko-Griffin and P. Bion Griffin, "Woman the hunter: The Agta," in *Woman the Gatherer,* ed. Frances Dahlberg (New Haven: Yale University Press, 1981); Agnes Estioko-Griffin, "Women hunters: The implications for Pleistocene prehistory and contemporary ethnography," in *Women in Asia and the Pacific,* ed. Madeleine J. Goodman (Honolulu: University of Hawaii Press, 1985); M. Goodman et al., "The compatibility of hunting and mothering among the Agta hunter-gatherers of the Philippines," *Sex Roles* 12 (1985): 1199–1209; Agnes Estioko-Griffin, "Daughters of the forest," *Natural History* 95 (1986).

20   K. L. Endicott, "The conditions of egalitarian male-female relationships in foraging societies," *Canberra Anthropology* 4 (1981): 1–10; Sheila McKell, "An axe to grind: More ripping yarns from Australian prehistory," in *Reader in Gender Archaeology,* eds. Kelley Hays-Gilpin and David S. Whitley (New York: Routledge, 1998); Jenny Green, "Utopian women," in *Fighters and Singers: The Lives of Some Australian Aboriginal Women,* eds. I. White, D. Barwick, and B. Meeham (Sydney: George Allen and Unwin, 1985), 59–61.

21   Vilmos Diószegi, *Tracing Shamans in Siberia: The Story of an Ethnographical Research Expedition* (Oosterhout, the Netherlands: Anthropological Publications, 1968), 140; Julie Cruikshank, *Life Lived Like a Story: Life Stories of Three Yukon Native Elders* (Lincoln: University of Nebraska Press, 1990), 227; William Thalbitzer, *The Ammassalik Eskimo Contributions to the Ethnology of the East Greenland Natives* (Copenhagen: Bianco Luno, 1915), 34; M. G. Levin and L. P. Potopov, *The Peoples of Siberia* (Chicago: University of Chicago Press, 1964), 600ff.; Lee Guemple, "Men and women, husbands and wives: The role of gender in traditional Inuit society," *Études Inuit Studies* 10 (1986): 1–2, 9–24.

22   Diane Bell, *Ngarrindjeri Wurruwarrin: A World That Is, Was, and Will Be* (North Melbourne: Spinifex, 1998), 342–343.

23   Norman Whitten, *Sacha Runa: Ethnicity and Adaptation of Ecuadorian Jungle Quichua* (Chicago: University of Chicago Press, 1976) and *Sicuanga Runa: The Other Side of Development in Amazonian Ecuador* (Urbana: University of Illinois Press, 1985).

24   Stacey Schaefer, *To Think With a Good Heart: Wixárika Women, Weavers, and Shamans* (Salt Lake City: University of Utah Press, 2002).

25   Guadalupe de la Cruz Ríos (1917–1999) taught Ramón yarn painting which they often worked on together, although many paintings were subsequently credited by collectors and museums solely to him.

26   Alfred Métraux, "The Guarani: The tropical forest tribe," *Handbook of South American Indians,* ed. Julian Steward (Washington, DC: Bureau of American Ethnology, 1948), 88; Bradford Keeney, *Guarani Shamans of the Forest* (Philadelphia: Ringing Rocks Press, 2000), 81–84.

27   Diana Riboli, "Shamanic rites of the Terai Chepangs," *East and West* 44 (1994): 327–352; "Shamanic visual art in Nepal," in *Tunsuriban: Shamanism in the Chepang of Southern and Central Nepal* (Kathmandu: Mandala Book Point, 2000). Feminine erasure has also occurred among women who were the wives of Euro-American politicians, diplomats, priests, corporate executives, and scholars. They were informally incorporated into their husband's careers as helpers or assistants. For more about the erasure of wives in Europe and North America see my essay "Works and wives: On the sexual division of textual labor," in *Women Writing Culture: Culture Writing Women,* eds. Ruth Behar and Deborah Gordon (Berkeley: University of California Press, 1995).

28   Géza Róheim's discussion of Hungarian *táltoses* appears in his essay "Hungarian shamanism," *Psychoanalysis and the Social Sciences* 3 (1951): 131–169.

29   For a discussion of female shamans in Hungary see Tekla Dömötör, "The problem of the Hungarian female *táltos*," in *Shamanism in Eurasia,* ed. Mihály Hoppál (Budapest: Akadémiai Kiadó, 1984); Mihály Hoppál, "The role of shamanism in Hungarian ethnic identity," *Danubian Historical Studies* 1 (1987): 34–43; Izabella Horváth, "A comparative study of the shamanistic motifs in Hungarian and Turkic folk tales," in *Shamanism in Performing Arts,* eds. Tae-gon Kim and Mihály Hoppál (Budapest: Akadémiai Kiadó, 1995), 159–170; László Kürti, "Eroticism, sexuality, and gender reversal in Hungarian culture," in *Gender Reversals and Gender Cultures,* ed. S. P. Ramet (London: Routledge, 1996).

30   The approving quotation of Róheim can be found in Eliade, *Shamanism,* 224–225.

31   See Eliade, *Shamanism,* 4–6. Some studies suggest that mediums and shamans are found in different types of societies. See Erika Bourguignon, *Religion, Altered States of Consciousness, and Social Change* (Columbus: Ohio State University Press, 1973) and Michael Winkelman, *Shamans, Priests, and Witches: A Cross-Cultural Study of Magico-Religious Practitioners* (Tempe: Arizona State University Press, 1992). The gendering of this difference began in the 1940s when ethnographers began to discuss the idea that ritualized possession states were a way for women to achieve social prestige. See Raymond Prince, "Foreword," in *Case Studies in Spirit Possession,* eds. Vincent Crapanzano and Vivian Garrison (New York: John Wiley and Sons, 1977), xi. The British anthropologist Ioan Lewis in his influential book *Ecstatic Religion* (Middlesex: Penguin Books, 1971) described what he saw as a worldwide pattern of possession cults as a form of indirect social and religious protest by women. More

recently, however, he backed away from this interpretation and in his book *Religion in Context* (Cambridge: Cambridge University Press, 1986) noted that "spirit possession" and "ecstatic flight of the soul" are serial phases in the assumption of the shamanistic career. As Wolfgang Jilek has remarked, "the possession state has been reserved for non-Western cultures and for cases not approved by Christian authorities" which is "an arbitrary convention indicative of Euro-centric bias." See his *Indian Healing: Shamanic Ceremonialism in the Pacific Northwest Today* (Surry, BC: Hancock House, 1982), 23. For a scholarly, though sympathetic, ethnography portraying recent trance possession or "channeling" practices among women in Santa Fe, New Mexico, see Michael Brown, *The Channeling Zone: American Spirituality in an Anxious Age* (Cambridge, MA: Harvard University Press, 1997). Also see Michael Harner, *The Way of the Shaman: A Guide to Power and Healing* (San Francisco: HarperSanFrancisco, 1980).

32   Susan Sered, *Priestess, Mother, Sacred Sister* (New York: Oxford University Press, 1994), 186–187. This dichotomy between transcendence, as beyond experience, outside oneself, and thereby unknowable, and its opposite, immanence, that which is experiential, present, or indwelling in form, is from the philosopher Immanuel Kant. Sered does not include shamanism in her category of "religions dominated by women." The ethnographic literature is studded with mantras to the prominence of women worldwide in so-called "possession cults." See Ian Hogbin, *Law and Order in Polynesia* (London: Christopher's, 1934), who notes how women are mediums consulted for diseases ascribed to possession by the spirits of ancestors. Reo Fortune, *Manus Religion* (Philadelphia: American Philosophical Society, 1953), 95, asserted that among the Manus of New Guinea, while women may be spiritually disenfranchised with the paternal Sir Ghost cult, they are spiritually enfranchised in possession cults.

33   Enid Nelson, "Gendered possession and communication among the Rejang of Sumatra," *Indonesia Circle* 67 (1995): 199–215; Ruth-Inge Heinze, *Trance and Healing in Southeast Asia Today* (Bangkok: White Lotus, 1988).

34   Åke Hultkrantz, *Shamanic Healing and Ritual Drama* (New York: Crossroad, 1992), 65. This statement about the lack of women shamans among Great Basin peoples is contradicted by the ethnographic work of Willard Park among the Northern Paiutes, *Shamanism in Western North America: A Study in Cultural Relationships* (Evanston, IL: Northwestern University Press, 1938). Park spent three summers gathering data on shamanism. One of his key informants was the famous shaman Rosie Plummer and her daughter, Daisy Lopez, who was undergoing shamanic apprenticeship at the time. Park also stated, "The shaman's calling is open to both sexes among nearly all of the tribes west of the Rocky Mountains" (p. 88). For a sensitive discussion of the possible reasons for male bias in describing aboriginal healing in Canada see James Waldram, D. Ann Herring, and T. Kue Young, *Aboriginal Health in Canada: Historical, Cultural, and Epidemiological Perspectives* (Toronto: University of Toronto Press, 1995).

35   Donald Callaway, Joel Janetski, and Omer Stewart, "Ute," in *Handbook of North American Indians,* vol. 11: *Great Basin,* ed. Warren L. D'Azevedo (Washington, DC: Smithsonian Institution, 1986); Robert Ruby and John Brown, *Myron Eells and the Puget Sound Indians* (Seattle: Superior Publishing, 1976); Pamela Amoss, *Coast Salish Spirit Dancing: The Survival of an Ancestral Religion* (Seattle: University of Washington Press, 1978); Sam Gill and Irene Sullivan, *Dictionary of Native American Mythology* (New York: Oxford University Press, 1992).

36   This sculpture, illustrated by Marius Barbeau, *Medicine Men on the North Pacific Coast* (Ottawa: National Museums of Canada, 1958), 33, may have been obtained in 1939 from the sculptor Amos Watson. Today it is part of the Reverend Raley collection at City Hall in Vancouver, Canada. For more about these figurines see John Swanton, *Contributions to the Ethnology of the Haida* (New York: G. E. Stechert, 1905); Carol Sheehan, *Pipes That Won't Smoke; Coal That Won't Burn: Haida Sculpture in Argillite* (Calgary: Glenbow Museum, 1981), 95–104.

37   See Edward Nelson, *The Eskimo About Bering Strait* (Washington, DC: Bureau of American Ethnology, 1899), 427; Therkel Mathiassen, "Diary extracts," *Intellectual Culture of the Caribou Eskimos*, ed. Knud Rasmussen, (1930), Copenhagen: Glydendalske Boghandel, Nordisk Forlag, 119–129. Vilhjalmur Stefansson, *My Life With the Eskimo* (New York: Collier Books, 1941), 392; Jaarich Oosten, "The diary of Therkel Mathiassen (1922–1923)," in *Shamanism in Eurasia,* ed. Mihály Hoppál (Göttingen: Edition Herodot, 1984), 2:384. The quotation is from Lillian Ackerman, "Gender status in Yup'ik society," *Études Inuit Studies* 14 (1990): 218–219.

38   Alfred Kroeber, "The Yurok religion," in *Handbook of the Indians of California,* ed. Alfred Kroeber (Washington, DC: Government Printing Office, 1925), 53–75. Robert Torrance asserted that among the Eskimo in Siberia, "The female shaman was the exception." See Torrance, *The Spiritual Quest* (Berkeley: University of California Press, 1994), 173.

Chapter Six
THE MYSTICAL UNION:
EROTICISM, ECSTASY, AND TRANCE

1   The concept of "shamanic states of consciousness" was coined by Michael Harner, *The Way of the Shaman: A Guide to Power and Healing* (San Francisco: HarperSanFrancisco, 1980), 25–50.

2   Occasionally scholars even combine these two terms into a single concept, "ecstatic trance." See Felicitas Goodman, *Maya Apocalypse: Seventeen Years with the Women of a Yucatan Village* (Bloomington: Indiana University Press, 2002), xvii-xviii. For an interesting recent discussion of shamanic trance see Diana Riboli, "Trances of initiation, incorporation, and movement: Three different typologies of the shamanic trance," *Shaman* 10 (2002): 161–177.

3   Laurel Kendall, "Of gods and men: Performance, possession, and flirtation in Korean shaman ritual," *Cahiers d'Extrême Asie* 6 (1991): 56.

4   In 1973 a team of researchers at the Johns Hopkins School of Medicine discovered that the human brain contained special opiate receptors. Other scientists then isolated a system of endorphins and encephalins located in areas of the brain connected with the emotions. See Nora Ahlberg, "Some psycho-physiological aspects of ecstasy in recent research," in *Religious Ecstasy,* ed. Nils Holm (Stockholm: Almquist and Wiksell, 1981); Raymond Prince, "Shamans and endorphins," *Ethos* 10 (1982): 409–423. Dancing and drumming produce endogenous opiates. This is due to a combination of prolonged rhythmic exercise, exhaustive anaerobic exercise, and high-intensity exercise activating the central opioid system that releases the peptide beta-endorphin. See P. Thoren et al., "Endorphins and exercise: Physiological mechanisms and clinical implications," *Medicine Science Sports Exercise* 22 (1990): 417–428.

5   See M. Ja. Zornickaja, "Dances of Yakut shamans," in *Shamanism in Siberia,* eds.

Vilmos Diószegi and Mihály Hoppál (Budapest: Akadémiai Kiadó, 1978), 131. It has been experimentally demonstrated that rhythmical stimulus alone is sufficient to bring about major changes in the electrical activity of the brains of normal people. See V. J. Walter and W. G. Walter, "The central effects of rhythmic sensory stimulation," *Electroencephalic Clinical Neurophysiology* 1 (1949): 57–86; Andrew Neher, "A physiological explanation of unusual behavior in ceremonies involving drums," *Human Biology* 34 (1962): 141–160. Dancing and drumming leading to collapse and unconsciousness indicate sympathetic system activation that leads to parasympathetic dominance. Such sympathetic-parasympathetic system activation is responsible for these as well as other features of the shamanic mystical experience. See Charles Laughlin, J. McManus, and E. d'Aquili, *Brain, Symbol, and Experience: Toward a Neurophenomenology of Consciousness* (New York: Columbia University Press, 1992).

6   Rodney Needham, "Percussion and transition," *Man* 2 (1967): 606–614; Thomas Johnston, "Auditory driving hallucinogens, and music-color synesthesia in Tsonga ritual," in *Drugs, Rituals and Altered States of Consciousness,* ed. Brian M. Du Toit (Rotterdam: A. A. Balkema, 1977); Barbara Lex, "The neurobiology of ritual trance," in *The Spectrum of Ritual: A Biogenetic Structural Analysis,* eds. E. d'Aquili, C. Laughlin, and J. McManus (New York: Columbia University Press, 1979); Sandra Harner and Warren Tryon, "Psychoimmunological effects of shamanic drumming," in *Northern Religions and Shamanism,* eds. M. Hoppál and J. Pentikäinen (Budapest: Akadémiai Kiadó, 1992).

7   Warren Ten Houten, "Hemispheric interaction in the brain and the propositional, compositional, and dialectical modes of thought," *Journal of Altered States of Consciousness* 4 (1978): 129–140; Arnold Mandell, "The neurochemistry of religious insight and ecstasy," in *Art of the Huichol Indians,* ed. Kathleen Berrin (San Francisco: Fine Arts Museum, 1978); "Toward a psychobiology of transcendence: God in the brain," in *The Psychobiology of Consciousness,* eds. Julian M. Davidson and Richard J. Davidson (New York: Plenum, 1980), and "Interhemispheric fusion," *Journal of Psychoactive Drugs* 17 (1985): 257–266.

8   Scientific research in energy medicine is reported during the meetings of the International Society for the Study of Subtle Energies and Energy Medicine, and published in the peer-reviewed journal *Subtle Energies.*

9   Margaret Fischer, "Shamanism in Alaska," in *Spirit Versus Scalpel,* eds. Leonard Loeb Adler and B. Runi Mukherji (Westport, CT: Bergin and Garvey, 1995), 142–143.

10 This discussion of bodily energy in South Africa is based on Richard Katz, *Boiling Energy: Community Healing Among the Kalahari Kung* (Cambridge, MA: Harvard University Press, 1982) and Richard Katz, Megan Biesele, and Verna St. Denis, *Healing Makes Our Hearts Happy: Spirituality and Cultural Transformation Among the Kalahari Ju/'hoansi* (Rochester, VT: Inner Traditions, 1997), 116.

11 Marjorie Shostak, *Nisa: The Life and Words of a !Kung Woman* (Cambridge, MA: Harvard University Press, 1983), 296.

12 Diana Riboli, who has worked among a number of ethnic groups in Nepal, with the Fon of Bénin, and with members of the ecstatic cult of the Anastenarides in northern Greece, notes that shamans often fall into uncontrollable trembling. See Diana Riboli, "Trances of initiation, incorporation, and movement: Three different typologies of the shamanic trance," *Shaman* 10 (2002): 165; Jerrold Levy, Raymond Neutra, and Dennis Parket, *Hand Trembling, Frenzy Witchcraft, and Moth Madness: A Study of Navajo Seizure Disorders* (Tucson: University of Arizona Press, 1987); M. D.

Topper, "The traditional Navajo medicine man: Therapist, counselor, and community leader," *Journal of Psychoanalytic Anthropology* 10 (1987): 217–249; Linda Ligon, "Mary Begay: Traditional Navajo medicine woman," *Herbs for Health,* Summer 1996, 34–40; Lori Arviso Alvord and Elizabeth Cohen Van Pelt, *The Scalpel and the Silver Bear: The First Navajo Woman Surgeon Combines Western Medicine and Traditional Healing* (New York: Bantam, 1999).

13   Bradford Kenney, *Walking Thunder: Diné Medicine Woman* (Philadelphia: Ringing Rocks Press, 2001), 124.

14   Knud Rasmussen, *Across Arctic America, Narrative of the Fifth Thule Expedition* (New York: Putnam, 1927), 34. See also Joan Halifax, *Shamanic Voices: A Survey of Visionary Narratives* (New York: E. P. Dutton, 1979), 13; Daniel Merkur, "Breath-soul and wind owner: The many and the one in Inuit religion," *American Indian Quarterly* 7 (1983): 23–39, and *Becoming Half Hidden: Shamanism and Initiation Among the Inuit* (Stockholm: Almquist and Wiksell, 1985).

15   Mantak Chi and Juan Li, *The Inner Structure of Tai Chi* (Huntington, NY: Healing Tao Books, 1996); Eva Wong, *The Shambhala Guide to Taoism* (Boston: Shambhala, 1997), 172–174.

16   Huston Smith, "Augmented power: Taoist hygiene and yoga," *World's Religions* (San Francisco: HarperSanFrancisco, 1991), 130–131; Wong Kiew Kit, *The Art of Chi Kung: Making the Most of Your Vital Energy* (Shattesbury, Dorset: Element, 1993). In Japan there are also three key energies: *tama, kami,* and *ki. Tama* is the animating life force we are all born with. It controls our human physical well-being when we are alive, and when we die it leaves our bodies, transforming itself into *kami* or spiritual energy. *Ki* is an enhanced life force we can develop during our lifetime by combining our natural human energy (*tama*) with the spiritual energy of the external world (*kami*). One is born with *tama,* comes to experience *kami,* but only slowly learns how to develop the transcendental cosmic energy known as *ki.* This feat is accomplished by allowing external cosmic energies to enter into the crown of the head at the point of the hair whorl. There the external cosmic energies mingle with internal human energies and pass down the spine to the sacrum. From there they rise as *ki,* filling the entire body with enhanced sexual energy that courses through the heart and solar plexus and out into the arms and fingertips. As this occurs one shudders. See Carmen Blacker, *The Catalpa Bow: A Study of Shamanistic Practices in Japan* (London: George Allen and Unwin, 1975), 34–50; Benito Ortolani, *The Japanese Theater: From Shamanistic Ritual to Contemporary Pluralism* (Princeton: Princeton University Press, 1990), 7–12. In Korea the word *ki* indicates both the driving force of life and life itself. A lack of *ki,* or "energy," brings on illness, which can be cured by supplying the client with extra *ki.* Korean shamans, since they are filled with overflowing *ki,* cure primarily by giving away some of their own subtle energy to their patients. See Hyun-Key Kim Hogarth, *Kut: Happiness Through Reciprocity* (Budapest: Akadémiai Kiadó, 1998), 102–103.

17   Mantak Chia and Maneewan Chia, *Healing Love Through the Tao* (Huntington, NY: Healing Tao Books, 1986). See also the description of sexual ecstasy in the Buddhist "diamond way" or "diamond thunderbolt" tradition in Huston Smith, *The Illustrated World's Religions: A Guide to Our Wisdom Traditions* (San Francisco: HarperSanFrancisco, 1994), 92–93.

18   For a full discussion of the historical and cultural connections between shamanism, tantra, and kundalini yoga see Claudia Müller-Ebeling, Christian Rätsch, and Surendra Bahadur Shahi, *Shamanism and Tantra in the Himalayas* (Rochester, VT: Inner

Traditions, 2002). Yoga is a method of meditation that has been traced back to the third millennium BCE. See Vivian Worthington, *A History of Yoga* (Boston: Routledge and Kegan Paul, 1989), 11. Its roots are found in the earlier shamanic practices found in South India, specifically those of indigenous Dravidian culture. A discussion of the tension between the visionary and yogic side of Buddhism, with its struggle to re-create and maintain the shamanic vision, and the clerical and scholarly side, with its attempt to develop a religious community as part of a hierarchical social order is found in Geoffrey Samuel's excellent book *Civilized Shamans: Buddhism in Tibetan Societies* (Washington, DC: Smithsonian Institution Press, 1993). For erotic flower and lightning symbolism in tantric yoga see Thomas Cleary, *The Ecstasy of Enlightenment: Teachings of Natural Tantra* (York Beach, ME: Samuel Weiser, 1998).

19   For a discussion of how sexual energy and orgasm are carefully encouraged and controlled through the practice of hatha yoga see Ajit Mookerjee and Madhu Khanna, *The Tantric Way: Art, Science, Ritual* (Boston: Graphic Society, 1977), 175–188. For kundalini yoga see Rachel McDermott, *Singing to the Goddess: Poems to Kali and Uma from Bengal* (Berkeley: University of California Press, 2001), 103–117, 167–169; Nik Douglas, *Spiritual Secrets of Tantra from the New Age to the New Millennium* (New York: Pocket Books, 1997).

20   Marilyn Mallory, *Christian Mysticism Transcending Techniques* (Amsterdam: Van Gorcum Assen, 1977); Ralph Hood and James Hall, "Gender differences in the description of erotic and mystical experiences," *Review of Religious Research* 21 (1980): 195–207; Barbara Newman, *From Virile Woman to Woman Christ: Studies in Medieval Religion and Literature* (Philadelphia: University of Pennsylvania Press, 1995). As a number of critics have recently noted, it is the continuing unwillingness of celibate Roman Catholic priests to integrate this spiritual understanding of sexuality into the official teachings of the church that is perhaps the most grievous failure in the history of Catholic Christianity. See Andrew Greeley and Mary Greeley Durkin, *How to Save the Catholic Church* (New York: Viking, 1984) and Ruth El Saffar, *Rapture Encaged: The Suppression of the Feminine in Western Culture* (London: Routledge, 1994).

21   The neurophsychologist James Prescott has found neurological connections between trance and female sexuality. For a report see Mary Long, "Visions of a new faith," *Science Digest* 89 (1981): 41; Robert Nadeau, *S/He Brain: Science, Sexual Politics, and the Myths of Feminism* (Westport, CT: Praeger, 1996), 50–53; Elizabeth Wilson, *Neural Geographies: Feminism and the Microstructure of Cognition* (New York: Routledge, 1998). Increased levels of the neurotransmitter dopamine in the bloodstream can bring on ecstasy by releasing a chemical, called phenyl ethylamine. This alters the pathways from the limbic system (the part of the brain that governs emotional responses) to the cerebral cortex (where thinking, planning, organizing, and communicating occur). In so doing, it affects the connections between the sex-seeking and sex-reactive areas of the limbic system that radiate throughout the brain. See Benjamin Walker, *Sex and the Supernatural* (London: Macdonald, 1970); William Sargant, "The ecstasy of sexual union," in *Man, Myth and Magic*, ed. Richard Cavendish (New York: Marshall Cavendish, 1983); Rita Carter, *Mapping the Mind* (Berkeley: University of California Press, 1998), 68–76; Bruce McEwen and Harold Schmeck, *The Hostage Brain* (New York: Rockefeller University Press, 1994), 26–32; Karen Jo Torjesen, *When Women Were Priests: Women's Leadership in the Early Church and the Scandal of their Subordination in the Rise of Christianity* (San Francisco: HarperSanFrancisco, 1995).

22   My experiences with the shamanic arts in North Asia and North America have encouraged me to engage in what has come to be known as "strategic essentialism." In the 1990s "essentialism" became a pejorative concept that was used to discredit the work of scholars who held the view that there were any key differences between women and men. The response to this strongly antiessentialist discourse, which had the effect of removing all sexual differences, became known among feminists as strategic essentialism. For a review of this debate see Jane Atkinson and Shelly Errington, *Power and Difference: Gender in Island Southeast Asia* (Stanford: Stanford University Press, 1990); Judith Butler, *Gender Trouble: Feminism and the Subversion of Identity* (New York: Routledge, 1990) and *Bodies that Matter: On the Discursive Limits of "Sex"* (New York: Routledge, 1993); Tania Modleski, *Feminism Without Women: Culture and Criticism in a "Postfeminist" Age* (New York: Routledge, 1991); Hannah Rachel Bell, *Men's Business, Women's Business: The Spiritual Role of Gender in the World's Oldest Culture* (Rochester, VT: Inner Traditions, 1998); C. De Lacoste-Utamsing and R. Holloway, "Sexual dimorphism in the human corpus callosum," *Science* 216 (1982): 1431–1432; Anne Moir and David Jessel, *Brain Sex: The Real Difference Between Men and Women* (New York: Carol Publishing, 1989), 47–49; Simon LeVay, *The Sexual Brain* (Cambridge, MA: MIT Press, 1994), 102; Bruce McEwen et al., "Steroid and thyroid hormones modulate a changing brain," *Journal of Steroid Biochemistry and Molecular Biology* 40 (1991): 1–14; Rita Carter, *Mapping the Mind* (21, 71).

23   Leo Sternberg, "Die Religion der Giljaken," *Archiv für Religion-swissenschaft* (1905) and "Divine election in primitive religion," *Congrès international des Américanistes, compte-rendu de la XXI session* (Göteborg: Göteborg Museum, 1924).

24   Marjorie Balzer, "The poetry of shamanism," in *Shamanism in Performing Arts,* eds. Tae-gon Kim and Mihály Hoppál (Budapest: Akadémiai Kiadó, 1995), 172.

25   Mihály Hoppál, "Shaman traditions in Siberia," in *Shaman Traditions in Transition,* ed. M. Hoppál (Budapest: International Society for Shamanistic Research, 2000), 10.

26   Conversely male shamans wear layers of female clothing during séances in order to take on the feminine dimension of the spirit world. See Alan Carter Covell, *Ecstasy: Shamanism in Korea* (Elizabeth, NJ: Holly International, 1983), 97–98; Hogarth, *Kut: Happiness Through Reciprocity,* 48, Matthias Eder, "Schamanismus in Japan," *Paideuma* 6 (1958): 367–380.

27   Melford Spiro, *Burmese Supernaturalism* (Philadelphia: Institute for the Study of Human Issues, 1967), 322.

Chapter Seven
RIDING THE WIND HORSE:
A SHAMANIC PERFORMANCE

1   See Sendenzhavyn Dulam, *Central Asian Shamanism and Shamanic Cosmology: Papers and Abstracts for the 5th Conference of the International Society for Shamanistic Research* (Ulaanbaatar, 1999).

2   Note that the Mongol term *udayan,* for a woman shaman, also has the meaning of "midwife" in Ordos Mongol. See Krystyna Chabros, *Beckoning Fortune: A Study of the Mongol Dalalga Ritual* (Wiesbaden: Otto Harrassowicz, 1992): 68. For a discussion of the entire class of sacred icons called *ongot* (sing. *ongon*) see Dorji Banzarov, "The black faith, or shamanism among the Mongols," *Mongolian Studies* 6 (1981):

53–91. This famous 1846 essay was originally a thesis for the *kandidat* degree at Kazan University, which was published in Russian in the *Learned Mémoires of Kazan University;* 3:53–120. The English translation of the original essay published in the journal *Mongolian Studies* was made by Jan Nattier and John Krueger. For more recent discussions see Magdalena Tatar, "Tragic and stranger *ongons* among the Altaic people," in *Altaic Studies* Papers at the 25th Meeting of the Permanent International Altaistic Conference at Uppsala, June 7–11, 1982 (Stockholm: Almquist and Wiksell, 1982); Ágnes Birtalan, "Some animal representations in Mongolian shaman invocations and folklore," *Shaman* 3 (1995): 99–111.

3   Bayar and the other Mongol shamans I interviewed described these silk streamers on their gowns as "snakes" or "vipers," but some shamans have reportedly said that they are "feathers" that enable them to fly on their spiritual journey. See Walther Heissig, "Mongol religions," in *The Encyclopedia of Religion,* ed. Mircea Eliade (New York: Macmillan, 1987), 55.

Chapter Eight
CROSSROADS BETWEEN WORLDS:
THE POWER OF DREAMING

1   See Timothy White, "Once upon a time shamans were dreamers," *Shaman's Drum* 61 (2002): 4. For further discussions of shamans as dreamers see Stanley Krippner, "Tribal shamans and their travels into dreamtime," in *Dreamtime and Dreamwork: Decoding the Language of the Night,* ed. Stanley Krippner (Los Angles: Tarcher, 1990); Waud Kracke, "Everyone who dreams has a bit of shaman: Culture and personal meanings of dreams: Evidence from the Amazon," *Psychiatric Journal of the University of Ottawa* 12 (1991): 65–72; Timothy Knab, *A War of Witches: A Journey into the Underworld of the Contemporary Aztecs* (San Francisco: HarperSanFrancisco, 1995); and Stanley Krippner et al., "Called to be dreamers: Initiatory and lucid dreams," *Shaman's Drum* 61 (2002): 19–27.

2   For more about these and other types of dreams see Harry Hunt, *The Multiplicity of Dreams: Memory, Imagination, and Consciousness* (New Haven: Yale University Press, 1989).

3   See Carl Jung, *Memories, Dreams, Reflections* (New York: Vintage, 1965); James Hillman, *The Dream and the Underworld* (New York: Harper and Row, 1979) and *Healing Fiction* (Barrytown, NY: Station Hill Press, 1983). For more details about these methods of working with dreams see Mary Watkins, *Waking Dreams* (Dallas: Spring, 1976).

4   Bernard Baars, *A Cognitive Theory of Consciousness* (Cambridge: Cambridge University Press, 1988); Harry Hunt, *On the Nature of Consciousness: Cognitive, Phenomenological, and Transpersonal Perspectives* (New Haven: Yale University Press, 1995); Rita Carter, *Mapping the Mind* (Berkeley: University of California Press, 1998).

5   See Namkhai Norbu, *Dream Yoga and the Practice of Natural Light* (Ithaca: Snow Lion, 1992).

6   Barbara Tedlock, "Lucid dreaming in Native America," in *Dream Cultures: Toward a Comparative History of Dreaming,* eds. David Shulman and Guy Stroumsa (New York: Oxford University Press, 1999). Stephen La Berge, *Lucid Dreaming: The Power of Being Awake and Aware in Your Dreams* (Los Angeles: Tarcher, 1985) is an excellent book on the topic.

7   Cecilia Green first suggested the concept of "lucid dreaming" in her classic book *Lucid Dreams* (Oxford: Institute of Psychophysical Research, 1968). For more information about the nature and universality of lucid dreams see George S. Sparrow, *Lucid Dreams: Dawning of the Clear Light* (Virginia Beach: A.R.E. Press, 1976); P. Tholey, "Techniques for inducing and manipulating lucid dreams," *Perceptual and Motor Skills* 57 (1983): 79–90; Jayne Gackenbach and Stephen La Berge, *Conscious Mind, Sleeping Brain: Perspectives on Lucid Dreaming* (New York: Plenum Press, 1988). For more about REM sleep and dream lucidity see F. Crick and G. Mitchison, "REM sleep and neural nets," *Journal of Mind and Behavior* 7 (1986): 229–249.

8   This account is abstracted from William Thalbitzer, *The Ammassalik Eskimo* (Copenhagen: Bianco Luno, 1914), 2:479–487.

9   Ruby Modesto (1913–1980) practiced as a healing shaman for many years. See Ruby Modesto and Guy Mount, *Not for Innocent Ears: Spiritual Traditions of a Desert Cahuilla Medicine Woman* (Arcata, CA: Sweetlight Books, 1980), 26.

10   See George Gillespie, "Lucid dreams in Tibetan Buddhism," in *Conscious Mind, Sleeping Brain*, eds. Jayne Gackenbach and Stephen La Berge (New York: Plenum Press, 1988); Larry Peters, *Ecstasy and Healing in Nepal* (Malibu: Undena Publications, 1981), 92–93; Serinity Young, *Dreaming in the Lotus: Buddhist Dream Narrative, Imagery, and Practice* (Boston: Wisdom Publications, 1999), 120–127.

11   Robert Laughlin, *Of Wonders Wild and New: Dreams from Zinacantán* (Washington, DC: Smithsonian Institution Press, 1976), 163–164.

12   Frank Linderman, *Pretty Shield: Medicine Woman of the Crows* (Lincoln: University of Nebraska Press, 1972), 21–23.

13   Ruth Benedict, "The vision in Plains culture," *American Anthropologist* 24 (1922): 1–23 and *The Concept of the Guardian Spirit in North America* (Menasha: American Anthropological Association, 1923); Jackson Steward Lincoln, *The Dream in Primitive Cultures* (London: Cresset Press, 1935). For narratives of feminine vision quests see Robin Ridington, "Stories of the vision quest among Dunne-za women," *Atlantis* 9 (1983): 68–78.

14   Alfred Bowers, *Mandan Social and Ceremonial Organization* (Chicago: University of Chicago Press, 1950).

15   Tela Star Hawk Lake, *Hawk Woman Dancing with the Moon* (New York: M. Evans, 1996), 57–58.

16   See Robert Lake (Medicine Grizzlybear), "Sorcery, psychic phenomena, and stress: Shamanic healing among the Yurok, Wintu, and Karok," *Shaman's Drum* 11 (1987): 39–46; "Tela Donahue Lake: Traditional Yurok 'Doctor,'" *Shaman's Drum* 15 (1989): 47–53; "Trials and tests of a native healer," *The Quest* 4 (1991): 18–28, and *Native Healer: Initiation into an Ancient Art* (Wheaton, IL: Quest Books, 1991).

17   Theresa Smith, *The Island of the Anishnaabeeg* (Moscow: University of Idaho Press, 1995), 30–32.

18   Ken Hedges, *Welcome the Caribou Man: Tsonakwa and Yolaikia* (San Diego: San Diego Museum of Man, 1992).

19   Barbara Tedlock, "Sharing and interpreting dreams in Amerindian nations," in *Dream Cultures: Toward a Comparative History of Dreaming*, eds. David Shulman and Guy Stroumsa (New York: Oxford University Press, 1999).

Chapter Ten
SONG OF THE CONEFLOWER:
HERBALISM AND PLANT POWER

1   There are various definitions of the word *herb*. Some people insist that an herb must have a woody stem and be used as a spice or medicine, thus eliminating all of the plants and bushes without woody stems. Others say it is an herbaceous rather than a woody plant, thus eliminating all bushes and trees. I consider an herb any useful plant having medicinal properties.

2   This narrative was abstracted from the folklorist Ella Elizabeth Clark's collection, *Indian Legends from the Northern Rockies* (Norman: University of Oklahoma Press, 1966), 56–58.

3   Claudia Müller-Ebeling, Christian Rätsch, and Surendra Bahadur Shahi, *Shamanism and Tantra in the Himalayas* (Rochester, VT: Inner Traditions, 2002), 166–167, 241.

4   Daniel Moerman, *Native American Ethnobotany* (Portland, OR: Timber Press, 1998); E. Barrie Kavash and Karen Baar, *American Indian Healing Arts* (New York: Bantam, 1999), 261. The Chehalis Indian Reservation, located in the state of Washington, hosted the "Salish and Sohaptan Cultures, Foods and Medicine Workshop," which I attended. The conference drew on the extensive knowledge and authentic food and medicines of the Salish nations along the Pacific Coast in British Columbia, Canada, south to southern Oregon, USA. For more information about this two-day public seminar on Salish and Sohaptan culture and foods and medicine in diabetes prevention and management in the Pacific Northwest of the United States and southwest Canada see www.cwis.org.

5   Clifford Geertz, *The Religion of Java* (New York: The Free Press of Glencoe, 1960); Linda Connor, Patsy Asch, and Timothy Asch, *Jero Tapakan: Balinese Healer* (New York: Cambridge University Press, 1986). Ana Mariella Bacigalupo, *La voz del kultrun en la modernidad: Tradición y cambio en la terapéutica de siete machi mapuche* (Santiago: Ediciones Universidad Catolica de Chile, 2001), 74–79.

6   Lydia Nakashima Degarrod, "From oral texts to images: The painting of Mapuche dreams of heaven," talk given at the Latin American Center, Harvard University, 1999.

7   For more about the belief that many plants have their own spirit, or "mother" that enables a shaman to acquire his or her powers see Luis Eduardo Luna, "The concept of plants as teachers among four mestizo shamans of Iquitos, Northeastern Peru," *Journal of Ethnopharmacology* 11 (1984): 135–156.

8   Müller-Ebeling, Rätsch, and Shahi, *Shamanism and Tantra*, 177.

9   Thomas Johnston, "Auditory driving, hallucinogens, and music-color synesthesia in Tsonga ritual," in *Drugs, Rituals and Altered States of Consciousness,* ed. Brian M. Du Toit (Rotterdam: A. A. Balkema, 1977).

10 Sigfrid Rafael Karsten, "Contributions to the sociology of the Indian tribes of Ecuador," *Acta academiae aboensis humaniora* 1 (1920): 1–35; "The religion of the Jibaro Indians of Ecuador," *Boletín de la academia nacional de historia* 3 (1922): 124–145; *The Civilization of the South American Indians, with Special Reference to Magic and Religion* (New York: Knopf, 1926); and *The Head-Hunters of Western Amazonas: The Life and Culture of the Jibaro Indians of Eastern Ecuador and Peru* (Helsinki: Societas Scientiarum Fennica, 1935); Bertrand Flornoy, *Jivaro* (London: Elek, 1953); Norman Whitten, *Sacha Runa: Ethnicity and Adaptation of Ecuadorian Jungle Quichua* (Chicago: University of Illinois Press, 1976); Pita Kelekna, "Sex

Asymmetry in Jivaroan Achuara Society," Ph.D. dissertation, University of New Mexico, 1981; and Philippe Descola, *Spears of Twilight: Three Years Among the Jivaro Indians of South America* (New York: New Press, 1996).

11 Richard Schultes and Alec Bright, "A native drawing of an hallucinogenic plant from Colombia," *Botanical Museum Leaflets Harvard University* 25 (1977): 151–159.

12 Herbert Rappaport and Margaret Rappaport, "The integration of scientific and traditional healing," *American Psychologist* 36 (1981): 774–781; David Young, Grant Ingram, and Linda Swartz, "A Cree healer attempts to improve the competitive position of native medicine," *Arctic Medical Research* 47 (1988): 313–316; David Gregory, "Traditional Indian healers in Northern Manitoba: An emerging relationship with the health care system," *Native Studies Review* 5 (1989): 163–174; James Overton, "Shamanism and clinical hypnosis: A brief comparative analysis," *Shaman* 6 (1998): 151–170; E. Barrie Kavasch and Karen Baar, *American Indian Healing Arts* (New York: Bantam, 1999); Frank Lipp, "A comparative analysis of Southern Mexican and Guatemalan shamans," in *Mesoamerican Healers*, eds. Brad R. Huber and Alan R. Sandstrom (Austin: University of Texas Press, 2001).

13 Barbara Tedlock, "Indigenous, Cosmopolitan and Integrative Medicine in the Americas," in *Indigenous Peoples and the Modern State,* eds. Duane Champagne, Susan Steiner, and Karen Torjesen (Walnut Creek, CA: Alta Mira Press, 2005).

Chapter Eleven
THE FLOWERY DREAM:
THE SHAMANIC USE OF PSYCHEDELICS

1 The research on hallucinogens in culture is vast. A good beginning can be found in the following books and essays: Peter Furst, *Flesh of the Gods: The Ritual Use of Hallucinogens* (New York: Praeger, 1972); Peter Furst, *Hallucinogens and Culture* (San Francisco: Chandler and Sharp, 1976); Richard Schultes, "An overview of hallucinogens in the Western hemisphere," in *Flesh of the Gods: The Ritual Use of Hallucinogens,* ed. Peter Furst (New York: Praeger, 1972); Michael Harner, ed., *Hallucinogens and Shamanism* (London: Oxford University Press, 1973); Weston La Barre, "Anthropological perspectives on hallucination and hallucinogens," in *Hallucinations,* eds. R. K. Siegel and L. J. West (New York: John Wiley, 1975); F. Hoffmeister and G. Stille, *Psychotropic Agents* (New York: Springer-Verlag, 1982); E. Brocca, "Xamanismo, alucinógenos y meloterapa," *Guatemala Indígena* 17 (1982): 159–168; Marlene Dobkin de Rios, *Hallucinogens: Cross-Cultural Perspectives* (Albuquerque: University of New Mexico Press, 1984); Terence McKenna, *The Archaic Revival* (San Francisco: HarperSanFrancisco, 1991) and *Food of the Gods* (New York: Bantam, 1992); Peter Stafford, *Psychedelics Encyclopedia* (Berkeley: Ronin Publishing, 1992); Jonathan Ott, *Pharmacotheon: Entheogenic Drugs, Their Plant Sources and History* (Kennewick, WA: Natural Products, 1996); Richard Evans Schultees, Albert Hofmann, and Christian Rätsch, *Plants of the Gods: Their Sacred, Healing and Hallucinogenic Powers* (Rochester, VT: Healing Arts Press, 2001).

2 Fray Bernardino de Sahagún, *Historia general de las cosas de la Nueva España* (Florentine Codex) (Mexico: Porrua, 1969); Schultes, "An overview of hallucinogens in the Western hemisphere," in *Flesh of the Gods,* ed. Peter Furst (1972): 9.

3 For more about hallucinogens as healing agents see Arnold Mandell, "Toward a psychobiology of transcendence: God in the brain," in *The Psychobiology of*

Consciousness, eds. Julian M. Davidson and Richard J. Davidson (New York: Plenum, 1980); R. Zanger, "Psycholytic therapy in Europe," *The Albert Hoffman Foundation Newsletter* 1 (1989); Michael Winkelman, "Therapeutic effects of hallucinogens," *The Anthropology of Consciousness* 2 (1991): 15–19; Carl Ruck, Jeremy Bigwood, Danny Staples, Jonathan Ott, and R. Gordon Wasson, "Entheogens," *Journal of Psychedelic Drugs* 11 (1979): 145–146; Thomas Riedlinger, "Preface," in *The Sacred Mushroom Seeker*, ed. Thomas Riedlinger (Rochester, VT: Park Street Press, 1990), 9; Frank Lipp, "Mixe concepts and uses of entheogenic mushrooms," in *The Sacred Mushroom Seeker*, ed. Thomas Riedlinger (Rochester, VT: Park Street Press, 1990), 151; Carl Ruck, "Mr. Wasson and the Greeks," in *The Sacred Mushroom Seeker*, ed. Thomas Riedlinger (Rochester, VT: Park Street Press, 1990), 225.

4   R. Gordon Wasson, "Persephone's quest," in R. Gordon Wasson et al., *Persephone's Quest: Entheogens and the Origins of Religion* (New Haven: Yale University Press, 1986), 68–71.

5   R. Gordon Wasson, "What was the soma of the Aryans," in *Flesh of the Gods: The Ritual Use of Hallucinogens*, ed. Peter Furst (New York: Praeger, 1972), 201; Elio Schaechter, *In the Company of Mushrooms: A Biologist's Tale* (Cambridge, MA: Harvard University Press, 1997), 193–194; R. Gordon Wasson, *The Wondrous Mushroom* (New York: McGraw-Hill, 1980). The suggestion that Lewis Carroll was inspired by the discussion of the Siberian mushroom cult is from *Ott, Pharmacotheon*, 329, 342. See also Mordecai Cubitt Cooke, *The Seven Sisters of Sleep: Popular History of the Seven Prevailing Narcotics of the World* (London: Blackwell, 1860).

6   Waldemar Jochelson, *The Koryak* (New York: Museum of Natural History, 1908); Henry N. Michael, ed., *Studies in Siberian Shamanism* (Toronto: University of Toronto Press, 1963); Vilmos Diószegi, *Tracing Shamans in Siberia* (Oosterhout: Anthropological Publications, 1968); Lauri Honko, "Role-taking of the shaman," *Temenos* 4 (1969): 44; L. G. Czigány, "The use of hallucinogens and the shamanistic tradition of the Finno-Ugrian people," *Slavonic and East European Review* 58 (1980): 212–217; W. Bauer, et al. *Der Fliegenpilz: Ein Kulturhistorisches Museum* (Köln: Wienand-Verlag, 1991); Maret Saar, "Ethnomycological data from Siberia and North-East Asia on the effect of Amanita Muscaria," *Journal of Ethnopharmacology* 31 (1991): 157–173; H. Geerken, "Fliegen Pilze? Merkungen and Anmerkungen zum Shamanismus in Sibirien and Andechs," *Integration: Zeitschrift für Geistbewegende Pflanzen und Kultur* 2 (1992): 109–114; Theodore Schurr, "Aboriginal Siberian Use of *Amanita muscaria* in shamanistic practices," *Curare* 18 (1995): 31–65; Mihály Hoppál, "Shamanhood among the Nenets," in *Shaman Traditions in Transition*, ed. M. Hoppál (Budapest: International Society for Shamanistic Research, 2000), 26–27. Among the Khanty (Ostyaks) a shaman fasts all day, goes to the sauna, and then eats three or seven fly agarics and goes to rest. Upon waking s/he begins to shamanize.

7   Tom Stimson, "The song of Mukhomor," *Shaman's Drum* 41 (1996): 61. The half-hour video can be ordered from him at 2313 South Elm Drive, Denver, CO 80222.

8   Keewaydinoqua, *Puhpohwee for the People: A Narrative Account of Some Uses of Fungi Among the Ahnishinaubeg* (Cambridge, MA: Botanical Museum of Harvard University, 1978); *Min: Anishinaabeg Ogimaawi-minan: Blue Berry: First Fruit of the People* (Miniss-Kitigan, MI: Miniss-Kitigan Drum, 1978), and "The legend of Miskwedo," *Journal of Psychedelic Drugs* 11 (1979): 29–31. There are actually four degrees in the midewiwin: first or weasel degree, followed by mink, hawk, and bear. Ojibwe generally called them in English "once grand-medicined," "twice grand-medicined," "three

times grand-medicined," and "four times grand-medicined." My grandmother told me that she had been four times grand-medicined.

9   S. F. De Borhegyi, "Miniature mushroom stones from Guatemala," *American Antiquity* 16 (1961): 498–504; B. Lowy, "New records of mushroom stones from Guatemala," *Mycologia* 63 (1971): 983–993; "Ethnomycological inferences from mushroom stones, Maya codices, and Tzutuhil legend," *Revista/Review Interamericana* 10 (1980): 94–103; R. Gordon Wasson, "Notes on the present status of ololiuhqui and the other hallucinogens of Mexico," in *The Psychedelic Reader,* eds. Gunther M. Weil, Ralph Metzner, and Timothy Leary (New York: University Books, 1965), 182–185, and *The Wondrous Mushroom: Mycolatry in Mesoamerica* (New York: McGraw-Hill, 1980), 31, 32, 215–220.

10   Sahagún, *Historia general;* Álvardo Estrada, *María Sabina: Her Life and Chants* (Santa Barbara: Ross-Erikson, 1981), 199.

11   These mushrooms are used today in a number of Aztec communities near Mexico City, in the vicinity of Popocatpétl and Iztaccíhuatl volcanoes, as well as in the state of Morelos and the mountains of Puebla. Mercedes de la Garza, *Sueño y alucinación en el nundo náhuatl y maya* (México: Universidad Nacional Autónoma de México, 1990), 217.

12   Salvador Roquet, *Operation Mazteca: A Study of Mushrooms and Other Mexican Hallucinogenic Plants* (Mexico City: Albert Schweitzer Association, 1971).

13   Frances Karttunen, *Between Worlds: Interpreters, Guides, and Survivors* (New Brunswick, NJ: Rutgers University Press, 1994), 235; Henry Munn, "The mushrooms of language," in *Hallucinogens and Shamanism,* ed. Michael Hamer (London: Oxford University Press, 1973), 94.

14   Munn, "The mushrooms of language," 107–108.

15   This quote is from her biography, which was taken down by a Mazatec neighbor and friend: Álvardo Estrada, *Vida de María Sabina la sabia de los hongos* (Mexico: Siglo Veintiuno Editores, 1977), 39. A documentary film about her life, *María Sabina: Mujer Espíritu,* by Nicolas Eshevaría, premiered in Mexico City in 1979. María Sabina (1900–1985) was described and profiled a number of times.

16   R. Gordon Wasson et al., *Maria Sabina and Her Mazatec Mushroom Velada* (New York: Harcourt Brace Jovanovich, 1974), xvii.

17   Ibid., *Maria Sabina,* 19, 57.

18   The origin story of peyote has been told and retold by many peoples, ranging from the Aztecs to the Tarahuma, Otomí, and Lipan Apache. See C. Burton Dustin, *Peyotism and New Mexico* (Farmington, NM: n.p., 1960), 7–8, and Alice Marriott and Carol Rachlin, *Peyote* (New York: New American Library, 1971), 14–15.

19   Richard Evans Schultes, "The appeal of peyote *(Lophophora williamsii)* as a medicine," *American Anthropologist* 40 (1938): 685–715; B. J. Albaugh and P. O. Anderson, "Peyote in the treatment of alcoholism among American Indians," *American Journal of Psychiatry* 131 (1975): 1247–1249; Michael Weiner, *Earth Medicine, Earth Food: Plant Remedies, Drugs, and Natural Foods of the North American Indians* (New York: Macmillan, 1980). In the early 1970s in Santa Catarina, Mexico, a Huichol woman shaman showed my friend the ethnographer Timothy Knab her peyote enema apparatus. The bulb was made from a deer's bladder and the tube from a hollow deer femur. She told him that she prepared the peyote by grinding it to a fine pulp and diluting it with water. Instead of taking the mixture by mouth she injected it into her rectum. In so doing she experienced its hallucinogenic effects immediately and avoided the unpleasant taste and nausea. See Peter Furst and Michael Coe, "Ritual enemas," *Natural History* 86 (1977): 91.

20   This description is based on my own experiences with peyote as well as those of other ethnographers, including Weston La Barre, *The Peyote Cult* (New Haven: Yale University Press, 1938); David Aberle, *The Peyote Religion Among the Navaho* (Chicago: Aldine, 1966); Peter Furst, "'To find our life: Peyote among the Huichol Indians of Mexico," in *Flesh of the Gods,* ed. Peter Furst (New York: Praeger, 1972); Bryce Boyer, Ruth Boyer, and Harry Basehart, "Shamanism and peyote use among the Apaches of the Mescalero Indian reservation," in *Hallucinogens and Shamanism,* ed. Michael Harner (London: Oxford University Press, 1973); Barbara Myerhoff, *Peyote Hunt* (Ithaca: Cornell University Press, 1974); Fernando Benitez, *In the Magic Land of Peyote* (Austin: University of Texas Press, 1975).

21   Paul Steinmetz, "Shamanic images in peyote visions," in *Religion in Native North America,* ed. Christopher Vecsey (Moscow: University of Idaho Press, 1990).

22   R. K. Siegel, *Hallucinations* (New York: John Wiley, 1975); J. D. Lewis-Williams and T. A. Dowson, "The signs of all times: Entoptic phenomena in Upper Paleolithic art," *Current Anthropology* 29 (1988): 201–245.

23   Medicinal and psychedelic uses of peyote were once the common property of a large number of Mexican peoples including the Aztecs, Coras, Huichols, Tepecanos, and Tarahumaras. Today, however, while a few Cora and Tarahumara shamans continue to use peyote, the Huichol are the primary bearers of peyote culture. See Stacey Schaefer and Peter Furst, "Introduction," in *People of the Peyote: Huichol Indian History, Religion and Survival,* eds. Stacey Schaefer and Peter Furst (Albuquerque: University of New Mexico Press, 1996), 23–25.

24   Stacey Schaefer, "The crossing of the souls," in *People of the Peyote: Huichol Indian History, Religion, and Survival,* eds. Stacey Schaefer and Peter Furst (Albuquerque: University of New Mexico Press, 1996), 158.

25   Ibid., 159–160.

26   Schaefer, *To Think with a Good Heart: Wixárika Women, Weavers, and Shamans* (Salt Lake City: University of Utah Press, 2002), 99–100.

27   In 1994 the governor of the state of San Luis Potosí established the ecological reserve of Wirikuta so that Huichols would be free to collect peyote and take it home. This legislation was intended to strengthen Article Four of the Mexican Constitution, and a clause in the International Vienna Treaty of Psychotropic Substances, in which indigenous peoples who use psychoactive plants in their religious ceremonies are exempt from legal prosecution. See Susana Valdez, "Huichol religious pilgrims jailed for possession of peyote," *Native Americas* 15 (1998): 12; Eduard Seler, "Wirikuta, the holy land of the Huichol Indians, declared an ecological reserve zone," *Mexicon* 5 (1995): 5–6; Susan Rinderle, "The Huichol Way: An endangered path to completion," *Native Americas* 17 (2000): 52–55.

28   James Mooney, *The Ghost-Dance Religion and the Sioux Outbreak of 1890* (Chicago: University of Chicago Press, 1965); Weston La Barre, *The Peyote Cult* (Norman: University of Oklahoma Press, 1989); Robert Preston and Carl Hammerschlag, "The Native American Church," in *Psychodynamic Perspectives on Religion, Sect, and Cult,* ed. David Halperin (Boston: John Wright, 1983), 93; Omer Stewart, *Peyote Religion: A History* (Norman: University of Oklahoma Press, 1987), 327–336; W. Blackmun, "Dissenting opinion in U. S. Supreme court case," *The United States Law Week* 58 (1990): 4443–4446; Peter Gorman, "Peyote justice in New Mexico," *High Times,* July 1992.

29   For more information about the artist see Daniel Swan, *Peyote Religious Art* (Jackson: University Press of Mississippi, 1999), 72–79.

30 Among the Apache and Arapaho, for example, women are not allowed to attend peyote rituals. The Northern Paiute and Washo allow women to participate, but during menstruation they must tie feathers on their wrists. See Edward Anderson, *Peyote: The Divine Cactus* (Tucson: University of Arizona Press, 1980), 5.

31 David Jones, *Sanapia: Comanche Medicine Woman* (Prospect Heights, IL: Waveland Press, 1972), 77.

32 Ibid., 81.

33 Bradford Keeney, *Walking Thunder: Diné Medicine Woman* (Philadelphia: Ringing Rocks Press, 2001), 106.

34 Marlene Dobkin de Rios, *Visionary Vine: Psychedelic Healing in the Peruvian Amazon* (Prospect Heights, IL: Waveland Press, 1972) and *Hallucinogens: Cross-Cultural Perspectives* (Albuquerque: University of New Mexico Press, 1984), 91–114; Douglas Sharon, "The San Pedro cactus in Peruvian folk healing," in *Flesh of the Gods,* ed. Peter Furst (New York: Praeger, 1972); Michael Winkelman and Walter Andritzky, *Sacred Plants: Consciousness and Healing* (Berlin: Verland and Vertrieb, 1996); Ott, *Pharmacotheon,* 88–89.

35 Douglas Sharon and Christopher Donnan, "The magic cactus: Ethnoarchaeological continuity in Peru," *Archaeology* 30 (1977): 374–381, *Wizard of the Four Winds* (New York: Free Press, 1978), 42, and *Shamanism and the Sacred Cactus* (San Diego: San Diego Museum of Man, 2000).

36 See Claudius Giese, "Curanderos," in *Traditionelle Heiler in Nord-Peru* (Hohenschaftlarn: Klaus Renner Verlag, 1989); Donald Joralemon and Douglas Sharon, *Sorcery and Shamanism: Curanderos and Clients in Northern Peru* (Salt Lake City: University of Utah Press, 1993); Mario Polía, *Las Lagunas de los encantos: medicina tradicional Andina del Perú septentrional* (Lima: Gráfica Bellida,1988).

37 Eduardo Calderon (1930–1995) was a Spanish-speaking *mestizo* with only tenuous ties to South American Indian culture. He first came to the attention of ethnographers in 1965 when he was working as an artist at the archaeological site of Chan-Chan near the city of Trujillo, Peru. Douglas Sharon wrote a biography of Eduardo's life and healing practices, *Wizard of the Four Winds* (1978). Later, with the help of his wife and another colleague, he made an ethnographic film and published the script of one of Eduardo's curing ceremonies: *Eduardo el Curandero: The Words of a Peruvian Healer* (Richmond, CA: North Atlantic Press, 1982), 45.

38 E. Wade Davis, "Sacred plants of the San Pedro cult," *Botanical Museum Leaflets, Harvard University* 29 (1983): 367–386; Donald Joralemon, "Symbolic Space and Ritual Time in a Peruvian Healing Ceremony," *Ethnic Technology Notes* 19 (San Diego: San Diego Museum of Man, 1984), 1–20; R. Donald Skillman, "Huachumero: Peruvian Curandero Jorge Merino Bravo," *Ethnic Technology Notes* 22 (San Diego: San Diego Museum of Man, 1990).

39 Mario Polía, *Las lagunas de los encantos* (Lima: Gráfica Bellida, 1988), 27–28; Bonnie Glass-Coffin, *The Gift of Life: Female Spirituality and Healing in Northern Peru* (Albuquerque: University of New Mexico Press, 1998), 139–163.

40 Glass-Coffin, *The Gift of Life,* 120–126.

41 Lizbeth Rymland, "Ecstasy in Ecuador: Experiences with curanderos and plant teachers," *Shaman's Drum* 34 (1994): 38–51.

Chapter Twelve
BUTTERFLIES IN THE MOONLIGHT:
BLOOD MAGIC

1 Randi Koeske, "Theoretical perspectives on menstrual cycle research," in *The Menstrual Cycle,* eds. A. Dan, E. Grahaman, and C. P. Beecher (New York: Springer, 1980), 2:8–24, and "Premenstrual emotionality: Is biology destiny? Lifting the curse of menstruation: Toward a feminist perspective on the menstrual cycle," *Women and Health* 8 (1983): 1–16.

2 Dena Taylor, *Red Flower: Rethinking Menstruation* (Caldwell, NJ: Blackburn Press, 1988); Louise Lander, *Images of Bleeding: Menstruation as Ideology* (New York: Orlando Press, 1988), 136–162.

3 Alma Gottlieb, "Menstrual cosmology among the Beng of Ivory Coast," in *Blood Magic: The Anthropology of Menstruation,* eds. Thomas Buckley and Alma Gottlieb (Berkeley: University of California Press, 1988), 58.

4 Ajit Mookerjee, *Kali: The Feminine Force* (Rochester, VT: Destiny Books, 1988), 32–42; Lara Owen, *Honoring Menstruation* (Freedom, CA: Crossing Press, 1998), 111; A. R. Radcliffe-Brown, *The Andaman Islanders* (Cambridge: Cambridge University Press, 1922), 295.

5 Susan Milbrath, "Decapitated lunar goddesses in Aztec art, myth, and ritual," *Ancient Mesoamerica* 8 (1997): 185–206.

6 Salvador Díaz Cínora, *Xochiquétzal: estudio de mitologia náhuatl* (México: Universidad Nacional Autónoma de México, 1990). See Doris Heyden, *Mitologia y simbolismo de la flora en el méxico prehispánico* (México: Universidad Nacional Autónoma de México, 1983), 106; Susan Rostas, "Mexican mythology divine androgyny but 'his' story: The female in Aztec mythology," in *The Woman's Companion to Mythology,* ed. Carolyne Larrington (London: Harper Collins, 1997), 376–378; Doris Heyden, "Metaphors, Nahualtocaitl, and other 'disguised' terms among the Aztecs," in *Symbol and Meaning Beyond the Closed Community,* ed. Gary Gossen (Albany, NY: Institute for Mesoamerican Studies, 1986), 36; Alan Sandstrom and Pamela Sandstrom, *Traditional Papermaking and Paper Cult Figures of Mexico* (Norman: University of Oklahoma Press, 1986), 204, 284; Louise Burkhart, "Flowery heaven: The aesthetic of paradise in Nahuatl devotional literature," *RES* 21 (1992): 88–109. Motecuzoma I instituted the practice of the Flowery Wars for the purpose of seeking captives for human sacrifice in order to obtain blood to feed the gods rather than for political victory on the battlefield.

7 Robert Zingg, *The Huichols Primitive Artists* (New York: G. E. Stechert, 1938), 247, 335; Stacey Schaefer, *To Think With a Good Heart: Wixárika Women, Weavers, and Shamans* (Salt Lake City: The University of Utah Press, 2002), 164–166. In Huichol culture five is the sacred number representing the four cosmological directions plus the center.

8 Brigitte Berthier, *La Dame-du-bord-de-l'eau* (Nanterre: Société d'Ethnologie, 1988); Hung-youn Cho, "An archetypal myth and its reality in Korean shamanism," in *Re-Discovery of Shamanic Heritage,* eds. Mihály Hoppál and Gábor Kósa (Budapest: Akadémiai Kiadó, 2004).

9 Laurie Lisle, *Portrait of an Artist. A Biography of Georgia O'Keeffe* (New York: Seaview Books, 1980), 190; Elinor Gadon, *The Once and Future Goddess* (San Francisco: Harper and Row, 1989), 318.

10   Joseph Shipley, *The Origins of English Words: A Discursive Dictionary of Indo-European Roots* (Baltimore: Johns Hopkins University Press, 1984).

11   Alexander Marshack, *The Roots of Civilization: The Cognitive Beginnings of Man's First Art, Symbol, and Notation* (New York: McGraw-Hill, 1972); Antal Bartha, "Myth and reality in the ancient culture of the northern peoples," in *Northern Religions and Shamanism*, eds. Mihály Hoppál and Juha Pentikäinen (Budapest: Akadémiai Kiadó, 1992), 21–25.

12   David S. Nivison, "The origin of the Chinese lunar lodge system," in *World Archaeoastronomy*, ed. Anthony Aveni (Cambridge: Cambridge University Press, 1989), 203–208; Derek Walters, *Chinese Astrology* (London: Watkins, 2002).

13   Helen Neuenswander, "Vestiges of early Maya time concepts in a contemporary Maya (Cubulco Achi) community: Implications for epigraphy," *Estudios de Cultura Maya* 13 (1981): 159; Duncan Earle and Dean Snow, "The origin of the 260-day calendar: The gestation hypothesis reconsidered in light of its use among the Quiche-Maya," in *Fifth Palenque Round Table*, eds. Merle Green Robertson and Virginia M. Fields (San Francisco: Pre-Columbian Art Research Institute, 1985), 242; Barbara Tedlock, *Time and the Highland Maya* (Albuquerque: University of New Mexico Press, 1982), 93; Merideth Paxton, *The Cosmos of the Yucatec Maya: Cycles and Steps from the Madrid Codex* (Albuquerque: University of New Mexico Press, 2001), 33, 48–61, 139–140; Jan Jacob Marie De Groot, *The Religious System of China* (Leiden: E.J. Brill, 1939), 4:397–405.

14   Linda Schele and Jeffrey Miller, *The Mirror, the Rabbit, and the Bundle: "Accession" Expressions from the Classic Maya Inscriptions* (Washington, DC: Dumbarton Oaks, 1983); Charles Wicke, "The Mesoamerican rabbit in the moon: An influence from Han China?" *Archaeoastronomy* 8 (1984): 47; Alfredo Lopez Austin, *The Rabbit on the Face of the Moon: Mythology in the Mesoamerican Tradition* (Salt Lake City: University of Utah Press, 1996); Susan Milbrath, *Star Gods of the Maya: Astronomy in Art, Folklore, and Calendars* (Austin: University of Texas Press, 1999), 32, 119–120.

15   Martha McClintok, "Menstrual synchrony and suppression," *Nature* 299 (1971): 244–245; Penelope Schuttle and Peter Redgrove, *The Wise Wound* (New York: Bantam, 1990); Chris Knight, "Menstrual synchrony and the Australian rainbow snake," in *Blood Magic: The Anthropology of Menstruation*, eds. Thomas Buckley and Alma Gottlieb (Berkeley: University of California Press, 1988), 234–350, and *Blood Relations: Menstruation and the Origins of Culture* (New Haven: Yale University Press, 1991), 400–401, 444–448; Ann Martha and Dorothy Myers Imel, *Goddesses in World Mythology* (Santa Barbara, CA: ABC-CLIO, 1993), 427.

16   This narrative is abstracted from F. D. McCarthy, "The string figures of Yirrkalla," in *Records of the American-Australian Scientific Expedition to Arnhem Land*, ed. C. P. Mountford (Melbourne: Melbourne University Press, 1960), 2:426.

17   June Gutmanis, *Kahuna La'au Lapa'au: The Practice of Hawaiian Herbal Medicine* (Aiea, Hawaii: Island Heritage Publishing, 1999), 31–32; Carolyn Patterson, "In the far Pacific at the birth of nations," *National Geographic* 179 (1986): 460–499.

18   Maureen Trudelle Schwarz, *Molded in the Image of Changing Woman: Navajo Views on the Human Body and Personhood* (Tucson: University of Arizona Press, 1997), 215.

19   Ibid., 191, 195.

20   This story is abstracted from J. R. Walker, *Lakota Belief and Ritual* (Lincoln: University of Nebraska Press, 1980), 109–112, and Robert Pickering, *Seeing the White Buffalo* (Denver: Denver Museum of Natural History Press, 1997), 16–20.

21   Alanson Skinner, *Social Life and Ceremonial Bundles of the Menomini Indians* (New York: American Museum of Natural History, 1913); Leonard Bloomfield, *Menominee Texts* (New York: American Ethnological Society, 1928); E. Barrie Kavasch and Karen Baar, *American Indian Healing Arts* (New York: Bantam, 1999), 57. This story is abstracted from Gerald Vizenor, *Summer in the Spring: Ojibwe Lyric Poems and Tribal Stories* (Minneapolis: Nodin Press, 1981), 68–70.

22   John Swanton, "Contributions to the Ethnology of Haida," *Memoirs of the American Museum of Natural History* 8 (1905): 49–50.

23   Lise Klein Kirsis, " 'She taught us how to Be': The cultural construction of birth and midwifery among the Koyukon Athabaskans of interior Alaska," *Arctic Anthropology* 33 (1996): 62–76; Clifford Geertz, *The Religion of Java* (New York: Free Press of Glencoe, 1960), 44; Stephan Beyer, *The Cult of Tara: Magic and Ritual in Tibet* (Berkeley: University of California Press, 1978).

24   R. Piddington, "Karadjeri initiation," *Oceania* 2 (1932); Rita Gross, "Menstruation and childbirth as ritual and religious experience among native Australians," in *Unspoken Worlds: Women's Religious Lives in Non-Western Culture,* eds. Nancy Falk and Rita M. Gross (New York: Harper and Row, 1980); Catherine Berndt, "Women and the 'secret life,' " in *Religion in Aboriginal Australia,* eds. Max Charlesworth et al. (Queensland: University of Queensland Press, 1984), 324.

25   Anne Carolyn Klein, *Meeting the Great Bliss Queen: Buddhists, Feminists, and the Art of the Self* (Boston: Beacon, 1995), 158–194.

26   Stephen Hugh-Jones, *The Palm and the Pleiades: Initiation and Cosmology in Northwest Amazonia* (Cambridge: Cambridge University Press, 1979), 125–131; Christine Hugh-Jones, *From the Milk River: Spatial and Temporal Processes in Northwest Amazonia* (Cambridge: Cambridge University Press, 1979), 137–138; Jean Jackson, "Coping with the dilemmas of affinity and female sexuality: Male rebirth in the central north-west Amazon," in *Denying Biology: Essays on Gender and Pseudo-Procreation,* eds. Warren Shapiro and Uli Linke (Lanham: University Press of America, 1996), 105.

27   Lucy Thompson, *To the American Indian* (Berkeley, CA: Heyday Books, 1991 [1916]); Thomas Buckley, "Menstruation and the power of Yurok women," in *Blood Magic: The Anthropology of Menstruation,* eds. Thomas Buckley and Alma Gottlieb (Berkeley: University of California Press, 1988), 187–209.

28   This account is a shortened first-person version adapted from Robert Spott and Alfred Kroeber, "Yurok shamanism," in *The California Indians,* ed. Alfred Kroeber (Berkeley: University of California Press, 1951), 535–539.

29   Thomas Buckley, "Yurok doctors and the concept of 'shamanism,' " in *California Indian Shamanism,* ed. Lowell John Bean (Berkeley: University of California Press, 1992), 140–141.

30   Tela Star Hawk Lake, *Hawk Woman Dancing with the Moon* (New York: M. Evans, 1996), 177–178; Pliny Earle Goddard, *Hupa Texts* (Berkeley: The University Press, 1904), 252–264.

31   Thomas Buckley, "Menstruation and the power of Yurok women," in *Blood Magic: The Anthropology of Menstruation,* eds. Thomas Buckley and Alma Gottlieb (Berkeley: University of California Press, 1988), 194–195.

32   William Thalbitzer, *The Ammassalik Eskimo* (Copenhagen: Bianco Luno, 1923), 2:454–457.

33   Elinor Gadon, *The Once and Future Goddess* (San Francisco: Harper and Row, 1980), 323. Judy Chicago's massive art piece featured a large triangular table set for thirty-

nine famous women of mythology and history. The first place was the primordial Goddess and the last place was for Georgia O'Keeffe. For more about the significance of Chicago's art and its controversial nature see her books *The Dinner Party: A Symbol of Our Heritage* (Garden City, NY: Doubleday, 1979) and *Through the Flower: My Struggle as a Woman Artist* (Garden City, NY: Doubleday, 1975) and her essay "Our heritage is our power," in *The Politics of Women's Spirituality*, ed. Charlene Spretnak (Garden City, NY: Doubleday, 1982).

Chapter Thirteen
THE SACRED, THE DANGEROUS, AND THE FORBIDDEN:
MENSTRUAL TABOOS AS FEMININE POWER

1 Marshall Sahlins, *The Use and Abuse of Biology: An Anthropological Critique of Sociobiology* (Ann Arbor: University of Michigan Press, 1977), 33. While there have long been controversies over the precise meaning of *mana* there has been general agreement that it is directly associated with chiefly power. See Valerio Valeri, *Kinship and Sacrifice: Ritual and Society in Ancient Hawaii* (Chicago: University of Chicago Press, 1985), 95–105; Nicholas Thomas, "Unstable categories: Tapu and gender in the Marquesas," *Journal of Pacific History* 22 (1987): 129; Brad Shore, "Mana and tapu," in *Developments in Polynesian Ethnology*, eds. Alan Howard and Robert Borofsky (Honolulu: University of Hawaii Press, 1989); Annette Weiner, *Inalienable Possessions: The Paradox of Keeping-While-Giving* (Berkeley: University of California Press, 1992), 65.

2 Judith Vander, *Songprints: The Musical Experience of Five Shoshone Women* (Urbana: University of Illinois Press, 1988), 13–14; Marla Powers, "Menstruation and reproduction: An Oglala case," *Signs* 6 (1980): 54–65; *Oglala Women in Myth, Ritual and Reality* (Chicago: University of Chicago Press, 1986) and "Mistress, mother, visionary spirit: The Lakota culture heroine," in *Religion in Native North America*, ed. Christopher Vecsey (Moscow: University of Idaho Press, 1990).

3 The origin of the term *trickster* as a character type widely found in Native American mythology has been traced to Daniel Brinton's 1885 article "The Hero-God of the Algonkians as a cheat and liar," in *Dictionary of Native American Mythology*, ed. Sam Gill (Denver, CO: ABC-CLIO, 1992), 308. The texts Kroeber gathered from women shamans are available in the manuscript division of the Bancroft Library, University of California at Berkeley. Sections of these materials were cited by Thomas Buckley, "Menstruation and the power of Yurok women," in *Blood Magic: The Anthropology of Menstruation*, eds. Thomas Buckley and Alma Gottlieb (Berkeley: University of California Press, 1988), 194–195.

4 This version of the myth is based on Tela Star Hawk Lake, *Hawk Woman Dancing in the Moon* (New York: M. Evans, 1996), 177–178.

5 Carl Jung, "On the psychology of the trickster figure," in *Psyche and Symbol*, ed. R. F. C. Hull (Princeton, NJ: Princeton University Press, 1990).

6 Amelia Bell, "Separate people: Speaking of Creek men and women," *American Anthropologist* 92 (1990): 332–345.

7 Gananath Obeyesekere, *The Cult of the Goddess Pattini* (Chicago: University of Chicago Press, 1984), 14–16; Karen Smyers, "Women and Shinto: The relations between purity and pollution," *Japanese Religions* 12 (1983): 7–19; Yoshida Teigo, "The feminine in Japanese folk religion: Polluted or divine?" in *Unwrapping Japan*, eds.

Eyal Ben-Ari, Brian Moeran, and James Valentine (Honolulu: University of Hawaii Press, 1990). For the distinction between clerical and shamanistic Buddhist traditions see Geoffrey Samuel, *Civilized Shamans: Buddhism in Tibetan Societies* (Washington, DC: Smithsonian Institution Press, 1993).

8   See Barbara Tedlock, "Works and wives: On the sexual division of textual labor," in *Women Writing Culture,* eds. Ruth Behar and Deborah Gordon (Berkeley: University of California Press, 1995), where I lay out the history of women ethnographers as "honorary males."

9   Ruth Landes, *The Ojibwa Woman* (New York: Columbia University Press, 1938), 5–6.

10 Ruth Underhill, *Red Man's Religion: Beliefs and Practices of the Indians North of Mexico* (Chicago: University of Chicago Press, 1965), 52.

11 Marina Warner, *Alone of All Her Sex: The Myth and the Cult of the Virgin Mary* (New York: Alfred Knopf, 1976), 268. For a parallel Australian discussion of the pollution metaphor for women's menstrual blood as an import from Judaeo-Christian beliefs see Diane Bell, *Ngarrindjeri Wurruwarrin: A World That Is, Was, and Will Be* (North Melbourne: Spinifex, 1998), 511–513. See also Barbara Walker, *The Woman's Encyclopedia of Myths and Secrets* (San Francisco: Harper and Row, 1983), 635–648. For insightful discussions of the strange evolution of the Roman Catholic Church's extraordinary negative views toward women's bodies see Charles Wood, "The doctor's dilemma: Sin, salvation, and the menstrual cycle in medieval thought," *Speculum* 56 (1981): 710–727, and Karen Jo Torjesen, *When Women Were Priests* (New York: HarperCollins, 1993). See also F. Young and A. Bacdayan, "Menstrual taboos and social rigidity," *Ethnology* 4 (1965): 225–240; William Stephens, "A cross-cultural study of the menstrual taboo, in *Cross-Cultural Approaches,* ed. Clellan S. Ford (New Haven: HRAF Press, 1967); Judy Grahn, *Blood, Bread, and Roses: How Menstruation Created the World* (Boston: Beacon, 1993); Carole Rayburn, "The body in religious experience," in *Handbook of Religious Experience,* ed. Ralph Hood (Birmingham: Religious Education Press, 1995).

12 Mircea Eliade, *Patterns in Comparative Religion* (Cleveland: World Publishing, 1963), 166; R. Wasserfall, "Menstruation and identity: The meaning of *niddah* for Moroccan women immigrants to Israel," in *People of the Body: Jews and Judaism from an Embodied Perspective,* ed. H. Eilberg-Schwartz (Albany: State University of New York Press, 1992).

13 Janice Delaney, J. Lipton, and E. Toth, *The Curse: A Cultural History of Menstruation* (New York: E. P. Dutton, 1976).

14 Penelope Shuttle and Peter Redgrove, *The Wise Wound: Eve's Curse (Menstruation) and Everywoman* (New York: R. Marek, 1978).

15 Freud's discussion of the "oceanic" feeling can be found in his essay "Civilization and its discontents," *The Standard Edition of the Complete Psychological Works of Sigmund Freud* (London: Hogarth Press, 1961). Margaret Mead devotes an entire chapter to "womb-envying patterns" in her classic book *Male and Female* (New York: Morrow, 1949), 78–104. See also Bruno Bettelheim, *Symbolic Wounds: Puberty Rites and the Envious Male* (Glencoe, IL: Free Press, 1954).

16 Maria Powers, "Menstruation and reproduction: An Oglala case," *Signs* 6 (1980): 57.

17 Joseph Bastien, *Healers of the Andes: Kallawaya Herbalists and Their Medicinal Plants* (Salt Lake City: University of Utah Press, 1987).

18 Ian Hogbin, *The Island of Menstruating Men: Religion in Wogeo, New Guinea* (Prospect Heights, IL: Waveland Press, 1970); Anna Meigs, *Food, Sex, and Pollution: A New Guinea Religion* (New Brunswick, NJ: Rutgers University Press, 1995), 14–16.

19 L. R. Hiatt, "Secret pseudo-procreative rites among Australian aborigines," in *Anthropology in Oceania,* eds. L. R. Hiatt and C. Jayawardena (Sydney: University Press, 1971).

20 Hogbin, *Island of Menstruating Men;* Ruth Lidz and Theodore Lidz, "Male menstruation: A ritual alternative to the Oedipal transition," in *Culture and Sexuality,* ed. Lois J. McDermott (New York: Simon and Schuster, 1996), 69–70.

21 Sir John Lubbock, *The Origin of Civilization and the Primitive Condition of Man: Mental and Social Condition of Savages* (New York: D. Appleton, 1895), 15–20; M. Godelier, "The origins of male domination," *New Left Review* 127 (1981): 3–17.

22 Eduardo Kohn, "Infidels, virgins and the black-robed priest: A backwoods history of Ecuador's Montaña region," *Ethnohistory* 49 (2002); Roger Loomis and Laura Loomis, *Medieval Romances* (New York: Random House, 1957), 251; Caitlín Matthews and John Matthews, *The Encyclopaedia of Celtic Wisdom* (New York: Barnes and Noble, 1994), 313.

23 Carroll Dunham, *Mamatoto: A Celebration of Birth* (New York: Penguin, 1991), 71; Ruth Underhill, *Red Man's Religion,* 59.

24 Alan Campbell, "Submitting," in *Shamanism: A Reader,* ed. Graham Harvey (London: Routledge, 2003), 137–138; Underhill, *Red Man's Religion,* 60–61; Kohn, "Infidels, virgins and the black-robed priest."

25 Lake, *Hawk Woman,* 142.

26 Felix Oinas, "Couvade in Estonia," in *Culture and Sexuality,* ed. Lois J. McDermott (New York: Simon and Schuster, 1996), 99.

27 Susan Sered, "Jewish healing in Boston," in *Religious Healing in Boston,* eds. Susan Sered and Linda Barnes (Cambridge, MA: Center for the Study of World Religions, Harvard University, 2001).

28 Lynn Gottlieb, *She Who Dwells Within* (San Francisco: HarperSanFrancisco, 1998); Joan Borysenko, "Tired of traditional worship, women across America are creating bold new forms of spiritual expression," *New Age,* 1999, 77.

Chapter Fourteen
CALLING FORTH THE SPIRITS:
BIRTH, RITUAL, AND THE MIDWIFE'S ART

1 Manuela Carneiro da Cunha, "Logique du mythe et de l'action: Le mouvement messianique Canela de 1963," *L'Homme* 13 (1973): 5–37; Michael Brown, "Beyond resistance: Comparative study of utopian renewal in Amazonia," *Amazonian Indians from Prehistory to the Present,* ed. Anna Roosevelt (Tucson: University of Arizona Press, 1994), 294–296.

2 The Nanai, or "Earth People," live in the Lower Amur basin of the Russian Far East. Gara Geiker (1914–1985) lived in the village of Daerga, Khabarovsk district. See Mihály Hoppál, *Das Buch Der Schamanen: Europa und Asien* (Luzern, Switzerland: Motovun Books, 2002), 58–59, 82–83; Ivan Lopatin, *The Cult of the Dead Among the Natives of the Amur Basin* (Gravenhage: Mouton, 1960); Lydia Black, "People of the Amur and maritime regions," in *Crossroads of Continents: Cultures of Siberia and Alaska,* eds. William Fitzhugh and Aron Cropwell (Washington, DC: Smithsonian Institution Press, 1988), 24–25; Tatiana Bulgakova, "The creation of new spirits in Nanai shamanism," *Shaman* 5 (1997): 5.

3 The Ul'ichi are neighbors of the Nanai. See Kira Van Deusen, "The flying tiger,

aboriginal women shamans, storytellers and embroidery artists in the Russian Far East," *Shaman* 4 (1996): 67, and "Ul'ichi shamans and storytellers: Field report, August 1995," *Shaman* 5 (1997): 155.

4   The Evenki, also known as the Tungus, are a Siberian group of between 30,000 and 36,000 individuals living in Russia, Mongolia, and China. See Nadezhda Bulatova, "*Alga,* an Evenki shamanic rite," *Shaman* 2 (1994); Hoppál, *Das Buch der Schamanen,* 58–59, 66–67.

5   Ruth-Inge Heinze, *Trance and Healing in Southeast Asia Today* (Bangkok: White Lotus, 1988); S. J. Tambiah, "The cosmological and performative significance of a Thai cult of healing through meditation," *Culture, Medicine and Psychiatry* 1 (1977): 97–132; Josiane Cauquelin, "The flower-soul in Nung shamanism," *Shaman* 4 (1996): 43.

6   Thelma Sullivan, "Pregnancy, childbirth, and the deification of the women who died in childbirth," *Estudios de Cultura Náhuatl* 6 (1966): 63–95; Brad Huber, "The recruitment of Nahua curers: Role conflict and gender," *Ethnology* 29 (1990): 159–176; Mónica del Villa and Elisa Ramírez, "El embarazo y el parto en la mujer mexica: textos nahuas de Thelma Sullivan," *Arqueología Mexicana* 5 (1998): 42–49.

7   Caroline Humphrey with Urgunge Onon, *Shamans and Elders: Experience, Knowledge, and Power Among the Daur Mongols* (Oxford: Clarendon Press, 1996), 51; Wu Bing-an, "Shamans in Manchuria," in *Shamanism: Past and Present,* eds. M. Hoppál and Ogto von Sadovszky (Budapest: Ethnographic Institute, 1989); Barbara Tedlock, *Time and the Highland Maya* (Albuquerque: University of New Mexico Press, 1992), 47–85; Robert Carlsen and Martin Prechtel, "Walking on two legs: Shamanism in Santiago Atitlán, Guatemala," in *Ancient Traditions: Shamanism in Central Asia and the Americas,* eds. G. Seaman and J. S. Day (Niwot: University Press of Colorado, 1994), 100–104.

8   The World Health Organization (WHO) and UNICEF use the phrase "traditional birth attendant" as a label for women who do not meet the international biomedical definition of a midwife. Among the researchers who have recognized childbirth as a shamanic practice and midwives as shamans are Ruth Boyer and Narcissus Gayton, *Apache Mothers and Daughters* (Norman: University of Oklahoma Press, 1992), 55; Jeannine Baker, "The shamanic dimension of childbirth," *Pre- and Perinatal Psychology Journal* 7 (1992): 5–20; Humphrey with Onon, *Shamans and Elders,* 320–323; and Andrei Golovnev and Gail Osherenko, *Siberian Survival: The Nenets and Their Story* (Ithaca: Cornell University Press, 1999), 38. For the categorizing of midwives as "empirical practitioners" see Brigitte Jordan, "Authoritative knowledge and its construction," in *Childbirth and Authoritative Knowledge: Cross-Cultural Perspectives,* eds. Robbie Davis-Floyd and Carolyn Sargent (Berkeley: University of California Press, 1997), 57; James Dow, "Central and North Mexican shamans," in *Mesoamerican Healers,* eds. Brad Huber and Alan Sandstrom (Austin: University of Texas Press, 2001). For midwives as empowered healers outside the biomedical paradigm see Carol McClain, "Ethno-Obstetrics in Ajijic," *Anthropological Quarterly* 40 (1975): 38–56. For a discussion of the problematics involved in the use of the term "traditional birth attendant," see Stacy Pigg, "Authority in translation: Finding, knowing, naming, and training 'traditional birth attendants' in Nepal," *Childbirth and Authoritative Knowledge: Cross-Cultural Perspectives,* eds. Robbie Davis-Floyd and Carolyn Sargent (Berkeley: University of California Press, 1997), and Robbie Davis-Floyd, "Mutual accommodation or biomedical hegemony? Anthropological perspectives on global issues in midwifery," *Midwifery Today,* spring 2000. In the late 1960s

Carol MacCormack learned that traditional indigenous midwives in Sierra Leone were the senior leaders of a women's religious cult, known as Sande. Members engage in complex female puberty rituals, communicate with spirits, and use intuition, touch healing, and other shamanic practices. Carol MacCormack, "Mende and Sherbro women in high office," *Canadian Journal of African Studies* 6 (1972): 151–164, and "Sande: The public face of a secret society," in *The New Religions of Africa*, ed. Bennetta Jules-Rosette (Norwood, NJ: Ablex, 1979). For an excellent general discussion of midwifery see Carol McClain, "Toward a comparative framework for the study of childbirth: A review of the literature," in *Anthropology of Human Birth*, ed. Margarita Kay (Philadelphia: F. A. Davis, 1982).

9   Lois Paul, "Recruitment to a ritual role: The midwife in a Maya community," *Ethos* 3 (1975): 449–462; "Careers of midwives in a Mayan community," in *Woman in Ritual and Symbolic Roles*, eds. J. Hock-Smith and A. Spring (New York: Plenum Press, 1978); Lois Paul and Benjamin Paul, "The Maya midwife as sacred specialist: A Guatemalan case," *American Ethnologist* 2 (1975): 131–148. Other ethnographers who also reported the midwife shamanic role among the Tzutujil include Nathaniel Tarn and Martin Prechtel, "Constant inconstancy: The feminine principle in Atiteco mythology," in *Symbol and Meaning Beyond the Closed Community: Essays in Mesoamerican Ideas*, ed. Gary Gossen (Albany, NY: Institute for Mesoamerican Studies, 1986); Martin Prechtel and Robert Carlsen, "Weaving and cosmos amongst the Tzutujil Mayas of Guatemala," *RES* 88 (1988): 122–132; Robert Carlsen and Martin Prechtel "Walking on two legs: Shamanism in Santiago Atitlan, Guatemala," in *Ancient Traditions: Shamanism in Central Asia and the Americas*, eds. Gary Seaman and Jane S. Day (Niwot: University Press of Colorado, 1994), 101.

10   Eva Hunt, "A Cuicatec girl's initiatory shamanic descent into the underworld," 1978, unpublished manuscript in the author's possession, and *The Transformation of the Hummingbird* (Ithaca: Cornell University Press, 1977).

11   Gerardo Reichel-Dolmatoff, *The Shaman and the Jaguar: A Study of Narcotic Drugs Among the Indians of Colombia* (Philadelphia: Temple University Press, 1975); Mary Miller and Karl Taube, *The Gods and Symbols of Ancient Mexico and the Maya* (London: Thames and Hudson, 1993), 102–104; Roy Willis, *World Mythology* (New York: Holt, 1993), 261.

12   This glyph is discussed in Stephen Houston and David Stuart, *The Way Glyph: Evidence for Co-essences among the Classic Maya* (Washington, DC: Center for Maya Research, 1989). Jaguars are important shamanic creatures who, like humans, occupy the top level of the food chain. Thus, people sought to identify themselves with these big cats. See Michael Coe, "Olmec jaguars and Olmec kings," in *The Cult of the Feline*, ed. Elizabeth Benson (Washington, DC: Dumbarton Oaks, 1972) and George Kubler, "Jaguars in the Valley of Mexico," in *The Cult of the Feline*.

13   This is a story told in the ancient book known as the *Popol Vuh*. See Dennis Tedlock, *Popol Vuh* (New York: Simon and Schuster, 1996). For more about this figurine see Linda Schele and Peter Mathews, *The Code of Kings: The Language of Seven Sacred Mayan Temples and Tombs* (New York: Scribner, 1998), 215; Mary Ellen Miller, *Maya Art and Architecture* (London: Thames and Hudson, 1999), 158–159; and Linda Schele, *Hidden Faces of the Maya* (New York: Alti, 1997), 164–165.

14   These cords, which are fastened to the rafters of a house, represent the passage of the child's spirit from the sky to the earth. The ceiling is the vault of the sky and the cords are the umbilicus of the house. This intimate connection between a house and a birthing rope is underscored by the word *na*, which means both "house" and

"mother" in Mayan languages. And although the origin of this vase is unknown, chemical analysis of the clay indicates that it was produced in the central Peten jungle of Guatemala. Unfortunately, during the long period of time the vessel was buried, the painting suffered considerable damage. Since so many portions of the hieroglyphic text were either totally obliterated or else illegible, and the few glyphs that remain are rare and poorly understood, I have chosen not to reproduce them here. My analysis centers on the narrative art and iconography of the vessel. For a detailed discussion of this vessel see Karl Taube, "The birth vase: Natal imagery in ancient Maya myth and ritual," in *The Maya Vase Book,* ed. Justin Kerr (New York: Kerr Associates, 1994).

15   In addition to this elderly rainbow goddess, Chak Chel, there is a younger goddess who serves as a midwife, Ix Chel or "Lady Rainbow." Her reign as perhaps the most prominent of all Mayan goddesses has spanned an immense period of time, beginning around 1000 BCE and continuing today. She is worshiped as the goddess of medicine and the goddess of the moon, as well as the patroness of weaving, pregnancy, and childbirth.

16   The quotation is from Marina Roseman, "Engaging the Spirits of Modernity," book manuscript in preparation. Mariana began her ethnographic work in Malaysia in the early 1980s and published a number of essays and books based on her astute observations of men's and women's healing roles. See her essay "The pragmatics of aesthetics: The performance of healing among the Senoi Temiar," *Social Science and Medicine* 27 (1988): 811–818, and her book *Healing Sounds from the Malaysian Rainforest: Temiar Music and Medicine* (Berkeley: University of California Press, 1991). Prior to Marina's work the evidence for shamanic midwifery in Asia consisted of scattered reports from Korea, the Philippines, and Indonesia. On Cheju Island, the largest island off the southern coast of the Korean peninsula, not only were most of the shamans women but 100 out of 128 also practiced obstetrics and pediatrics. See Chu-kun Chang, "An introduction to Korean shamanism," in *Shamanism: The Spirit World of Korea,* eds. Richard W. I. Guisso and Cbai-shin Yu (Berkeley: Asian Humanities Press, 1988), 37; Donn Hart, "From pregnancy through birth in a Bisayan Filipino village," in *Southeast Asian Birth Customs,* eds. Donn Hart, Phya Anuman Rajadhon, and Richard Coughlin (New Haven: Human Relations Area Files Press, 1965), 24–25.

17   Clifford Geertz, *The Religion of Java* (New York: Free Press of Glencoe, 1960), 43–44, 86–87. Turmeric has been used for centuries for the treatment of inflammation. Its efficacy is due to its high vitamin C content and anti-inflammatory properties. See Michael Murray and Joseph Pizzorno, in *Encyclopedia of Natural Medicine* (Rocklin, CA: Prima Publishing, 1991), 190.

18   Eighty thousand Saami, once called "Lapps," live in Norway, Sweden, Finland, and the Kola Peninsula of Russia. Hoppál, *Das Buch Der Schamanen,* 58–61; V. M. Mikhailovskii, "Shamanism in Siberia and European Russia," *Journal of the Anthropological Institute of Great Britain and Ireland* 24 (1895): 62–100, 126–58; Ernst Manker, *Die lappische Zaubertrommel: Eine ethnologische Monographie* (Stockholm: Acta Lapponica, 1938) and *"Seite* cult and drum magic of the Lapps," in *Folk Beliefs and Shamanistic Traditions in Siberia,* ed. Vilmos Diószegi (Budapest: Akadémiai Kiadó, 1996), 4; Louise Bäckman, "The Akkas: A study of four goddesses in the religion of the Saamis (Lapps)," in *Current Progress in the Methodology of the Science of Religions,* ed. Witold Tyloch (Warsaw: Polish Scientific Publishers, 1984); Peg Weiss, *Kandinsky and Old Russia: The Artist as Ethnographer and Shaman* (New Haven: Yale

University Press, 1995), 80–85. The word *sar* is derived from the verb *saaret,* meaning "to separate," "split," or "divide."

19   The Selkup are an Altayan people closely related to the Ket. Today there are approximately 2,000 Selkups living in the Russian Federation. O. Nahodil, "Mother cult in Siberia," in *Popular Beliefs and Folklore Tradition in Siberia,* ed. Vilmos Diószegi (The Hague: Mouton, 1968); Hoppál, *Das Buch der Schamanen,* 58–59, 63.

20   Van Deusen, "The flying tiger," 49–50.

Chapter Fifteen
TIED TO THE FABRIC OF THE SKY:
WEAVERS AND CELESTIAL GODDESSES

1   An excellent history of women and weaving in the Old World was written by Elizabeth Wayland Barber, *Women's Work: The First 20,000 Years: Women, Cloth, and Society in Early Times* (New York: W. W. Norton, 1994). A parallel history for the New World has yet to be composed. There are a number of key sources for such a work including Marie Watson-Franke, "A woman's profession in Guajiro culture: Weaving," *Anthropologica* 37 (1974): 25–40; Lena Bjerregaard, *Techniques of Guatemalan Weaving* (New York: Van Nostrand, 1977); Norbert Sperlich and Elizabeth Sperlich, *Guatemalan Backstrap Weaving* (Norman: University of Oklahoma Press, 1980); Walter Morris, *A Millennium of Weaving in Chiapas* (San Cristóbal de Las Casas: Sna Jolobil, 1984); Stacey Schaefer, *Becoming a Weaver: The Women's Path in Huichol Culture* (Ann Arbor: University Microfilms, 1990); Elizabeth Brumfiel, "Weaving and cooking: Women's production in Aztec Mexico," in *Engendering Archaeology,* eds. Joan M. Gero and Margaret W. Conkey (Oxford: Basil Blackwell, 1991).

2   This riddle appears in Bernadino de Sahagún, *General History of the Things of New Spain: Florentine Codex,* eds. Arthur Anderson and Charles Dibble (Santa Fe: School of American Research, 1950), 6:240. The spindle in the whorl, as a metaphor for coitus, was discussed by Thelma Sullivan, "Tlazolteotl-Ixcuina: The great spinner and weaver," in *The Art and Iconography of Late Post-Classic Central Mexico,* ed. Elizabeth Boone (Washington, DC: Dumbarton Oaks, 1982), 14.

3   Françoise Dussart, "Warlpiri Women Yawulyu Ceremonies," Ph.D. dissertation, Australian National University (1988), 188; Peter Buck, *The Coming of the Maori* (Wellington: Maori Purposes Board, 1950), 462; Annette Weiner, *Inalienable Possessions: The Paradox of Keeping-While-Giving* (Berkeley: University of California Press, 1992), 50. The Huichol of Mexico paint a visually similar fertility symbol, known as a "god eye," on the face of the sacred bundle representing the first woman shaman, Grandmother Growth. And each year pilgrims create woven god eyes and leave them at the edge of a sacred spring in peyote country. They are offerings for Grandmother Growth's daughter, Stuluwiákame, the goddess of childbirth. See Robert Zingg, *The Huichols: Primitive Artists* (New York: G. E. Stechert, 1938), 323. In North and South Asia the eye is a symbol of the womb. See Wendy Doniger, *Splitting the Difference: Gender and Myth in Ancient Greece and India* (Chicago: University of Chicago Press, 1999), 106. Eye-shaped amulets representing the womb, known as *milagros* in the Spanish-speaking world, are left as fertility offerings at shrines. See Martha Egan, *Milagros: Votive Offerings from the Americas* (Santa Fe: Museum of New Mexico Press, 1991) and Eileen Oktavec, *Answered Prayers: Miracles and Milagros Along the Border* (Tucson: University of Arizona Press, 1995).

4   Caroline Humphrey with Urgunge Onon, *Shamans and Elders: Experience, Knowledge, and Power Among the Daur Mongols* (Oxford: Clarendon Press, 1986), 269–270. This was confirmed for me during my research in Mongolia.

5   Margot Schevill, *The Maya Textile Tradition* (New York: Harry Abrams, 1997); Julia Hendon, "Hilado y tejido en la época prehispánica: Tecnología y relaciones sociales de la producción textil," in *La indumentaría y el tejido mayaas a través del tiempo* (Guatemala: Museo Ixchel del Traje Indígena, 1992).

6   Discussions of the cosmology of weaving and the loom in Mexico include Stacey Schaefer, "The loom and time in the Huichol world," *Journal of Latin American Lore* 15 (1990): 179–194 and *To Think with a Good Heart: Wixárika Women, Weavers, and Shamans* (Salt Lake City: University of Utah Press, 2002); Sharisse McCafferty and Geoffrey McCafferty, "Spinning and weaving as female gender identity in post-classic Mexico," in *Reader in Gender Archaeology*, eds. Kelly Hays-Gilpin and David Whitley (New York: Routledge, 1998).

7   Similar statements have been published by Nathaniel Tarn and Martín Prechtel, "Constant inconstancy: The feminine principle in Atiteco mythology," in *Symbol and Meaning Beyond the Closed Community*, ed. Gary Gossen (Albany, NY: Institute for Mesoamerican Studies, 1986), 176–177; Irma Otzoy, "Identidad y trajes maya," *Mesoamérica* 23 (1992): 95–112; and Allen Christenson, *Art and Society in a Highland Maya Community: The Altarpieces of Santiago Atitlán* (Austin: University of Texas Press, 2001), 85.

8   See Joyce Marcus, "Monte Albán's Tomb 7," in *The Cloud People*, eds. Kent Flannery and Joyce Marcus (New York: Academic Press, 1983), 283–285, for a discussion of the possibility that the carved bones deal with genealogy and historical events related to the occupants of the tomb. A reinterpretation of the evidence for the gender and sex of the main individual in the tomb was published by Geoffrey McCafferty and Sharisse McCafferty, "Engendering tomb 7 at Monte Albán: Respinning an old yarn," *Current Anthropology* 35 (1994): 143–166.

9   For an astute discussion of the goddess known as both Lady Nine Reed and Lady Ten Reed see Jill Leslie Furst, *Codex Vindobonensis Mexicanus I: A Commentary* (Albany, NY: Institute for Mesoamerican Studies, 1978), 137.

10   A turquoise-and-gold pectoral found in a nearby tomb includes the round shield with horizontal arrows that constitute the Mesoamerican sign of war. Irene Nicholson, *Mexican and Central American Mythology* (New York: Peter Bedrick Books, 1967), 73.

11   Karl Taube, "The Teotihuacán spider woman," *Journal of Latin American Lore* 9 (1983): 107–189; Sam Gill and Irene Sullivan, *Dictionary of Native American Mythology* (New York: Oxford University Press, 1992), 282, 333.

12   For longer versions of this myth see Leslie White, *The Acoma Indians* (Washington, DC: Government Printing Office, 1932); Matthew Stirling, *Origin Myth of Acoma and Other Records* (Washington, DC: Smithsonian Institution, 1942).

13   Washington Matthews, *Navaho Legends* (Boston: Houghton, Mifflin, 1897); Gladys Reichard, *Spider Woman: A Story of Navajo Weavers and Chanters* (New York: Macmillan, 1934), frontispiece.

14   Aileen O'Bryan, *The Diné: Origin Myths of the Navajo Indians* (Washington, DC: Government Printing Office, 1956), 38.

15   Lana Troy, *Patterns of Queenship: In Ancient Egyptian Myth and History* (Uppsala: Acta Univeersitatis Upsaliensis, 1986); Ann Martha and Dorothy Myers Imel, *Goddesses in World Mythology* (Santa Barbara, CA: ABC-CLIO, 1993); Barbara Lesko, *The Remarkable Women of Ancient Egypt* (Providence, RI: BC Scribe, 1996).

16 Fu Yuguang, "The worldview of the Manchu shamanism," in *Shamans and Cultures*, eds. Mihály Hoppál and Keith Howard (Budapest: Akadémiai Kiadó, 1993); David Pankenier, "The mandate of heaven," *Archaeology,* March/April (1997), 26–33. Triple goddesses of childbirth are also present in native North America. At Cochiti and other Keresan-speaking pueblos in the Southwest human creation was accomplished by a great mother with the help of her twin daughters. Midwives still worship this triple deity and women in childbirth call upon her for strength. See Ruth Benedict, *Tales of the Cochiti Indians* (Washington, DC: Smithsonian Institution, 1931).

17 Humphrey with Onon, *Shamans and Elders,* 291.

18 Odongowa, "Ancient Daur shamanism," in *The Northern Ethnic Groups* (in Chinese) (1991), 7–8; cited in Humphrey with Onon, *Shamans and Elders,* 293.

19 Mircea Eliade, *Shamanism: Archaic Technique of Ecstacy* (New York: Bolingen Foundation, 1964), 505.

20 For a critique of Eliade together with more information on the womb goddess in the sky, see Humphrey with Onon, *Shamans and Elders,* 286–301, and Caroline Humphrey, "Shamanic practices and the state in northern Asia: Views from the center and periphery," in *Shamanism, History, and the State,* eds. Nicholas Thomas and Caroline Humphrey (Ann Arbor: University of Michigan Press, 1994), 21–28.

21 See Laurel Kendall, "Changing gender relations: The Korean case," in *Korean Women, View from the Inner Room,* eds. Laurel Kendall and Mark Peterson (New Haven: East Rock Press, 1983) and *Shamans, Housewives, and Other Restless Spirits* (Honolulu: Hawaii Press, 1985), 124–131.

22 Carol Laderman, *Wives and Midwives: Childbirth and Nutrition in Rural Malaysia* (Berkeley: University of California Press, 1983), 132.

23 Schaefer, *Becoming a Weaver,* 189. This same quote, with slightly different wording, also appears in Schaefer, *To Think With a Good Heart,* 89.

Chapter Seventeen
UNITING SEPARATE REALMS:
GENDER SHIFTING IN SHAMANISM

1 Anne Bolin, "Transcending and transgendering: Male-to-female transsexuals, dichotomy and diversity," in *Third Sex, Third Gender,* ed. Gilbert Herdt (New York: Zone Books, 1996); Leslie Feinberg, *Transgender Warriors: Making History from Joan of Ark to Rupaul* (Boston: Beacon, 1996).

2 Rosemary Joyce, *Gender and Power in Prehispanic Mesoamerica* (Austin: University of Texas Press, 2000), 198–199; Mary Miller and Karl Taube, *The Gods and Symbols of Ancient Mexico and the Maya* (London: Thames and Hudson, 1993), 81.

3 Bernardino de Sahagún, *General History of the Things of New Spain: Florentine Codex,* eds. Arthur Anderson and Charles Dibble (Santa Fe: School of American Research, 1950).

4 The Russian ethnographer Maria Czaplicka in *Aboriginal Siberia: A Study in Social Anthropology* (Oxford: Clarendon Press, 1914) suggested that shamans were neither male nor female, but rather belonged to a third class. Bernard Saladin d'Anglure further developed her idea in several recent articles: "Du foetus au chamane: la construction d'un troisième sexe," *Études Inuit Studies* 10 (1986): 25–113, "Penser le 'féminin' chamanique, ou le 'tiers-sexe' des chamanes inuit," *Recherches amérindiennes au Québec* 19 (1988): 19–50; "La 'troisième' sexe," *Ethnologie* 23 (1992):

836–844; and "The shaman's share, or Inuit sexual communism in the Canadian central arctic," *Anthropologica* 35 (1993): 59–103.

5 Charles Callender and Lee Kochems, "The North American berdache," *Current Anthropology* 24 (1983); Sue-Ellen Jacobs and Jason Cromwell, "Visions and revisions of reality: Reflections on sex, sexuality, gender, and gender variance," *Journal of Homosexuality* 23 (1992): 43–69; Sue-Ellen Jacobs, Wesley Thomas, and Sabine Lang, *Two-Spirit People: Native American Gender Identity, Sexuality, and Spirituality* (Urbana: University of Illinois Press, 1997); Will Roscoe, *Changing Ones: Third and Fourth Genders in Native North America* (New York: St. Martin's Press, 1998).

6 Lydia Black, "The Konyag (the inhabitants of the Island of Kodiak) by Iosaf [Bolotov] (1794–1799) and by Gideon (1804–1807)," *Arctic Anthropology* 14 (1977): 79–108; Waldemar Bogoras, *The Chuckchee* (New York: G. E. Stecheret, 1904), 448–457, and "Chuckchee," in *Handbook of American Indian Languages*, ed. Franz Boas (Washington, DC: US Government Printing Office, 1922).

7 Piers Vitebsky, *The Shaman: Voyages of the Soul, Trance, Ecstacy, and Healing from Siberia to the Amazon* (Boston: Little, Brown and Comapny, 1995), 93; Marjorie Balzer, "Sacred genders in Siberia: Shamans, bear festivals, and androgyny," in *Gender Reversals and Gender Cultures: Anthropological and Historical Perspectives*, ed. Sabrina Petra Ramet (London: Routledge, 1996), 69.

8 Claude Lévi-Strauss, "The effectiveness of symbols," in *Structural Anthropology*, trans. Claire Jacobson and Brooke Schoepf (New York: Anchor, 1963); Gerardo Reichel-Dolmatoff, *Amazonian Cosmos: The Sexual and Religious Symbolism of the Tukano Indians* (Chicago: University of Chicago Press, 1971); Henry Munn, "The mushrooms of language," in *Hallucinogens and Shamanism*, ed. Michael Harner (New York: Oxford University Press, 1973), 107–108; Robert Ryan, *The Strong Eye of Shamanism* (Rochester, VT: Inner Traditions, 1999).

9 The quote is from Peter Furst, "To find our life: Peyote among the Huichol Indians of Mexico," in *Flesh of the Gods: The Ritual Use of Hallucinogens*, ed. Peter Furst (New York: Praeger, 1972), 160–161. This ceremony of tying the cord can be seen toward the end of his documentary film, *To Find Our Life: The Peyote Pilgrimage of the Huichols of Mexico* (Los Angeles: Latin American Center, University of California at Los Angeles, 1969).

10 Vicki Noble described her own experience as "a state of emptiness," only to learn that lamas who combine Buddhism with shamanist teaching prohibit nursing women from religious activities. See Vicki Noble, *Shakti Woman: Feeling Our Fire, Healing Our World* (San Francisco: HarperSanFrancisco, 1991), 140. This is ironic since milk is the supreme product offered to gods, spirits, and ancestors in much of the world. Mongol shamans say that "milk-minded persons" *(süsedkiltei kömün)* are "good" or "kind-hearted" persons. See Caroline Humphrey, "Women and ideology in hierarchical societies in East Asia," in *Persons and Powers of Women in Diverse Cultures*, ed. Shirley Ardener (New York: Berg, 1992), 184.

11 Don Pollock, "Culina shamanism: Gender, power, and knowledge," in *Portals of Power: Shamanism in South America*, eds. E. Jean Matteson Langdon and Gerhard Baer (Albuquerque: University of New Mexico Press, 1992); Lucy Thompson, *To the American Indian* (Berkeley, CA: Heyday Books, 1991 [1916]) and "The training and practices of Yurok female spiritual doctors," *Shaman's Drum* 26 (1991): 32–35; Thomas Buckley, "Yurok doctors and the concept of shamanism," in *California Indian Shamanism*, ed. Lowell John Bean (Menlo Park, CA: Ballena Press, 1992).

12 Ana Mariella Bacigalupo, "The exorcising sounds of warfare: Shamanic healing and

the struggle to remain Mapuche," *Anthropology of Consciousness* 9 (1998): 1–16, and "Shamanism as reflexive discourse: Gender, sexuality and power in the Mapuche religious experience," in *Gender/Bodies/Religions,* ed. Sylvia Marcos (Cuernavaca, Mexico: ALER Publications, 2000).

13 Martha Binford, "Julia: An East African diviner," in *Unspoken Worlds: Women's Religious Lives in Non-Western Culture,* eds. Nancy Falk and Rita M. Gross (New York: Harper and Row, 1980).

Chapter Eighteen
BRAVE ACTS AND VISIONS:
WOMEN WARRIORS AND PROPHETS

1 See Marjorie Balzer, "Introduction," in *Soviet Anthropology and Archaeology* 28 (1989): 3–8.

2 In Southeast Asia pregnant women make offerings to the spirits of women who died in childbirth. See Ruth-Inge Heinze, *Trance and Healing in Southeast Asia Today* (Bangkok: White Lotus, 1988), 393.

3 Marjorie Shostak, *Nisa: The Life and Words of a !Kung Woman* (Cambridge, MA: Harvard University Press, 1981), 180–181.

4 Megan Biesele, "An ideal of unassisted birth: Hunting, healing, and transformation among the Kalahari Ju/'hoansi," in *Childbirth and Authoritative Knowledge,* eds. R. Davis-Floyd and C. Sargent (Berkeley: University of California Press, 1997), 480.

5 See Bernard Ortiz de Montellano, "Empirical Aztec medicine," *Science* 188 (1975): 215–220, and *Aztec Medicine, Health, and Nutrition* (New Brunswick, NJ: Rutgers University Press, 1990), 191.

6 Cecelia Klein, "The shield women: Resolution of an Aztec gender paradox," in *Current Topics in Aztec Studies,* eds. Alana Cordy-Collins and Douglas Sharon (San Diego: San Diego Museum of Man, 1995).

7 The word *Amazon* has been traced variously to Armenian, Kalmuck (a Mongol language), Phoenician, and Scythian. While the ancient Greeks were not sure of the etymology of this borrowed word, it was said to mean "without a breast." Supposedly young women had their right breasts excised in childhood or burned off with a red-hot iron so that it would be easier for them to draw a bow or hurl a javelin. See Stanley Alpern, *Amazons of Black Sparta: The Women Warriors of Dahomey* (New York: New York University Press, 1998), 4.

8 Renate Rolle, *Die Welt der Skythen* (Frankfurt: Bucher Report, 1980), 94–99; Sharon MacDonald, Pat Holden, and Shirley Ardener, *Images of Women in Peace and War* (Madison: University of Wisconsin Press, 1987); Bettina Arnold, "The deposed princess of Vix: The need for an engendered European prehistory," in *The Archaeology of Gender,* eds. Dale Walde and Noreen Willows (Calgary: Archaeological Association of the University of Calgary, 1991), 366.

9 Jeannine Davis-Kimball, "Warrior women of the Eurasian steppes," *Archaeology* 50 (1997): 44–48.

10 Jeannine Davis-Kimball, *Warrior Women: An Archaeologist's Search for History's Hidden Heroines* (New York: Warner Books, 2002), 47–49.

11 The Tang dynasty stretched from 618 until 907 CE. Inazo Nitobe, *Bushido: The Warrior Code* (Burbank, CA: Ohara Publications, 1979); Antonia Fraser, *The Warrior Queens* (New York: Knopf, 1988); Anonymous, "Female warriors unearthed," *China*

Today, October 1993, 64; Catharina Blomberg, *The Heart of the Warrior: Origins and Religious Background of the Samurai System in Feudal Japan* (Sandgate: Japan Library, 1994); David Jones, *Women Warriors: A History* (Washington, DC: Brassey's, 1997).

12 Richard Burton, *Mission to Gelele, King of Dahome* (New York: Praeger, 1966 [1864]), 2:63–85; Melville Herskovits, *Dahomey: An Ancient West African Kingdom* (New York: J. J. Augustin, 1938); Stanley Diamond, *Dahomey: A Proto State in West Africa* (Ann Arbor: University Microfilms, 1951).

13 Stanley Alpern, *Amazons of Black Sparta* (New York: New York University Press, 1998).

14 Sabine Jell-Bahlsen, "Female power: Water priestesses of the Oru-Igbo," in *Sisterhood, Feminisms and Power,* ed. Obioma Nnaemeka (Trenton: Africa World Press, 1998). The idea of palm fronds signaling ritual dedication is not restricted to Igboland. In Lagos, when riots were imminent after the aborted elections of 1993, many individuals covered their cars with palm fronds as a prophylactic against vandalism.

15 Priscilla Buffalohead, "Farmers, warriors, traders: A fresh look at Ojibway women," *Minnesota History* 48 (1983): 236–244. Nancy Ward (Nan-ye-hi, 1738–1822) is frequently referred to as the last "beloved woman" of the Cherokees. While many sources use the terms "beloved woman" and "war woman" interchangeably, Cherokees distinguished these titles between pre- and postmenopausal women. "Beloved Women" were postmenopausal, while "War Women" were younger. See Karen Kilcup, *Native American Women's Writing 1800–1924* (Oxford: Blackwell, 2000), 26.

16 Edwin Thompson Denig, "Biography of Woman Chief," in *Of the Crow Nation,* ed. Edwin Thompson Denig (Washington, DC: Bureau of American Ethnology, 1953), 61–68; Jessica Salmonson, *The Encyclopedia of Amazons: Women Warriors from Antiquity to the Modern Era* (New York: Anchor, 1992), 270.

17 Frank Linderman, *Pretty Shield: Medicine Woman of the Crows* (Lincoln: University of Nebraska Press, 1972).

18 The term "two-spirit" was coined in 1990 at a First Nations gay and lesbian conference in Winnipeg, Canada. It includes gays and lesbians as well as transvestites, transsexuals, and transgender people, who in the past were referred to by the French term *berdache,* a word that is now considered to be not only inappropriate but also insulting. As a generic term, "two-spirit" indicates persons who are not heterosexual or who are ambivalent in terms of gender or sexual preference. Native people who use this term say that it separates them from non-native gays and lesbians, downplays the negative homosexual persona, and emphasizes the spiritual aspect of their lives. See Will Roscoe, *Changing Ones: Third and Fourth Genders in Native North America* (New York: St. Martin's Press, 1998), 124; Sue-Ellen Jacobs, Wesley Thomas, and Sabine Lang, *Two-Spirit People: Native American Gender Identity, Sexuality, and Spirituality* (Urbana: University of Illinois Press, 1997); Claude Schaeffer, "The Kutenai female berdache: Courier, guide, prophetess, and warrior," *Ethnohistory* 12 (1965): 193–236; "*Kauxuma Nupika* (Gone to the Spirits)," *The Encyclopedia of Native American Religion* (New York: Facts on File, 1992), 114.

19 Eve Ball, *In the Days of Victorio: Recollections of a Warm Springs Apache* (Tucson: University of Arizona Press, 1970), 15.

20 Salmonson, *The Encyclopedia of Amazons,* 224–225; Jones, *Women Warriors: A History,* 208.

21 Caroline James, *Nez Perce Women in Transition 1877–1990* (Moscow, ID: University of Idaho Press, 1996), 126.

22 Truman Michelson, "On the origin of the so-called Dream Dance of the central Algonkians," *American Anthropologist* 25 (1923): 277–278; Alanson Skinner, "A

further note on the origin of the Dream Dance of the Central Algonkian and southern Siouan Indians," *American Anthropologist* 25 (1923): 427–428; James Clifton, *The Prairie People: Continuity and Change in Potawatomi Indian Culture* (Lawrence: Regents Press of Kansas, 1977); James Slotkin, *The Menominee Powwow: A Study in Cultural Decay* (Milwaukee, 1957).

23   She was killed in a war that bears her name, Mut Mandong. See Douglas Johnson, *Nuer Prophets: A History of Prophecy from the Upper Nile in the Nineteenth and Twentieth Centuries* (Oxford: Clarendon Press, 1994), 249, 270–281.

24   Peter Roe, "The Josho Nahuanbo are all wet and undercooked: Shipibo views of the whiteman and the Incas in myth, legend, and history," in *Rethinking History and Myth,* ed. Jonathan D. Hill (Urbana: University of Illinois Press, 1988), 128, 203. For more information about this woman shaman and her remarkable pottery design see Angelika Gebhart-Sayer, "The geometric designs of the Shipibo-Conibo in ritual context," *Journal of Latin American Lore* 11 (1985): 150–153.

25   Robert Lawlor, *Voices of the First Day: Awakening in the Aboriginal Dreamtime* (Rochester, VT: Inner Traditions, 1991), 335.

26   Frederick Franck, *An Encounter with Oomoto "The Great Origin": A Faith Rooted in the Ancient Mysticism and the Traditional Arts of Japan* (West Nyack, NY: Cross Currents, 1975), 22–28.

27   Margaret Nowak and Stephen Durrant, *The Tale of the Nishan Shamaness: A Manchu Folk Epic* (Seattle: University of Washington Press, 1977); Emily Ooms, *Women and Millenarian Protest in Meiji Japan* (Ithaca: Cornell University Press, 1993).

Chapter Nineteen
REKINDLING THE FLAME:
SHAMANIC REVITALIZATION AND RECONSTRUCTION

1   See Michael Harner, *The Way of the Shaman: A Guide to Power and Healing* (Toronto: Bantam, 1980) and his Web site, http://www.shamanicstudies.com.

2   Marjorie Balzer, "Dilemmas of the spirit: Religion and atheism in the Yakut-Sakha republic," in *Religious Policy in the Soviet Union,* ed. Sabrina Peta Ramet (Cambridge: Cambridge University Press, 1993) and "Shamanism and the politics of culture: An anthropological view of the 1992 international conference on shamanism, Yakutsk," *Shaman* 1 (1993): 71–96.

3   This prayer is from M. B. Kenin-Lopsan, *Shamanic Songs and Myths of Tuva* (Budapest: Akadémiai Kiadó, 1997), 34–35. Ever since the thirteenth century when Chinggis Khan conquered Tuva and Mongolians colonized the area, Tuvans have shared many linguistic and cultural features with Mongolians.

4   Nadia Stepanova, *L'invocatrice degli Dei: Storie di vita di una sciamana buriata raccontate a Sicilia D'Arista* (Milan, Italy: Zenia Edizioni, 1998), 79–101; C. Allione, "Nadia Stepanova, Buryatian shaman," *Mystic Fire Video,* 1995; Kira Van Deusen, "Buryat shamans and their stories," *Shamanism* 10 (1997): 11–15, and "In black and white: Contemporary Buriat shamans," *Shaman* 7 (1999): 153–166.

5   Marjorie Balzer, "The poetry of shamanism," in *Shamanism in Performing Arts,* eds. Tae-gon Kim and Mihály Hoppál (Budapest: Akadémiai Kiadó, 1995), 173.

6   These figures are from a 1992 sociological study that was made public during the conference on shamanism. See Marjorie Balzer, "Changing images of the shaman: Folklore and Politics in the Sakhá Republic Yakutia," *Shaman* 4 (1996): 14.

7   Mihály Hoppál, 'Tracing shamanism in Tuva: A history of studies," in *Shamanic Songs and Myths of Tuva,* ed. M. B. Kenin-Lopsan (Budapest: Akadémiai Kiadó, 1997), 133; David Brown, "Traditional healing returns to Tuva: In the Soviets' wake, a shamans' clinic is thriving in Northeast Asia," *Washington Post,* available on the internet at www.fotuva.org/misc/shamanism/clinic.html.

8   Kira Van Deusen, "New legends in the rebirth of Khakass shamanic culture," *Anthropology of East Europe Review* 16 (1998): 35–38.

9   Richard C. Kagan, "The Chinese Approach to Shamanism," *Chinese Sociology and Anthropology* 12 (1980); Shi Kun, "Shamanistic studies in China: A preliminary survey of the last decade," *Shaman* 1 (1993): 47–57; Mihály Hoppál, "Shamanism at the turn of the century," conference paper presented at the Fifth International Conference of the Society for Shamanistic Research, Ulaanbaatar, Mongolia, 1999; Gábor Kósa, "In search of the spirits: Shamanism in China before the Tan Dynasty. Part one," *Shaman* 8 (2000):131–179, "Some recent Chinese works on shamanism," *Shaman* 9 (2001): 77–81, and " 'Open Wide, Oh, Heaven's Door!' Shamanism in China before the Tang Dynasty. Part two," *Shaman* 9 (2001): 169–197; Hong Zhang and Constantine Hriskos, "Contemporary Chinese shamanism: The reinvention of tradition," *Cultural Survival Quarterly* 27 (2003): 55–57.

10   Marjorie Balzer, "Changing images of the shaman: Folklore and politics in the Sakhá Republic Yakutia," *Shaman* 4 (1996): 5–16; Uradyn Bulag, *Nationalism and Hybridity in Mongolia* (Oxford: Clarendon Press, 1998), 82–83, 86–88.

11   Kenin-Lopsan, *Shamanic Songs,* 29, 39, 107, 110, 114–15.

12   For more about Celtic shamanic spirituality see Nigel Pennick, *The Sacred World of the Celts: An Illustrated Guide to Celtic Spirituality and Mythology* (Rochester, VT. Inner Traditions, 1998); Hilda Davidson, *The Seer in Celtic and Other Traditions* (Edinburgh: John Donald, 1989); Mary Condren, *The Serpent and Goddess: Women, Religion, and Power in Celtic Ireland* (San Francisco: Harper and Row, 1989). For descriptions of the current revitalization of Celtic shamanism see Caítlin and John Matthews, *Taliesin: Shamanism and the Bardic Mysteries in Britain and Ireland* (London: Aquarian, 1991) and their *Encyclopaedia of Celtic Wisdom* (New York: Barnes and Noble, 1994); Tom Cowan, *Fire in the Head: Shamanism and the Celtic Spirit* (San Francisco: HarperSanFrancisco, 1993); Ward Rutherford, *Celtic Lore: The History of the Druids and Their Timeless Traditions* (London: Thorsons, 1993); D. J. Conway, *Advanced Celtic Shamanism* (Freedom, CA: Crossing Press, 2000).

13   Margaret Adler, *Drawing Down the Moon: Witches, Druids, Goddess-Worshippers and Other Pagans in America Today* (Boston: Beacon, 1986), 430–434; Scott Cunningham, *Wicca: A Guide for the Solitary Practitioner* (St. Paul, MN: Llewellyn, 1988), 4; T. M. Luhrmann, *Persuasions of the Witch's Craft: Ritual Magic in Contemporary England* (Cambridge, MA: Harvard University Press, 1989), 134, 329; Starhawk, *The Spiral Dance: A Rebirth of the Ancient Religion of the Great Goddess* (San Francisco: Harper and Row, 1989), 40. Kathryn Rountree profiles the current feminist witchcraft movement in New Zealand in her Ph.D. dissertation and several key essays. See "The new witch of the West: Feminists reclaim the crone," *Journal of Popular Culture* 30 (1997): 211–229, and "The politics of the goddess: Feminist spirituality and the essentialism debate," *Social Analysis* 43 (1999): 138–165.

14   Marija Gimbutas, *The Goddesses and Gods of Old Europe: Myths and Cult Images* (Berkeley, CA: University of California Press, 1974); L. Jencson, "Neopaganism and the Great Mother Goddess," *Anthropology Today* 5 (1989): 2–4; Lynn Meskell, "Goddesses, Gimbutas and 'New Age' archaeology," *Antiquity* 69 (1995): 74–86, and "Oh

my goddess! Archaeology, sexuality and ecofeminism," *Archaeological Dialogues* 2 (1998): 126–142; Starhawk, *The Spiral Dance: A Rebirth of the Ancient Religion of the Great Goddess* (San Francisco: Harper and Row, 1989), 16. Primal religions have recently been distinguished from "universal" or "developed" religions by scholars in religious studies. They feel, and I agree, that it is a better alternative than the older terms *tribal, traditional,* or *pre-literate* religions. See D. Pratt, *Religion: A First Encounter* (Auckland: Longman Paul, 1993), 19–30; Carol Christ, "Why women need the Goddess: Phenomenological, psychological and political reflections," in *The Politics of Women's Spirituality: Essays on the Rise of Spiritual Power within the Feminist Movement,* ed. C. Spretnak (New York: Doubleday, 1982).

15   For discussions of Nordic shamanism see Emest Moyne, *"Raising the Wind." The Legend of Lapland and Finland: Wizards in Literature* (University of Delaware Press, 1981); Jane Mack, "Shetland Finn-Men: Interpretations of shamanism?" and Bo Sommarström, "Shamanism and paranormal perception in the Saami Tradition," both in *Northern Religions and Shamanism,* eds. M. Hoppál and Juha Pentikäinen (Budapest: Akadémiai Kiadó, 1992); Kaledon Naddair, "Pictish and Keltic shamanism," in *Voices from the Circle: The Heritage of Western Paganism,* eds. P. Jones and C. Matthews (Wellingborough, Northamptonshire: Aquarian, 1990); Philip Shallcrass, "Druidry today," in *Paganism Today: Wiccans, Druids, the Goddess and the Ancient Earth Traditions for the Twenty-first Century,* eds. G. Harvey and C. Hardman (London: Thorsons, 1995).

16   Jenny Blain, *Nine Worlds of Seid-Magic: Ecstasy and Neo-shamanism in North European Paganism* (London: Routledge, 2002), 6; Merete Demant Jakobsen, *Shamanism: Traditional and Contemporary Approaches to the Mastery of Spirits and Healing* (New York: Berghahn Books, 1999), 225–228; Galina Lindquist, *Shamanic Performances on the Urban Scene: Neo-Shamanism in Contemporary Sweden* (Stockholm: Stockholm Studies in Social Anthropology, 1997).

17   Robert Wallis, *Shamans/Neo-Shamans: Ecstasy, Alternative Archaeologies and Contemporary Pagans* (London: Routledge, 2003), 125.

18   Diana Paxson, "The return of the Völva: Recovering the practice of Seidh," *Mountain Thunder* (1993). Also available online at www.hrafnar.org/articles/seidh.html.

19   For more information about Seidr see Jenny Blain, "Seiðr, a women's magic: Shamanism, journeying and healing in Norse heathenism," paper given at the Canadian Anthropology Society at the University of Toronto, 1998, "Seiðr as a shamanistic practice: Reconstituting a tradition of ambiguity," *Shaman* 7 (1999): 99–121, and *Nine Worlds of Seid-Magic.*

20   This quotation is from Craig Brown, the president of the National Federation of Spiritual Healers, which is located at Old Manor Farm Studio, Church Street, Sudbury-on-Thames, Middlesex TW 16 RG. It is registered as charity no. 211133. The organization's Web site can be found at www.nfsh.org.uk.

21   For more information see www.shamansociety.org.

22   Elisabeth Brooke has written two accessible books on the history of women healers through the ages: *Women Healers: Portraits of Herbalists, Physicians, and Midwives* (Rochester, VT: Inner Traditions, 1995) and *Medicine Women: A Pictorial History of Women Healers* (Wheaton, IL: Quest Books, 1997). In her first book she included a short chapter on women shamans but she limited them to crones, women past the age of childbearing who no longer menstruate. This unfortunately follows the masculine view of women in shamanism. Menstruating women, as I have shown in chapter twelve, can also be powerful shamans.

Illustration Sources
and Permissions

Except as otherwise noted, redrawings have been done by the author

1   Pen and ink drawing by Del Ashkewe, reproduced by permission of the Royal Ontario Museum.
2   Reproduced courtesy of the Phoebe Apperson Hearst Museum of Anthropology and the Regents of the University of California.
3   Redrawn from an image in *Codex Borbonicus* (folios 21 and 22).
4   Redrawn from sketches of Paleolithic figurines made by Catherine McCoid in possession of the author.
5   Redrawn from a photograph in Ivar Lismer, *Man, God and Magic* (1961: 210).
6   Redrawn from André Leroi-Gourhan, *Préhistoire de l'art occidental* (1965: 100).
7   Redrawn from an illustration by J. D. Lewis-Williams, "Ethnography and Iconography," *Man* (1980: 132).
8   Detail redrawn from Mary Leakey's photograph in *Africa's Vanishing Art* (1982: n.p.).
9   Black-and-white line drawing based on Ruth Annajqtuusi Tulurialik's color-pencil illustration in *Qikaaluktut: Images of Inuit Life* (Oxford University Press, 1986, n.p.)
10 Detail redrawn from a photograph of Lintel 25 Yaxchilán, Mexico Structure 23. c. AD 725.
11 Japanese figurine of a woman shaman. From Miki Fumio (1960) Haniwa: The Clay Sculpture of Protohistoric Japan. (Boston: Charles E. Tuttle [NB 1667 M513].)
12 Detail from a contemporary Mongolian art work (artist unknown). Painting in author's possession.
13, 14 Drawings by collection of Niedersächsische Staats-und Universitätsbibliothek, Göttingen.

15   Drawing by the Huichol shaman Ulu Temay (Arrow Man). Book reproduced by permission of Susana Valadez, Centro Indigena Huichol.

16   Image of Koryak woman shaman reproduced by permission of the American Museum of Natural History, New York, New York.

17   Redrawn from a photograph in Josephine Flood, *Rock Art of the Dreamtime* (Australia: Angus and Robertson, 1997: 281).

18   Late-nineteenth century drawing, artist unknown, from Kotzebue Sound Alaska. Department of Anthropology, National Museum of Natural History.

19   Detail of a photograph by Peter T. Furst in the author's possession.

20   Courtesy of the Museum of Anthropology, Vancouver, Canada.

21   Redrawn from an illustration by an unknown artist in M. Ja. Zornickaja, "Dances of Yakut shamans," in *Shamanism in Siberia* (Budapest: Akadémiai Kiadó, 1996: 131, fig. 2).

22   Redrawn from an illustration in Mantak and Maneewan Chia, *Healing Love through the Tao* (Huntington, NY: Healing Tao Books, 1986: 277).

23   Photograph by Barbara Kerr of a Mayan Late Classic Period (600-900 CE) shell.

24, 25 Photographs by Dennis Tedlock (1999).

26, 27 Drawings of Mongolian folk image in author's possession.

28   Photograph by Dennis Tedlock (1999).

29   Photograph by Barbara Tedlock (1999).

30   Photograph from William Thalbitzer, *The Ammassalik Eskimo* (Copenhagen: Bianco Luno, 1914, vol. 2: 482).

31   Reproduced by permission of Robert Lake-Thom (Medicine Grizzlybear Lake).

32   From the author's collection.

33   Redrawing based on Richard Evans Schultes, "A native drawing of an hallucinogenic plant from Colombia," *Botanical Museum Leaflets* 25 (1977: 152).

34   Drawings from Siberian rock art sites in the author's possession.

35   Reproduced with permission from the Tina and R. Gordon Wasson Ethnomycological Collection Archives, Harvard University, Cambridge, MA.

36   Detail redrawn from sixteenth-century screen fold book, *Codex Vindobonensis* (folio 24).

37   Reproduced with permission from the Tina and R. Gordon Wasson Ethnomycological Collection Archives, Harvard University, Cambridge, MA.

38   Redrawing based on an illustration in Gerardo Reichel-Domatoff, *Shamanism and Art of the Eastern Tukanan Indians* (Leiden: E. J. Brill, 1987: Plate 31).

39   Reproduced by permission of the National Museum of the American Indian, George Gustave Heye Center, [no. 3/3612A].

40   Courtesy of the photographer, Bonnie Glass-Coffin.

41   Photograph (1986), courtesy of Bonnie Glass-Coffin.

42, 43 Photographs by Lizbeth Rymland reproduced from *Shaman's Drum* vol. 34 (1994: 43, 44).

44   Redrawn from sixteenth-century manuscript, *Codex Vaticanus B* (n.p.).

45   Redrawn from Linda Schele's sketch in *The Mirror, the Rabbit, and the Bundle* (1983: figure 18d).

46   Redrawn from an illustration by F. D. McCarthy, "The string figures of Yirrkalla," in *Records of the American-Australian Scientific Expedition to Arnhem Land* (1960: 426).

47   Reproduced by permission of Northern California Collection: Humboldt State University Library.

48 Huichol culture, Nayarit or Jalisco, Mexico. The Husband Assists in the Birth of a Child. mid twentieth century. Yarn, 23¾ × 23¾ in. Reproduced by permission of The Fine Arts Museums of San Francisco, Gift of Peter F. Young. 74.21.14.

49 Drawn by Barbara Tedlock (2002).

50 Precolumbian, Mexico, Campeche, Jaina, Maya, Ceramic figure. Late Classic, clay: H. 26.0 cm. Reproduced by permission of Princeton University Art Museum. Gift of J. Lionberger Davis, Class of 1900.

51, 52, 53 Drawings by Jamie Borowicz (2000), in author's possession.

54 Redrawn from a photograph of a seventeenth-century drumhead in the author's possession.

55 Redrawn from early sixteenth-century screen fold book *Codex Mendoza* (folio 68 recto).

56 Redrawn from Françoise Dussart, *Warlpiri Women Yawulyu Ceremonies*. Ph.D. dissertation, Australian National University (1988: 188).

57 Photograph by Barbara Tedlock (1992).

58, 59, 60 Redrawn from photographs in Alfonso Caso, *El tesoro de Monte Albán* (1969, vol. 3 p. 895, 932).

61 Redrawn detail from Late Postclassic screen fold book, *Codex Fejérváry Mayer,* (folio 35).

62 Photograph by Morin Dawaa (1987), by permission of Caroline Humphrey.

63 Detail redrawn from sixteenth-century screen fold book *Codex Mendoza,* (folio 57 recto).

64 Redrawn from photograph in Donald Lathrap, "Shipibo Tourist Art," in *Ethnic and Tourist Arts* (Berkeley: University of California Press, 1986: 203).

Index

Shamans *(cont.)*
62; calling/selection of, 21,
22–25, 55–56, 186, 208–9, 276;
characteristics/nature of, 21,
23–24, 27; eclipse of women, 59,
60–75; first, 3–4, 24; and flying
dream as nucleus of shamanism,
72; functions and social position
of, 14–27, 43–45, 207–8;
hereditary, 22–23, 54, 94; in
history, 40–59; indigenous terms
for, 24–25; initiation of, 11–12,
16, 123, 124, 185–90, 202–4,
209–12, 262; inspirational,
22–23; male-female teams of,
54–55; myth of man the hunter-,
64–65; North Asia as heartland
of, 62; obscuring and denial of
tradition of, 4–5; origins of, 14; in
prehistory, 28–39, 41; sexual
rivalry among, 55–59; and
shamanic
revitalization/reconstruction,
270–82; and shamanic traditions,
281–82; souls of dead, 213; terms
for, 24–25, 70; as tricksters,
26–27; willful misreading of
evidence about, 62–64;
worldviews of, 20–21
Shangana-Tsonga culture, 139
Shawnee indians, 161
Shintoism, 195
Shipibo culture, 266
Shirokogoroff, Sergei, 62
Shoshoni culture, 73–74
Shostak, Marjorie, 256–57
Siberia, 24, 27, 51, 90, 203, 206; and
eclipse of female shamanism,
62–65, 69; gender shifting in,
250, 251; and origins of
shamanism, 14; and psychedelics,
146; shamanic revitalization in,
270, 271–74, 275–76; and
shamanic worldviews, 21; warriors
and prophets in, 255–56; and

women shamans in prehistory,
28–29, 34. *See also specific culture*
Simbaña, Mama Juana, 168–69, 170
Sitting-in-the-Water Grizzly Bear,
263
Skeletal materials: sexing of, 29–30
Sky goddesses, 232–36
Smith, Kitty, 69
Smithsonian Museum, 29
Snakes, 113, 199, 208, 228, 238, 276.
See also Serpents
Society for Shamanic Practitioners,
281
Soffer, Olga, 66–67
The Song of Mukhomor (video), 147
Soul flight, 45, 62, 72, 73, 145, 212,
252
Souls, 122, 238; ancestral, 238; of
animals, 221, 222; and childbirth,
206, 207, 222, 230; of dead
shamans, 213; and dreams, 111,
118; and eclipse of female
shamanism, 62, 72, 73; and
gender shifting, 249, 252; and
midwifery, 212, 221, 222; and
psychedelics, 145, 154; and
shamanic revitalization, 274; and
shamanic worldviews, 20; and
weaving, 225, 230; and women
shamans in history, 41, 45, 52.
See also Soul flight
South Africa, 36–37, 83–84, 256–57,
271. *See also* San culture
South America, 70, 213
Southeast Asia, 27, 73, 203, 207,
218–20, 234–35
Southesk, earl of, 52
Southwest United States: and women
shamans in history, 53–54
Speaking of the blood, 11, 25, 26, 79,
80, 123, 124
Spells, 15, 23
Spider Woman, 181, 182, 231–32
Spiders, 116–17, 208, 230, 231–32,
269

Yeshey Tsogyel (Great Bliss Queen),
  185
Yoga, 88
Yolngu culture, 179–80
Yukaghir culture, 63

Yurok culture, 24, 115, 186–88, 193,
  253

Zapotec culture, 148
Zuni culture, 53–54

ABOUT THE AUTHOR

BARBARA TEDLOCK, PH.D., is the granddaughter of an Ojibwe mid-wife and herbalist and was trained and initiated as a shaman by the K'iche' Maya of highland Guatemala. She is currently Distinguished Professor of Anthropology at SUNY Buffalo and Research Associate at the School of American Research in Santa Fe, New Mexico. For many years she co-edited *The American Anthropologist* with her husband, Dennis Tedlock.

She is the author of numerous essays and four previous books: *The Beautiful and the Dangerous: Encounters with the Zuni Indians; Dreaming: Anthropological and Psychological Interpretations; Time and the Highland Maya;* and *Teachings from the American Earth: Indian Religion and Philosophy* (with Dennis Tedlock).

Her honors include the 2002 SUNY Chancellor's Research Recognition Award for her research among Mayan and Mongolian shamans, and fellowships from the National Endowment for the Humanities, the National Institutes of Health, and the Center for the Study of World Religions at Harvard University. She has also received Mellon and Fulbright Foundation Fellowships, a Weatherhead Resident Fellowship at the School of American Research, and Senior Research Fellowships from both the American Council of Learned Societies and the Institute for Advanced Study at Princeton.